ART NOUVEAU
ARCHITECTURE

ART NOUVEAU ARCHITECTURE

ANNE ANDERSON

THE CROWOOD PRESS

First published in 2020 by
The Crowood Press Ltd
Ramsbury, Marlborough
Wiltshire SN8 2HR

enquiries@crowood.com
www.crowood.com

British Library Cataloguing-in-Publication Data
A catalogue record for this book is available from the British Library.

ISBN 978 1 78500 767 5

Frontispiece: Ödön Lechner, with Sándor Baumgarten, Postal Savings Bank, Hold u. 4, Pest (1900–01)

Acknowledgements:
Many thanks to Scott Anderson, my husband, for helping with the images. They were mostly taken by both of us on our Travel Editions tours. The image of the Villino Ruggeri, Pesaro, was kindly supplied by Foto di Andrea Speziali, Associazione Italia Liberty – http://www.italialiberty.it

Typeset by Derek Doyle & Associates, Shaw Heath
Printed and bound in India by Parksons Graphics

Contents

THE ART NOUVEAU CITY ROUTE LISTS OVER seventy cities that judge their Art Nouveau legacy to be of cultural significance. These cities range as far west as Lima and Mexico City and to the east, Moscow and Kecskemét. Recognizing Art Nouveau's 'millennial moment', the route was founded in 2000; the pan-world significance of Art Nouveau's quest for modernity on the eve of the twentieth century was also recognized in a major exhibition at the V&A. The growing enthusiasm for Art Nouveau, amongst both academics and tourists, had already resulted in the founding of the European Reseau Art Nouveau Network (RANN) in 1998. This currently comprises twenty-three European cities that are all committed to protecting, studying and raising awareness of their remarkable heritage: among these are Ålesund, Norway; Averio, Portugal; Bad Nauheim, Germany; Barcelona, Catalonia; Brussels, Belgium; Glasgow, Scotland; Havana, Cuba; Helsinki, Finland; La Chaux-de-Fonds, Switzerland; Ljubljana, Slovenia; Nancy, France; Regione Lombardia (Milan and Lake Como), Italy; Szeged, Southern Hungary; Riga, Latvia; and Terrassa, Catalonia.

Brussels, the 'cradle' of Art Nouveau, Barcelona, Glasgow and Riga have all benefited from this fervour for Art Nouveau with specialist tours and architectural walks abounding. Many books, both general surveys and detailed monographs on individual architects, have been published. Previous writers have dealt with the new art and architecture of the 1890s–1900s by city or country[1]. This approach has been taken in order to discuss the local conditions, cultural, economic and political, that stimulated the search for a modern idiom.

However, given the overwhelming number of cities in many different countries in the Art Nouveau Route, my appraisal must be selective. To a certain extent it concentrates on cities I have come to know well: Brussels, Paris, Nancy, Budapest, Barcelona, Milan, Turin, Porto and Aveiro. It evaluates the new architectural idioms through many different building types ranging from civic and commercial to domestic. By looking at houses and apartments, schools and hospitals, and shops and restaurants, we can see how architects responded to the demands of modern life. Greater attention has also been given to the role played by the so-called applied arts; stained glass, ceramics and metalwork. Many surveys fail to mention the many artisans and craftsmen whose work made Art Nouveau, or Jugendstil as it is known in German-speaking countries, so distinctive.

Chapter 2 surveys all the terminology associated with the New Art. Indeed, in order to avoid confusion, the term Art Nouveau is used specifically for Belgian and French forms. At the time, English magazines such as *The Studio* (1893–) coined the term New Art to categorize the developments taking place in London and Glasgow. Throughout this volume, therefore, the moniker New Art is adopted as a neutral term to describe an international impulse that strove through art and architecture to express modernity. Focusing on the terminology, this survey starts in England with the Arts and Crafts and the Aesthetic movements, recognized as the precursors of the New Art. England does develop its own New Art idioms, especially in the graphic arts, but the most significant architectural contribution comes from Glasgow. The centres for Art Nouveau (Brussels, Paris and

Nancy) are followed by Jugendstil (Darmstadt, Hagen, Weimar) and Secession (Munich and Vienna). Magyar Szecesszió, Catalan Modernisme, Italian Stile Liberty and Portugal's Arte Nova expand the field into areas often neglected in general surveys. Moreover, much of the current research is not published in English, making access to information doubly hard.

Allied to literary Decadence and Symbolism in the fine arts, the New Art sought to express the anxieties aroused by modern life. A symbolic language evolved, based on flora and fauna that expressed complex ideas in a visual form. Artists drew on a wide range of ancient sources, myths and legends as well as the Bible, to create a symbolic language that was universal. Exploring the concept of architecture as language, Chapter 3 unpicks these motifs and explains their meaning.

Understandably, the new architecture was driven by innovative technologies and materials (iron/steel, concrete, glass and ceramics). The role of new building materials is covered in Chapter 4; the New Art owes its very existence to mass-produced materials, industrial processes and technical innovations. The stress laid on ornamentation, stained glass, ceramics and metalwork brought the applied arts closer to the fine arts. Wider opportunities led many artists into different fields of endeavour; artists no longer simply painted, they designed posters, textiles, tiles and stained glass. As polymaths, artist-craftsmen strove to be like their Renaissance forebears.

Chapter 5 singles out iconic buildings that mark a turning point or epitomize the style of an outstanding architect, landmarks in the literal sense. Many iconic buildings have been lost, through wartime destruction or post-war development. During the 1950s and 1960s, when all things 'Victorian' were scorned, it was hard to protect buildings from developers and speculators.

The most famous victim was Victor Horta's Maison du Peuple or the People's House (1896–99), Brussels. Commissioned by the Belgian Workers' Party, the Maison du Peuple embodied Art Nouveau's democratic ethos or 'Art for the People'. With offices, meeting rooms and an auditorium that could seat 300 people, it was a 'true ship of socialist ideology'. It spawned a People's House in every Belgian city; the notion also inspired the Municipal House in Prague (1905–12, Osvald Polívka and Antonín Balšánek), which combines a concert hall with restaurants. The demolition of Horta's Maison du Peuple in 1965, despite an international protest mounted by over 700 architects, has been condemned as an 'architectural crime' and the 'assassination of Victor Horta'. Among the other great losses must be counted August Endell's Elvira Studio, Munich (1898), destroyed by allied bombing in 1944 and much more recently Charles Rennie Mackintosh's Glasgow School of Art (1896–1906) destroyed by fire in 2014 and 2018.

Finally, the Epilogue considers how Art Nouveau/ Jugendstil evolved into post-war intellectually driven Modernism, as epitomized by the Bauhaus and fashionable Art Deco.

Notes

1. Massini, Lara-Vinca, *Art Nouveau*, London: Thames and Hudson, 1984; Greenhalgh, Paul (ed.), *Art Nouveau 1890–1914*, London: V&A Publications, 2000; Russell, Frank (ed.), *Art Nouveau Architecture*, London: Academy Editions, 1979; Sembach, Klaus Jurgen, *Art Nouveau; Utopia: Reconciling the Irreconcilable*, Köln: Benedikt Taschen, 1991; Fahr-Becker, Gabriele, *Art Nouveau*, Potsdam: h. f. Ullmann, 2015.

Chapter One

New Art for a New Century

Before considering individual architects or buildings, this introductory chapter considers some key themes. How did the new style come about and how can we define it? Art Nouveau, literally the New Art, went by different names in different countries. Individuality is the key factor, with each architect pursuing his own agenda and creating his own style. The New Art was an artistic movement rather than a stylistic straight jacket. Peter Behrens (1868–1940), a leading German architect and designer, declared 'the style of an era does not mean specific forms in a specific form of art . . . each art form is a mere contribution to the style. Yet a style is the symbol of an overall feeling, of an era's attitude to life, and is only visible within the universe of all the arts'[1].

In other words, to understand the aims of the New Art we must examine all aspects of life at the close of the nineteenth century. Buildings cannot be studied in isolation but embedded in the culture that created them. The desire to respond to modern life can be tracked through all the arts, literature, music, painting and sculpture as well as architecture and the so-called decorative or applied arts. Many architects took a holistic approach, as they believed art, in the broadest sense of the word, enhanced life.

International exhibitions and a plethora of new magazines devoted to the arts allowed artists and architects to keep abreast of new developments. They enabled an international dialogue. The New Art was shaped by many factors especially Japonisme, an interest in all forms of Oriental art. When opened to trade with the West in 1853, Japan was not industrialized.

Many admired Japanese society: to Western eyes their culture successfully integrated art and life, with beautiful objects (ceramics, lacquer work, textiles) used daily.

On the eve of the twentieth century, artists wanted to create art forms that were relevant to the times and to widen the definition of art to encompass objects used daily. The concept of design was born, that utilitarian objects should be stylish as well as functional. The architect widened his remit to include all aspects of a building and its interior. Homes were to be beautiful, as the goal was a 'Life lived in Art'.

A Style for Modern Life

From many strands, a New Art arose; 'a movement, a style, a way of life, a culture, an enterprise that belonged to modern times'[2]. The New Art articulated the pressures of modern life, particularly the rapid changes taking place in society due to new technologies and the increasing emancipation of women. Traditional male and female roles were brought into question; female sexuality, a taboo subject, became a hot topic. The New Art responded to rising nationalism, an identity crisis having been brought about by industrialization, urbanization and internationalism. A crisis in conventional faith led to many seeking alternatives, spiritualism and mysticism. As a cultural phenomenon the New Art dared to break with convention: this was the shock of the new.

Architects and designers were united by the mission to create a modern style that expressed the zeitgeist, the spirit of the age. The divisions that separated the different genres of art, painting, sculpture, architecture and the decorative or applied arts were torn down. Architects now engaged in all facets of design, from window catches to wallpapers. Structure and ornament were conceived as an entity.

This New Art was both a local and global phenomenon, as seen in the myriad alternative terms coined at the time. It is known as Art Nouveau in France and Belgium. Jugendstil, literally 'youth style' in Germany, Scandinavia and the Baltic countries. Munich, Vienna, Berlin and Budapest witnessed a Secession, a younger generation breaking away from traditional institutions. In Italy, Stile Liberty expressed Italian unification (*Risorgimento*), while in Catalonia Modernista architects were driven by a desire to forge an identity distinct from Castilian Spain. Clearly these different terms do not simply reflect linguistic alternatives; German Jugendstil is stylistically very different to Belgian/French Art Nouveau, while Catalonian Modernisme is framed by local, nationalistic imperatives.

Crane, 'Triton's spear', *Flora's Feast A Masque of Flowers*, London: Cassell & Co., (1889).

Origins

The sources for the stylistic evolution of Art Nouveau/Jugendstil can be found in later Pre-Raphaelite and Symbolist paintings, especially those of Dante Gabriel Rossetti (1828–82) and Edward Burne-Jones (1833–98); the later wallpaper and fabric patterns of William Morris (1834–96); the graphic designs of Walter Crane (1845–1915); Japonisme; and the craft revival. As a leading spokesperson for both the Arts and Crafts and the New Art, following Morris' death in 1896, the role of Crane was crucial. His designs for illustrated books, notably *Flora's Feast A Masque of Flowers* (1889), and his wallpapers, *Woodnotes* (1887, V&A) and *Fairy Garden* (1890, V&A) are often identified as 'proto-Art Nouveau'. *Peacock Garden* (1889) won a Gold Medal at the 1889 Paris Exposition Universelle. Now acknowledged as the pre-eminent Art Nouveau architect, Belgian architect Victor Horta (1861–1947) was familiar with Crane's books and wallpapers, providing a link between London and

Horta, l'Hotel Frison, Sablon, Brussels (1894).

Eiffel Tower, entrance to the Exposition Universelle, Paris (1887–89).

Brussels. Horta's l'Hotel Tassel (1892–93) is recognized as the first expression of the new architectural style. His 'biomorphic whiplash' epitomizes the curvilinear vocabulary associated with Belgian and French Art Nouveau. Brussels, rather than Paris, is seen as the 'cradle' of the New Art.

In France, a turning point was reached at the 1889 Paris Exposition Universelle. The Eiffel Tower encapsulates a new era of iron and glass, materials that were transformed from utilitarian into beautiful architectural forms. These materials, already commonplace for railway stations and warehouses, were now daringly used in civic and domestic buildings. Iron provided not only the structure but also the embellishment in the form of balconies and awnings. Ceramics were used both externally and internally, and stained glass brought colour and light. The defining technology was electric light or 'artificial sunshine'; some six million light bulbs were used at the 1900 Paris Exposition Universelle.

STOLLWERCK'SCHE CHOKOLADE.

Trade card for Stollwerck's Chocolate, Palace of Electricity, Exposition Universelle, Paris (1900).

von Hansen, Parliament, Ringstrasse, Vienna (1874–83).

Breaking with the Past?

All the New Art movements shared one priority, the desire to come up with something fresh that broke with rehashed historical styles that were seen to be both outmoded and inappropriate. According to Franco-German entrepreneur Samuel Siegfried Bing (1838–1905), the originator of the term *l'Art Nouveau*, innovators were driven by 'the hatred of stagnation' that had paralysed art for the best part of the century[3]. Historicism, which saw the revival of architectural styles as diverse as neo-Romanesque and neo-Rococo, had dominated the mid-nineteenth century; the famous Ring in Vienna exemplifies this architectural melange with a neo-Attic parliament (1874–83, Theophil Edvard von Hansen), a neo-Gothic city hall (1872–83, Friedrich Schmidt) and a neo-Renaissance opera house (1861–69, August Sicard von Sicardsburg and Eduard van der Nüll). In the era of 'Iron and Glass', a period often referred to as the Second Industrial Revolution (c.1870–1914), such architectural forms seemed entirely misplaced.

While all agreed that historic styles were no longer relevant to modern life, it was still possible to learn from the past. Horta argued one should 'study the past as much as one can, to discover its acquired truths, the fundamental principles, to use them as part of a common heritage of knowledge'. But 'he had no right to copy'[4]. Horta would have consulted the publications of French architectural theorist, Eugène Emmanuel Viollet-le-Duc (1814–79), who spent his life studying Gothic architecture. His first-hand knowledge came from restoring many iconic buildings damaged during the French Revolution: Notre-Dame de Paris, Amiens Cathedral and Carcassonne. Viollet-le-Duc's encyclopaedic *Dictionnaire raisonné de l'architecture française du XIe au XVIe siècle* (Reasoned Dictionary of French Architecture 11th–16th century) (1854–68), which contained a wealth of exact structural data plus extensive design analysis, provided the intellectual impetus for the French Gothic Revival. He championed the Gothic as he believed it to be the national style of France: 'What we want, *messieurs*, is the return of an art

Schmidt, City Hall,
Ringstrasse, Vienna
(1872–83).

which was born in our country. . . Leave to Rome what belongs to Rome, and to Athens what belongs to Athens. Rome didn't want our Gothic (and was perhaps the only one in Europe to reject it) and they were right, because when one has the good fortune to possess a national architecture, the best thing is to keep it'[5]. This desire to create a 'national style' underpins the differing manifestations of Art Nouveau and Jugendstil. In Nancy, eighteenth-century Rococo forms provided a tangible link to a previous golden age, while Catalonian Modernisme drew on both its medieval and Islamic past.

The influence of neo-Rococo can be clearly seen in Horta's designs for furniture; 'The most widespread style of interior decoration from 1830 almost to the end of the century, the domestic qualities of its rounded and comfortable forms outweighed the virtues of Gothic, the Renaissance and Classicism'[6]. Horta's style was likened to 'Louis XV, but slimmer and more austere, a Calvinist Louis XV'[7]. Comparisons to neo-Rococo scrolls and curlicues or Gothic fan vaulting suggested continuity, an evolution or re-imagining, rather than an abrupt break with the past. Seen in this way, Art Nouveau could be viewed as a natural progression and accepted into the great pantheon of European styles.

Horta, chair designed for l'Hotel Aubecq, Brussels (1899–1902).
Musée Fin-de-Siècle, Brussels.

DOUZIÈME ENTRETIEN   (fig. 18)

SALLE VOÛTÉE

Viollet-le-Duc, design for a concert hall (1864) published in
Entretiens sur l'architecture et Dictionnaire du mobilier (1863–72).

Rational Architecture

Viollet-le-Duc argued Gothic principles could be
expressed in modern materials – cast iron, brick and
tiles. These materials should be used honestly, they
'should indicate their function by the form they are
given; that stone clearly appears as stone, iron as iron,
wood as wood; that these materials as well as taking the
forms which suit their nature, are in harmony with each
other'[8]. He advocated the use of iron skeletal frames,
providing they kept the original balance of forces found
in medieval structures. Honesty demanded that supporting iron beams should be exposed. The exterior
façade ought to reflect the interior plan; practicality
and convenience outweighed symmetry. Above all he

argued architectural forms should be adapted to their
function, rather than conforming to a style. Viollet-le-
Duc's concept of 'rational architecture' had a profound
impact on succeeding generations. His *Entretiens sur
l'architecture et Dictionnaire du mobilier* (Conversations on Architecture and Dictionary of Furniture),
published 1858–72, translated into English as *Dis-
courses on Architecture* (1874–81), systematized his
architectural philosophy. The concept of 'form follows
function' would be invoked by many Modernist architects, although the phrase is attributed to Chicago
architect Louis Sullivan (1856–1924).

Nature as a Cipher for Change

To shake off 'old memories', the way to rejuvenate all
branches of the arts was to take nature as a 'trust-
worthy guide'[9]. Many designers equated the natural
world with modernity, seeing human civilization as
a 'cosmic regime of advance, following evolutionist
tendencies . . . with movement through time and the
physical and metaphysical transformation of society';
their 'ideologically driven-vision of nature' embodied the struggle of human existence[10]. Phytomorphic
or plant-forms were abstracted into sinuous flowing
lines seen to embody energy or the life force. The cycle
of death and rejuvenation appealed to the *fin de siècle*
mindset, the dying century on the cusp of renewal.

    The line, curvilinear and linear, defines both Art
Nouveau and Jugendstil. Horta and Hector Guimard
(1867–1942) epitomize Art Nouveau's floral/curvi-
linear language, with its reliance on *coup de fouet* or
whiplash curls. The posters of Czech-born Alphonse
Mucha (1860–1939), with their Pre-Raphaelite-in-
spired femmes fatales caught in a tangle of plant
forms, have come to exemplify the style. With her
downcast eyes and enigmatic smile, his sculpture *La
Nature* (1899–1900, Musée Fin-de-Siècle, Brussels)
embodies the *femme idéale* of the *fin de siècle*. Shown
at numerous international exhibitions, *La Nature*
was transformed into an icon. The Parisian jeweller
René Lalique (1860–1945) exploited the concept of

Guimard, entrance to Castel Béranger, 16th arrondissement, Paris (1895–98).

Mucha, bronze sculpture *La Nature* (1899–1900), Musée Fin-de-Siècle, Brussels.

Hankar, Maison Ciamberlani, Rue Defacqz 48, Saint-Gilles, Brussels (1897).

metamorphosis, the female form caught on the cusp of transformation. Although a *femme fragile* emerging from a flower appears benign, transmuted into dragonflies or serpents Lalique's *femmes fatales* are clearly dangerous. Broadly speaking the most excessive floral forms appear to peter out after 1905, as a more restrained linearity takes over.

Contemporaries of Horta in Brussels, Paul Hankar (1859–1901), Henry van de Velde (1863–1957) and Gustave Serrurier-Bovy (1858–1910) had already opted for a controlled use of line and abstract forms such as compass-inscribed profiles and geometric shapes. This use of line was inspired by Japonisme, while the sobriety was instilled by the English Arts and Crafts movement. The geometric idiom was absorbed by the architects and designers of the Vienna Secession, notably Otto Wagner (1841–1918) and Josef Hoffmann (1870–1956), who were also influenced by the refined linearity of the Glasgow school led by Charles Rennie Mackintosh (1868–1928). At the time Bing noted two parallel currents, 'the system of floral elements' and a system of 'purely ornamental lines'[11]. The Belgian/French curvilinear school, the 'French twist' as it was nicknamed in America, and the Scottish/German/Viennese linear-geometric school are now defined as Floral Art Nouveau and Geometric or Perpendicular Art Nouveau/Jugendstil. With Mackintosh and Hoffmann favouring the square, the grid or checkerboard came to dominate their way of thinking. The linear approach is seen as pre-figuring both post-War Art Deco and Modernism.

The International National Style

Driven by a nationalistic impulse, theorists encouraged architects and designers to invent their own brand of Modernism rather than importing foreign forms; Alexander Koch (1860–1939), founder of the influential arts magazine *Deutsche Kunst und Dekoration* (1897–1935), feared German artists and craftsmen were 'being held spellbound by a foreign language of form; the idiom of a domestic,

Bing, 'Industrial Design. Gourd tendrils on a chequered ground', *Artistic Japan Illustrations and Essays*, No.4, August 1888, plate DD.

individually German art language is in danger of being lost'[12]. Following the 1900 Paris Exposition, architectural historian and theorist, Hermann Muthesius (1861–1927) began to search for a new *Volkskunst*, a people's art that was distinctly German and not dependent on the delicate Rococo-inspired forms of Belgian-French Art Nouveau. Germany needed to develop its own modern style. This was a matter of national pride as well as economic survival. Searching for 'Germanness' inevitably encouraged an interest in folk art and the handicrafts.

The search for a modern national style was often directed by a visionary architect; Horta in Brussels; Guimard in Paris; Mackintosh in Glasgow; Wagner and Hoffmann in Vienna; Joseph Maria Olbrich (1867–1908) and Peter Behrens in Darmstadt; Ödön

Eisenstein, Lyebedinskiy apartment building, Alberta iela 4 (Alberta Street), Riga (c.1904).

Lechner in Budapest (1845–1914); Lluís Domènech i Montaner (1850–1923) and Antoni Gaudí i Cornet (1852–1926) in Barcelona and Louis Sullivan in Chicago all developed their own distinctive voice or brand[13]. Working in partnership, Herman Gesellius (1874–1916), Armas Lindgren (1872–1929), and Eliel Saarinen (1873–1950) shaped the Jugendstil architecture of the Finnish capital, Helsinki. Riga was transformed by Konstantīns Pēkšēns (1859–1928) and Russian-born Mikhail Osipovich Eisenstein (1861–1921). The Latvian capital Riga boasts the highest concentration of Art Nouveau/Jugendstil architecture anywhere in the world. Roughly one-third of all the buildings, mostly multi-storey apartments, in the centre of Riga are in the new style. This building boom (1904–14) was fuelled by economic prosperity. It also reflects the 'Latvian National Awakening', the desire to express a distinct Latvian identity through art and architecture.

Encompassing a great variety of personal expressions, consistently anti-rationalist, flamboyant and even subversive, the New Art's strength lies in its diversity and divergencies. Creative freedom, allowing the imagination full reign, sanctioned 'each individual

to impress his personality upon the places in which he passes his life'[14]. In contrast Art Deco, which fully emerged after the First World War, is characterized by international conformity. Based on straight lines and geometric forms, a machine aesthetic that celebrates speed, Art Deco buildings look much the same whether in New York, Miami, Napier (New Zealand) or London. The New Art was bound to be denigrated by post-war era rationalists and Modernists who lauded functionalism and objected to unnecessary ornamentation.

International Exhibitions and the Media

National differences become apparent at the international exhibitions held in Barcelona (1888), Paris (1889), Chicago (1893), Venice Biennale (1895), Brussels (1897), Paris (1900), Vienna (1900), Glasgow (1901), and Turin (1902), an exemplary 'modern' city[15]. Art Nouveau made its debut at the 1897 Brussels International Exhibition; twenty-seven countries participated. The attendance figures exceeded 7.5 million people. Although Leopold, King of the

Hankar, Palace of the Colonies, International Exposition, Tervuren, Brussels (1897).

Wagner, 'Golden House', apartment block on Wienzeile, Naschmarkt, Vienna (1898).

Olbrich, Ernst Ludwig Haus, Mathildenhöhe, Darmstadt (1900–01).

Sneyers, Marjolaine, rue de la Madeleine, Brussels (1904).

Belgians, was not a fan of Art Nouveau, he appreciated its potential; it was both eye-catching and provocative. It was Edmond van Eetvelde, General Administrator of Foreign Affairs of the Congo Free State, who opened Leopold's eyes to Art Nouveau. As a result, he commissioned the Colonial Palace at Tervuren to celebrate the opportunities offered by the Congo, at that time his personal fiefdom. The exhibition's four sections were entrusted to Hankar, van de Velde, Serrurier-Bovy and Georges Hobé. A hall of honour designed by Hankar was dedicated to chryselephantine sculpture: here you could admire the combination of ivory carving with silver or bronze, a concept perfected by Pierre-Charles Van der Stappen and Philippe Wolfers. Henri Privat-Livemont, nicknamed the Belgian Mucha, produced posters for the exposition.

Exhibitions generated an international dialogue; Wagner encountered Hankar's *l'Art nouveau géométrique* at the Colonial Palace. On returning to Vienna, Wagner developed his own Modernist idiom exemplified by the so-called Golden House, Wienzeile 38. Olbrich, who developed his style working on Wagner's Wiener Stadtbahn projects, left for Darmstadt in 1899, playing a major role in the development of German Jugendstil. Encountering the work of Olbrich and Hoffmann at the Prima Esposizione Internazionale d'Arte Decorativa Moderna (First International Exposition of Modern Decorative Arts) held in Turin (1902), Léon Sneyers (1877–1949) and Paul Hamesse (1877–1956), Hankar's protégés, took Jugendstil/Secession geometric-linear forms back to Brussels. This complicated toing and froing illustrates the complex relationship between different design schools.

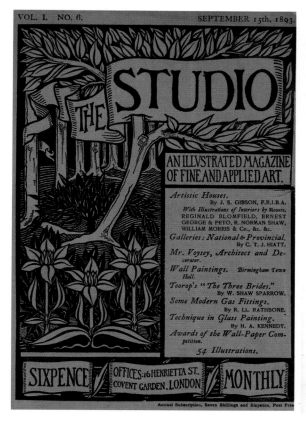

The Studio, Vol. 1, 15 September 1893, cover designed by Aubrey Beardsley.

Jugend, front cover, 30 May 1896, designed by Hans Pfaff.

Magazines

New magazines also played a significant role in spreading the word. Launched in 1893, *The Studio: An Illustrated Magazine of Fine and Applied Art*, which gave almost equal weight to the fine and decorative arts, ushered in a new generation of avant-garde magazines. Following his retirement from the wool and silk trades, Charles Holme (1848–1923), the founder and editor, devoted his energies to promoting modern art. Travelling extensively, 'the idea of an art magazine crystallized around his recurring observation that the chief barrier between countries was language'[16]. The first edition carried articles on the illustrator Aubrey Beardsley (1872–98) and the Arts and Crafts architect C. F. A. Voysey (1857–1941). Also published in Paris, the magazine was international

in scope, promoting both the Arts and Crafts and the New Art; it introduced Voysey and Mackintosh to a European audience. The American edition, *The International Studio* had its own editorial staff. It carried different content although many articles from the English edition were reprinted. It was published in New York by John Lane & Company from May 1897; it is an important source for documenting the international exhibitions.

Support for modernity flourished with astonishing vigor. In Berlin the art critic Julius Meier-Graefe (1867–1935) and the poet Richard Dehmel founded *Pan* (1895–1900), a literary and visual arts magazine. In January 1896 *Jugend: Illustrierte Wochenschrift für Kunst und Leben* (*Youth: The illustrated weekly magazine of art and lifestyle*) was launched in Munich; it gave its name to the New Art movement in Germany, Jugendstil. Drawing inspiration from international currents, its founder George Hirth (1841–1916) endorsed a national rebirth of the arts. Darmstadt had its own 'media activist', Alexander Koch. Marrying the daughter of Carl Hochstätter, a wallpaper manufacturer, Koch took a keen interest in contemporary interior design, developing several influential trade journals. The *Tapeten-Zeitung* (Wall-paper News) appeared from 1888, while *Zeitschrift für Innendekoration* (Interior Decoration) launched two years later. Van de Velde contributed to *Innendekoration*, highlighting the transnational character of the New Art; for a few years a French language edition of the journal was available. Koch himself showed a preference for British design, being especially fond of Mackintosh and the Arts and Crafts architect Mackay Hugh Baillie Scott (1865–1945). In the first issue of *Deutsche Kunst und Dekoration*, launched in 1897, Koch urged his readers to integrate art into their daily lives. Following Arts and Crafts precepts, he railed against shoddy mass-produced commodities, advocating craftsmanship and the use of high-quality materials.

Gesamtkunstwerk, or Total Artwork

While for many consumers the New Art was just another passing fashion, for those who fully embraced the ethos it was a lifestyle choice. The New Art was all-encompassing, a *'Renouveau dans l'Art'* – 'the Revival of Art' that sought to revitalize literature and music, painting and sculpture, architecture and interior décor, dress and jewellery[17]. All artistic manifestations now had equal rank.

A life lived in art could only be achieved by uniting all the arts, a synthesis expressed as a gesamtkunstwerk. This ethos sought to unify all the elements of a building into a complete whole; a building as a 'total artwork'. An architectural term, its origins lie in the aesthetic ideals of the German opera composer Richard Wagner (1813–83). In his 1849 essays 'Art and Revolution' and 'The Artwork of the Future', he speaks of unifying all works of art through the

theatre, a synthesis of the poetic, visual, musical and dramatic arts. The individual arts are subordinated to a common purpose, creating a totally immersive experience. Thus, the perfect interior was to engage all the senses of the body: sight, hearing, touch, smell and even taste. The concept of the 'total artwork' transformed both public institutions and private homes. Paintings, furniture, metalwork, ceramics, glass and textiles were integrated into a harmonious ensemble. In Vienna the *Raumkunst* concept (room art) privileged 'beautiful space'; this way of thinking encouraged fewer objects. Decluttering meant individual objects could be properly appreciated and experienced; they became 'key notes'.

The quest for unity encouraged architects to design or control all aspects of interior décor, especially furniture and lighting. Exteriors, interiors, furnishings, and even the landscape were to be orchestrated by the vision of one man – the architect. This impulse can be traced back to the neo-Classical architect Robert Adam (1728–92) and the neo-Gothic architect Augustus Welby Pugin (1812–52) who fashioned completely unified ensembles, extending to the choice or design of table silver, china and glassware.

However, a building and every aspect of its design did not have to be the work of a single hand. Some architects chose to collaborate, bringing in colleagues to design furniture, fabrics and light fittings, for example architect Philip Webb (1831–1915) working alongside Morris & Co. Nevertheless, the goal was the same: to create a stylistically harmonious work of art. Each project, which could be likened to a musical composition, was to be unique. Mackintosh exemplifies this desire to achieve an over-arching harmonization, or *toutes ensemble*, which could extend to the choice of cutlery and table linens.

Perfection or Tyranny?

While the gesamtkunstwerk expressed the originality of the architect-designer, it rarely allowed the patron to exert his own preferences. Baillie Scott feared the

Henry van de Velde, 'Reformed Dress', *Deutsche Kunst und Dekoration*, Band X, April–Sept 1902, p.378.

homeowner might ruin his conception: 'It is a painful thing for an architect to design a mantlepiece for which he dares not hope to choose the ornaments, and which may become a resting place for he knows not what atrocities in china and glass'[18].

In their own homes, architect-designers even attempted to integrate the occupants through dress and accessories. Maria van der Velde, wife of the architect, was harmonized through the patterns on her attire to the point where one speculates that she was trapped in the gesamtkunstwerk[19]! The Viennese architect and designer Adolf Loos (1870–1933) loathed the gesamtkunstwerk as pursued by his contemporaries Josef Hoffmann and Koloman Moser (1868–1918), founders of the Wiener Werkstätte (Vienna Workshops). Loos penned a salutatory warning; in the *Poor Little Rich Man* (1900), a rich man, having everything but art in his life, transforms his house into a work of art. His architect, who extols the virtues of the gesamtkunstwerk, designs every detail of the rich man's home, covering every surface with elaborate ornament; he anticipates everything, even the pattern on the rich man's slippers. But when the rich man's family ply him with birthday presents, bought at the most approved establishments, the architect, summoned to find correct places for them

Hokusai, *The Great Wave off Kanagawa* (1829–33), private collection.

in his composition, is furious. His client has dared to accept presents about which he, the architect, has not been consulted, for the house was finished, as was his client: he was complete!

The Cult of Japan

The taste for Japanese art was 'the most important single external influence on the European decorative and applied arts in the second half of the nineteenth century'[20]. This influence falls into clearly defined phases. During the 1850s and 1860s it was an enthusiasm shared by connoisseurs and collectors. By the 1870s Japonisme was in full swing amongst the fashion conscious, underpinning the so-called Art or Aesthetic movement (c.1860–1890); designers either tried to capture the spirit of Japanese design or appropriated indicative motifs – bamboo, cranes, fans, carp and patterns derived from silk kimonos popped up on ceramics, metalwork and textiles. Absorbed into popular culture, Japonisme became a craze and every household, high or low, was bedecked with Japanese paper fans and parasols and blue and white china.

Japonisme was given a new lease of life in the 1890s thanks to the Parisian dealer Samuel Bing, the decisive turning point for Art Nouveau/Jugendstil being the exhibition 'Maitres de l'estampe japonaise' held at the École des Beaux-Arts, Paris from 25 April to 22 May 1890. Unlike several earlier exhibitions, where a range of Japanese art and crafts objects had been shown together, Bing used this opportunity to concentrate exclusively on the art of the *ukiyo-e* (floating world) woodcut with a display of over a thousand illustrated books and individual prints.

Turning Japanese

With the signing of the first commercial treaty between Japan and America in 1854, more than 200 years of Japanese seclusion came to an end. Import shops quickly sprung up in Paris: J. G. Houssaye's À la porte chinoise (At the Chinese Gate) was established on Rue Vivienne by 1855. Avant-garde artists were fascinated by *ukiyo-e* woodcut prints by Katsushika Hokusai (1760–1849) and Utagawa Hiroshige (1797–1858). They admired the bold asymmetrical compositions, the clarity of line and colour, and the lightness and airiness of Japanese prints. So novel was the art of East Asia that the distinction between Japanese and Chinese traditions was blurred into the catch-all term, Japonisme.

At the 1862 London International Exhibition, the retired first Consul-General to Japan, Sir Rutherford Alcock (1809–97) showed his personal collection. It created a sensation. The exotic Japanese treasures – handcrafted pottery, lacquer, netsuke (button-like toggles) and inrō (crafted boxes) – seemed exquisite to the eyes of a public weary of tawdry mass-produced wares. Farmer and Rogers purchased much of the collection for resale in their new 'Oriental Warehouse'. Arthur Lasenby Liberty (1843–1917), who joined the company in 1862, found his vocation: 'It was the only shop in London that then dealt in things from the East. The products of Japan were then an absolute novelty, and they attracted the attention of the artistic world'[21]. Liberty opened his own establishment on Regent Street in 1875; the first catalogue, disseminating Oriental wares and styles to a wide audience, was issued in 1881.

The most popular commodities were textiles, notably silks. Brocades and embroidery offered a rich source of traditional patterns, many of which also bore a symbolic resonance. Normally a single motif is repeated: the 'Wave Crest' (*Seigaiha*), rows of concentric arches forming a fan pattern, represented good luck; 'Hemp Leaf' (*Asanoha*), which resembles a hemp leaf, recalled durability, while 'Tortoise Shell' (*Kikkou*) symbolized longevity. The *mon* tradition, where objects are adopted as crests, identifying a person or family, influenced Mackintosh and his wife Margaret Macdonald Mackintosh (1864–1933). The best-known crest is the Imperial Seal of Japan or Chrysanthemum Flower Seal, a sixteen-petal chrysanthemum with sixteen tips of another row of petals showing behind. The architect Edward William Godwin (1833–86) adapted the Crane crest of the Mori clan for his peacock wallpaper (1872, V&A).

Godwin, Whistler and Dresser

Godwin, one of the leaders of the Aesthetic movement, made the quantum leap from polychromatic 'Ruskinian Gothic' (Northampton Guild Hall, 1861–64) to Anglo-Japanese. Godwin's fame rests on two commissions, the White House on Tite Street, Chelsea (1877–78, demolished in the 1960s) for the painter James McNeill Whistler (1834–1903), another well-known connoisseur of Japanese prints, and the interiors of Oscar Wilde's (1854–1900) house, also on Tite Street (1884–85). Godwin invoked the spirit of Japanese art, coordinating individual rooms through the variation of a single colour. Wilde's white dining room was one of the first of its kind; the poet and playwright described the dining room chairs as 'sonnets in ivory' and the table as a 'masterpiece in pearl'[22]. The spirit of Japan, linearity and minimalism, is expressed in a black cabinet Godwin designed for himself in 1867 (V&A). The grid, based on Japanese checker and grille patterns, was also adopted for the glazing bars of the windows for Whistler's White House and Keats House, also on Tite Street (1879–80), for the artist Frank Miles. Another source for the grid was the *shoji*, a door, window or room divider, traditionally a lattice of wood or bamboo covered with translucent paper. The checkerboard/grid also underpins Hankar's geometric Art Nouveau, Mackintosh's Glasgow style and Hoffmann's Viennese Secession forms.

While on display at the 1862 London International Exhibition the designer and theorist Christopher Dresser (1834–1904) was able to see Japanese *objets d'art* at first hand. In 1877 Dresser was one of the first artists to visit Japan; he was commissioned by Tiffany of New York to acquire Japanese objects on their behalf. Dresser recorded his impressions in *Japan, its Architecture, Art and Art-Manufactures* (1882). In 1879 Dresser went into partnership with Charles Holme, opening 'a new and very expensive emporium of Oriental manufactures'. In 1882 Holme would visit Japan himself in the company of Liberty and the artist Alfred East, who had been commissioned to paint the landscape and its people.

Godwin, sideboard, made by William Watt & Co. (1867–70), V&A, London.

Samuel Bing

Retiring from his business dealings, Holme became a champion of modern design, founding *The Studio* magazine in 1893. Bing's career follows a similar trajectory, initially promoting oriental art before founding L'Art Nouveau in 1895. Bing's promotion of Japanese art was crucial to the development of Art Nouveau; his monthly journal, *Le Japon Artistique*, first published in 1888, ran to three volumes. Published in French, English, and German editions, the articles considered a wide variety of Japanese arts including architecture, painting, woodblock printing, pottery, and even poetry and theatre. The magazine's reproductions served as models for artists and designers. Nearly every issue has plant and flower images – gourd, fern, iris, lily, peony, chrysanthemum – with an emphasis on stalk forms. Cranes, swallows, butterflies or splayed fans are set against check, grille or other patterns.

Bing, *Artistic Japan*, front cover, Vol.1, May 1888.

Masters of the Japanese Print

A turning point was initiated by Bing's 'Maitres de l'estampe japonaise' (1890) as both European artists and the general public discovered the works of the Japanese masters. Bing showcased the full range of *ukiyo-e*, presenting the art of the woodcut within an evolutionary historical framework. The later masters,

Moronobu, *Two Lovers* (c.1675–80) Met Museum, NY.

Hokusai, Hiroshige and Kunisada, were preceded by the 'classical' generation, Torii Kiyonaga (1752–1815) and Kitagawa Utamaro (c.1753–1806). To these were added a whole new stratum, the 'primitive' artists Suzuki Harunobu (1724–70), Isoda Koryūsai (1735–90), and above all Hishikawa Moronobu (1618–94). Their works appeared more graphically conceived than those of later printmakers, relying on strength of line and even further divorced from European illusionistic art, eschewing the naturalistic use of colour and paying little respect to perspective. In addition to pictorial minimalism, Moronobu used a broad sinuous line, referred to as his 'singing line', to delineate the curvature of the human form, as seen in his *shunga* (erotica). The effect of this line was further pronounced by his preference for black and white. Commenting on Moronobu, Bing observed, 'At no later time can one find a richer, livelier, firmer stroke. His graphic compositions are as sculptural reliefs. The stroke speaks alone but says it all; the stroke alone suffices to convey form, far better than the most skilful shading'[23]. According to Klaus Berger, Moronobu's curvilinear graphic forms 'paved the way for the convoluted arabesque of Jugendstil and Art Nouveau; his abstract linear patterns led to the posters of Toulouse-Lautrec and the ornamental patterning of Gustav Klimt'[24].

The exhibition Maitres de l'estampe japonaise attracted artists from home and abroad; Mucha from Prague, Edvard Munch from Norway, Jan Toorop from Holland and August Endell from Munich. Apparently, they all fell 'under the spell of the power of line that they had discovered in the Japanese "primitives"'[25]. For those unable to travel to Paris, Bing's expansionist spirit led him to show his best Hokusais in London (1890) and his masterpieces in Boston (1894). In 1893, another extravaganza organized by Bing showcased Utamaro and Hiroshige at the gallery

Guimard, *banquette de fumoir* for the billiard room of Albert Roy (1897–98), Musée d'Orsay.

Domènech i Montaner, Hospital de Santa Creu i Sant Pau, Barcelona (1902–30).

of Paul Durand-Ruel, the great impresario of the Impressionists, revealing the link between Japanese woodcuts and modern painting.

In the years following Bing's exhibitions, the New Art blossomed. The asymmetrical linear forms of Guimard, the creator of the Paris Métro, were clearly informed by the 'pure line' of Japanese art:

> Line in Guimard, just as in his Japanese guides, is a living incarnation of natural laws. Thus, in an old Japanese manual, there is a catalogue of eighteen different types of line, with such descriptions as 'floating silk thread', 'ropes', 'water lines' or 'bent metal wire'. . . [Guimard] had an inborn sense of the inner tension of line.[26]

The expressive power of the line inevitably led to abstraction, arabesques dominating his textiles, furniture, stained glass and metalwork for the Castel Béranger, Paris (1895–98). His *banquette de fumoir* for the billiard room of the pharmacist Albert Roy (1897–98), now in the Musée d'Orsay, Paris, appears to have been inspired by Hokusai's famous print *Under the Wave off Kanagawa* (1830–33). Japonisme allowed architects and designers to cast off Historicism and imitation.

Democratic Style

It has been claimed that the New Art was a truly democratic style as it went beyond elite, enlightened avant-garde circles, reshaping the lives of ordinary people. It was in all senses popular, encompassing posters and printers and even commercial packaging; boxes of biscuits or packets of tea now carried distinctive Mucha-style women with masses of hair and elusive expressions. Public buildings were transformed:

schools, hospitals, town halls and railway stations were all modernized. This was not just a question of functionality or utility but also beauty. Streets were transformed with stunning façades, covered with tiles, mosaics and sculptures. Department stores and cafés were now palaces of art. Art transformed all aspects of life. This is seen most clearly in Barcelona, where Modernisme was a social and political as well as artistic movement. Domènech was both an architect and a politican with a single desire to regenerate and modernize his country. While the latest European models were to be imported, everything that could be identified with Catalan culture had to be recovered: its history, its culture, its language, in effect its identity. Modernista objects carry symbols of Catalan identity, the national flag and St George, the patron saint of Catalonia, alongside dragons and roses, predominate. A mythic past was reinvented in the name of patriotism. Thus, Catalonia Modernisme was expressly Art for the People. Domènech buildings spoke to this democratic ideal. The Hospital de Sant Pau and the Palau de la Música Catalana in Barcelona and the Insitut Pere Matta in Reus are all public institutions: a hospital, concert hall and psychiatric centre. The health of the nation, both physical and spiritual, was an expression of the will to modernize. However, these institutions were not funded by the State but through numerous associations and individual philanthropists. There is not a single town or city in Catalonia without a Modernist building of some kind: a factory, a school or apartment block. As champions of modernity, architects and designers were determined to embrace the twentieth century.

Decline

While Paris 1900 marks the apex of Art Nouveau, it also signals a decline. According to Bing, 'the insistent scourge of tortured, swollen and tentacular lines grew more and more aggravated thus causing an abuse most harmful to the reputation of L'Art Nouveau'[27]. 'Counterfeited by the army of profit-seekers', the style was bastardized and exploited by commercial manufacturers, the market flooded with crudely designed and poorly made commodities. The 'leaders of industry' were responsible for exaggerating forms, lines 'interlacing in all directions, writhing into fantastic expansions, meeting in snail-spirals'; a gullible public accepted 'this product under the official title which assured its success'[28]. Art Nouveau became equated with eccentricity and excess.

There was bound to be a reaction amongst the upper echelons. Art critics argued that rather than copying French stylistic forms, nations needed to develop their own modern idiom. Such national trends, Glasgow style, Jugendstil, Secession and Liberty, were fully expressed at Turin 1902. This shift could be said to give the New Art a second wind, with architects moving away from curvilinear to linear and geometric forms, precursors of Art Deco and Modernism.

DAS DEUTSCHE REICH.

Behrens, Hamburger Vorhalle des Deutschen Reiches, at the Prima Esposizione Internazionale d'Arte Decorativa Moderna, Turin, 1902. *Deutsch Kunst und Dekoration*, Band X, April–Sept 1902, p.599.

Notes

1. Fahr-Becker, Gabriele, *Art Nouveau*, Potsdam: h. f. Ullmann, 2015, p.6.
2. Berger, Klaus, *Japonisme in Western Painting from Whistler to Matisse*, Cambridge: Cambridge University Press, 1993, p.238.
3. Bing, Samuel, 'l'Art Nouveau', *The Craftsman*, Vol. V, No.1, October 1903, p.229, reprinted in Robert Koch, *Artistic America, Tiffany Glass and Art Nouveau*, Cambridge, Mass and London: MIT Press.
4. Dierkens-Aubry, F., *The Horta Museum*, Saint-Gilles, Brussels: Musea Nostra, 1990, p.37.
5. Viollet-le-Duc, Eugène, *Du style Gothique au Dix-Neuvieme Siècle* (June 1846) at Project Gutenberg, accessed July 2019.
6. Thornton, Peter, *Authentic Decor: The Domestic Interior 1620–1920*, London: Crescent Books, 1993, p.216.
7. *Le Peuple*, 1899, referring to Maison du Peuple; Dierkens-Aubry, p.40.
8. *Entretien*, p.472; Dierkens-Aubry, p.32.
9. Bing, 1903, p.229.
10. Greenhalgh, Paul (ed.), *Art Nouveau 1890–1914*, London: V&A Publications, 2000, p.21.
11. Bing, 1903, p.236.
12. Ulmer, Renate, *Jugendstil in Darmstadt*, Darmstadt: Eduard Roether Verlag, 1997, p.52.
13. Howard, Jeremy, *Art Nouveau: International and National Styles in Europe*, Manchester/New York: Manchester University, 1996.
14. Bing, 1903, p.236.
15. The headquarters of Fiat Automobiles was established in Turin in 1899.
16. Holme, Bryan, *The Studio: A Bibliography. The First Fifty Years 1893–1943*. London: Simms and Reed, 1978, p.5.
17. Bing, Samuel, 'l'Art Nouveau', *The Architectural Record*, Vol. 12, 1902, p.216, reprinted in Robert Koch, *Artistic America, Tiffany Glass and Art Nouveau*, Cambridge, Mass and London: MIT Press.
18. Baillie Scott, Mackay Hugh, 'The Fireplace of the Suburban House', *The Studio*, Vol. 6, 1896, p.105.
19. Anderson, Anne, '"She weaves by night and day, a magic web with colours gay": trapped in the Gesamtkunstwerk or the dangers of unifying dress and interiors', Alla Myzelev and John Potvin (eds.), *Fashion, Interior Design and the Contours of Modern Identity*, Aldershot: Ashgate, 2010, pp.43–66.
20. Aslin, Elizabeth, *E. W. Godwin Furniture and Interior Decoration*, London: The Fine Arts Society, 1986, p.9.
21. Ashmore, Sonia, 'Lasenby Liberty (1843–1917) and Japan', Hugh Cortazzi (ed.), *Britain and Japan: Biographical Portraits, Vol. IV*, London: Routledge and the Japan Society, 2002, p.144.
22. Aslin, p.19.
23. Berger, p.188.
24. Berger, p.190.
25. Berger, p.188.
26. Dore Ashton, *Le Monde*, 22 May 1970, quoted Berger, p.239.
27. Bing, 1903, p.240.
28. Bing, 1903, pp.234–35.

Chapter Two

New Art: Art Nouveau, Jugendstil, Secession, Modernisme or Liberty

T HE PLETHORA OF NAMES BY WHICH THE New Art is known is born out of its national and regional variations. French Art Nouveau takes its name from Samuel Bing's Maison l'Art Nouveau, a commercial gallery opened in Paris (1895; destroyed). Nancy, the capital of Lorraine, is noted for its own Art Nouveau school, École de Nancy, officially founded in 1901. In German-speaking areas, including Scandinavia, the new design ethos is termed Jugendstil (Youth-style) after the avant-garde magazine *Jugend* (1896). Munich (1892), Vienna (1897) and Berlin (1898) witnessed a breakaway from conservative art institutions; Georg Hirth coined the term Secession (*Sezessionismus*) to characterize this dissent. The first German artists to 'secede' broke away from the Munich Artists' Association in 1892. Secession was prompted in Berlin when a landscape by Walter Leistikow was rejected by the state-run Association of Berlin Artists; Leistikow was at the forefront in promoting modern art. Similarly, in Vienna, a group led by Gustav Klimt (1862–1918) resigned from the Association of Austrian Artists, housed in the Vienna Künstlerhaus, in 1897.

In Darmstadt, reform came from above rather than below, when Grand Duke Ernst Ludwig (1868–1937) invited seven avant-garde artists to form a colony on the Mathildenhöhe; here the aim was economic as well as cultural rejuvenation. The Darmstädter Künstlerkolonie also fostered local identity, repositioning Darmstadt as a forward-looking, modern city, within the newly formed Reich.

In Italy Stile Floreale was also dubbed Liberty style after the famous London store, Liberty of Regent Street, which had done so much since its founding in 1875 to promote artistic fabrics, ceramics and metalwork. But Liberty, meaning 'liberation', carried an obvious connotation given Italy's recent unification.

While all architects and designers turned to nature in search of a metaphor for modernity, each developed their own idiom. With individuality the driving force, Mackintosh, Horta, Guimard, Lechner and Gaudí all stand out as developing their own distinctive style that has left its mark on their native city. In evolving their own artistic language, they were all keenly aware of the design reforms associated with the English Aesthetic movement and the emergence of the Arts and Crafts.

Le Style Anglais: The Aesthetic Movement and Arts and Crafts

In England, one of the first nations to industrialize, the catalysts for change were John Ruskin (1819–1900) and William Morris. Furnishing his new home, Red House, Bexleyheath (1859, Philip Webb), Morris was faced with commercial designs, all too often badly made, that lacked artistry. Rallying his friends, who numbered architects and artists, Morris established his own commercial decorating firm, initially named Morris, Marshall, Faulker & Co. (1861–75). Later this would become simply Morris & Co. (1875–1940). As beauty was a 'positive necessity of life', he was determined to transform the world with beautiful things[1]. Inevitably things lovingly crafted would be more expensive than those mass produced by machine, a conundrum that dogged the Arts and Crafts movement.

For Morris, who gave his first public lecture on the decorative arts in 1877, architecture or the 'art of house-building begins it all'; it stood to reason that 'if we want art to begin at home… Have nothing in your houses that you do not know to be useful or believe to be beautiful'[2]. Morris's concept of 'art in the home' raised the status of wallpapers, curtains and carpets. Elevated to works of art they became the remit of the artist rather than the manufacturer. Design reform led artists down two very different paths: those who saw the answer in a return to the handicrafts and those who sought an alliance between art and industry. Christopher Dresser, England's foremost industrial designer, fully accepted the implications of mechanized production and stressed the importance of good design. The application of art to industry offered the artist new opportunities. Designing provided a good source of income and a means of establishing a reputation. Voysey began and ended his career designing 'flat patterns'. Renowned as an Arts and Crafts architect, Voysey was a very successful industrial designer. Selling patterns supplemented his income, especially in the lean years before he had established his reputation and after his practice declined c.1910. He sold his first wallpaper design in 1883; by the end of the decade his reputation was established at home and abroad.

The Aesthetic Movement

Commercial manufacturers realized the potential of 'Art at Home', commissioning designs or establishing specialist workshops. By the 1870s, the consumer could procure art wallpapers, art glass, art pottery and artistic dress. Any commodity with pretentions acquired the label 'art'. Walter Hamilton's *The Aesthetic Movement in England* (1882) argued it was about educating taste and cultivating an individual style. Oscar Wilde, the self-appointed spokesperson of the 'English Renaissance of Art', took it upon himself to educate both British and American audiences. At the heart of this design revolution lay the

House Beautiful, the desire to surround oneself with 'beautiful objects of everyday use'. German scholar Jakob von Falke (1825–93) deemed it a 'woman's aesthetic mission' to create a beautiful home, as an appreciation of the 'lesser or industrial arts' would cultivate good taste; 'it humanizes us and idealizes our life'[3]. The mantra became 'Art for Life's Sake'.

By the early 1880s taste had become a contentious issue. Lacking expertise, the wealthy could turn to their architect or interior decorator, a profession that was just emerging. Many relied on the plethora of domestic advice manuals that instructed the owner on the dos and don'ts of decorating a house. Architect and furniture designer Charles Locke Eastlake (1836–1906) led the way with *Hints on Household Taste* (1868). American journalist Clarence Cook's *House Beautiful*: *Essays on Beds and Tables, Stools and Candlesticks* (1878) gave its name to the entire vogue. These publications elevated interior decorating into an art form, a means of self-expression. Arranging a room was likened to painting a composition or orchestrating a symphony. The watch word was harmony, as *objets d'art*, an oriental blue and white vase, a piece of Venetian glass or a delicate embroidery, were to be arranged to form a pleasing whole. Decorative unity was largely achieved through complementary colours or tones. Art Nouveau/Jugendstil architects and designers developed this concept into the gesamtkunstwerk, in which every aspect of the interior was integrated into a 'total artwork'.

Arts and Crafts

The art industries created a consumer boom that was at odds with the ethical values implicit in the Arts and Crafts movement. A reformist ideology, born out of the impact of the Industrial Revolution and urban expansion, it sought a revival of the crafts claiming the machine had reduced men to slaves. The division of labour meant that few had pride in their work and they certainly rarely enjoyed it. It was no longer necessary to understand the relationship between materials, design and production. Conversely, the craftsman understood the properties and limits of the material he worked in. A true architect needed to understand the art of building, to be a practising craftsman. Philip Webb led the way, embracing all aspects of design and execution, from the pointing of brickwork, the design of staircase rails to window fittings. By extension furniture and furnishings were now considered integral to the overall scheme, falling within the architect's remit. According to Baillie Scott, 'each piece of furniture is a thing to be considered not entirely alone, but qualities depend in every case on the proper relation to a complete scheme when this furniture finds itself happily at home in a little world of colour and form'[4].

Ideally, design and making were undertaken by the same person but this was a tall order; it was more practical for an architect to build up a team of craftsmen. The interdependence of design and craft encouraged workshop practice, the designer working alongside the craftsman. Restoring the status of handwork was essential; skills that had been lost, due to industrialization, needed to be revived. With making a group process, the founding of brotherhoods or guilds became a natural outcome. The quality of the life of the worker was imperative, restoring pride and sense of accomplishment. Words were put into action with the founding of the Art Workers' Guild (1884), which provided a forum for discussing the relationship between architecture and the applied arts, and the Arts and Crafts Exhibition Society (1887).

The Century Guild

The Century Guild, a collective of artists who coalesced under the guidance of architect Arthur Heygate Mackmurdo (1851–1942), sought to unify the arts emphasizing their inter-dependence[5]. In his own words, Mackmurdo hoped the Guild would 'render all branches of art the sphere no longer of the tradesman but of the artist' and would 'restore building, decoration, glass painting, pottery, wood carving

and metalwork to their rightful place beside painting and sculpture'[6]. Clearly inspired by Morris & Co., the Guild offered a complete service covering all aspects of furnishing; textiles, wallpapers, light fittings, furniture and stained glass. Many of Mackmurdo's designs for wallpapers, textiles and metalwork were based on plant forms; created in the 1880s, they are recognized as precursors of New Art organic forms. Mackmurdo also mastered several crafts, including cabinet making and metalworking.

The Guild published its own magazine, *The Hobby Horse* (1884–94), which set new standards in terms of typography and graphics. This provided a platform

Mackmurdo, chair with fretted back (c.1881), William Morris Gallery, Walthamstow.

for expressing ideas and theories, promoting an alliance between artists and craftsmen and valorizing the handcrafted over mechanized production. As a publication devoted to the place of art in society, it inspired many imitators, notably *The Studio* (1893), *Jugend* (1896) and *Deutsche Kunst und Dekoration* (1897).

The Arts and Crafts emphasis on simplicity and utility created an antipathy to the perceived excesses of Belgian/French Art Nouveau; it was derided as 'squirm', 'macaroni style' or the 'decorative disease'. The dictum, 'Less is More' had been abandoned in favour of 'Decoration for its own Sake'. Touching on taboo subjects it was condemned as unwholesome, being seen at its worst in the androgynous graphic art of Aubrey Beardsley. Art Nouveau was also judged to be unethical as it stimulated a commodity culture, encouraging consumerism and materialism, invariably relied on factory production and rarely cared for the quality of the life of the worker. As a mainstream fashion it was seen to pander to feminine desires, notably the pleasures and self-gratification of shopping. Yet many Art Nouveau and Jugendstil architects and designers were inspired by the tenets of Ruskin and Morris, as well as the architects associated with the Arts and Crafts, notably Voysey and Baillie Scott.

Hermann Muthesius and the English House

Promising so much, the Arts and Crafts house was meticulously researched by architect Hermann Muthesius (1861–1927), who as cultural and technical attaché of the Prussian embassy in London from 1896 to 1903 was instructed to report on the English way of life, particularly architectural developments. Muthesius' mission for the Imperial German Government was tantamount to cultural espionage undertaken on behalf of 'a divided and backward country which had become a major power'[7]. Muthesius' final summation published as *Das englische Haus* (1904–05) privileged function, advocating honesty in construction and truth to materials as alternatives to ostentatious Historicism and excessive ornament. The cultural superiority of the English house lay in its comfort, convenience and practicality. *Das englische Haus* was both an historic survey and a program for domestic architectural reform. Muthesius also foresaw the potential of a craft revival, as higher standards would be of national economic benefit.

Voysey, Norney Grange, Shackleford, Surrey (1897).

Baillie Scott, Blackwell, Bowness, Lake Windermere (1898–1900).

Baillie Scott in Germany

Muthesius favoured Mackintosh and Baillie Scott, as using vernacular precedents they had evolved a quintessentially English 'cottage' style: both had a 'distinct personal trademark'[8]. Baillie Scott was popular on the Continent; in 1897, Ernst Ludwig, Grand Duke of Hesse and by Rhine, commissioned Baillie Scott and Charles Robert Ashbee (1863–1942) to transform the dining and drawing rooms of the Neues Palais,

Darmstadt[9]. Promoting local industry, the breakfast room was furnished by Julius Glückert, a furniture manufacturer who soon recognized the potential of the New Art. Renate Ulmer regards Ernst Ludwig's experiment as 'trend-setting', declaring the Grand Duke to be one of the first princes to 'bring the new style to life in his own quarters'[10].

Ernst Ludwig's preference for the English Arts and Crafts should not surprise us; his mother was Princess Alice, the second daughter of Queen Victoria.

Baillie Scott, 'Sitting Room in the Neues Palais', Darmstadt, from 'Some Furniture for the New Palace, Darmstadt', *The Studio*, Vol.14, 1898.

Baillie Scott, windows for the music room, Villa Kahn-Starre, Manheim, Germany (1904–05) Museum Künstlerkolonie, Darmstadt.

On his many trips to England, he would have been able to familiarize himself with current trends in the arts. Moreover, his wife Victoria Melita, his first cousin, was also a granddaughter of Queen Victoria; she supported her husband's endeavours and actively collaborated on the project to decorate the Neues Palais and the family's summer residence, Wolfsgarten[11]. Here the Grand Duke and Duchess organized lively parties introducing family members to new artistic trends and crafts, such as pokerwork wood-burning and furniture carving. Facilitating the New Art demonstrated their progressive outlook. The couple clearly wanted to impress their brother-in-law, Tsar Nicholas II. Royal endorsements encouraged other patrons; Dr R. Kahn-Starre commissioned a music room and boudoir for his Villa Kahn-Starre, Manheim, Germany. A double window provided an opportunity for stained glass, 'designed not to unduly obstruct the light' (c.1904–05, Museum Künstlerkolonie, Darmstadt)[12].

The *Landhaus*

As architectural historian Nikolaus Pevsner recognized, Muthesius was 'a connecting link between the English style of the nineties and Germany'; he was against the extreme individualism of Jugendstil, favouring *baukunst* (building) over *Stilarchitektur* (style). He developed his own suburban country house type, the *Landhaus*, a distillation of German vernacular architectural forms, as seen in Haus Cramer, Dahlem, Berlin (1911–13). Its multi-storey hall with large fireplace, so commonly found in the Arts and Crafts house, formed the social heart of the dwelling.

The multi-national survey *Das Moderne Landhaus und Seine Innere Ausstattung* (The modern country house and its interior) (1904), and *Landhaus und Garten* (Country House and Garden) (1907) also documented and promoted his own houses. The concept of the suburban country house formed the basis of the Darmstadt Künstlerkolonie's first exhibition (1901) on the Mathildenhöhe. However, while the English home was a private retreat, a place

Olbrich, Großes Haus Glückert, Mathildenhöhe, Darmstadt (1900–01).

to call one's own, in Germany the home came to be associated with the homeland, *Heimat*. This 'value-laden concept' signified national unity and identity. *Heimat* expressed 'a sense of belonging and the inheritance of a shared past... its roots were in the German soil and the German homestead, and in the bitter struggles for the survival of the German race'[13]. Reform had to generate a German culture of art and design.

New Art in London and Even Beyond

Oscar Wilde would have been the natural leader of an English New Art movement but following his conviction in 1895, there was a moral backlash against Aestheticism from which Art Nouveau sprang[14]. The New Art did surface in London, but it is often to be found in a commercial context, most notably the Harrod's Meat Hall (1902), its Doulton tiles designed

Neatby, Harrods Meat Hall, Knightsbridge, London (1902).

Neatby, Royal Arcade, Norwich (1899).

by William James Neatby (1860–1910). Best known for his terracotta and tiles, Neatby also designed wallpapers for Jeffrey & Co. and John Line & Sons. Beginning his career with the Burmantoft Pottery, Leeds, Neatby was headhunted by Doulton & Co. as director of its architectural department; his innovative designs brought the New Art to Bristol (Everard Printing works, 1900) and Norwich (Royal Arcade, 1899). The architect of the Royal Arcade, George John Skipper (1856–1948), introduced a modern dimension to the ancient city. Rather tongue in cheek, John Betjeman declared 'he was to Norwich what Gaudí was to Barcelona'![15] However, we should really credit Neatby with dropping a 'fragment from the Arabian Nights… into the heart of the old city'[16].

Skipper worked in the so-called 'Free style', an individualistic adaption of traditional forms that grew out of the Queen Anne revival associated with the architects Richard Norman Shaw (1831–1912), William Eden Nesfield (1835–88) and J. J. Stevenson (1831–1908). Sometimes known as 'Olde English', architects freely reworked vernacular and Georgian forms to create a distinctive, largely domestic, architectural style: fine red brickwork with terracotta panels and tile-hung upper stories; crisply-painted white woodwork; oriel windows and corner towers; picturesque massing and asymmetric façades and Flemish accents such as stepped gables. Deep, hooded

Townsend, Whitechapel Art Gallery, Whitechapel High St, Shadwell, London (1901).

porches were borrowed from eighteenth-century Baroque precursors. Free style added Byzantine and Romanesque sources to this eclectic mix. Free style even looked to America, particularly the work of Henry Hobson Richardson (1838–86), who created 'Richardson Romanesque'. Richardson, Louis Sullivan and Frank Lloyd Wright (1867–1959) form the 'trinity of American architecture'. Charles Harrison Townsend (1851–1928) in London and Edgar Wood (1860–1935) in Manchester and Huddersfield created notable Free style buildings. Architectural historian John Archer concludes that Wood blended the Arts and Crafts with New Art forms: 'In Wood's architecture the influences of both the Arts and Crafts movement and Art Nouveau are clearly apparent, the former by his revival of the vernacular traditions of Lancashire and West Riding buildings, and the latter by his use of elongated forms and interwoven motifs'[17]. His notable buildings include Banney Royd, Edgerton, Huddersfield (1901); Lindley Clock Tower, Huddersfield (1902); Long Street Methodist Church, Middleton (1899, now the Edgar Wood Centre); Church of Christ, Scientist, Manchester (1903) and the Modernist flat-roofed Royd House, Hale (1916), which he built for himself.

Townsend is best known for the Bishopsgate Institute, near Liverpool Street Station, London (1895); the Whitechapel Art Gallery (1901); the Horniman Museum, Forest Hill, London (1898–1901, extended, 1911) and St Mary the Virgin, Great Warley, Essex, often referred to as 'Vienna in Essex' in recognition of its unique New Art interior designed by William Reynolds-Stephens (1862–1943).

Liberty of Regent Street

Liberty's also responded to popular demand selling 'populuxe' goods including Moorcroft's Florian Ware pottery introduced in 1898 and Della Robbia Pottery of Birkenhead, founded by the painter Harold Rathbone and the sculptor Conrad Dressler in 1894. Liberty's successful importation of European pewter, Kayser Sohn of Krefeld-Bockum and Osiris-Metallwarenfabrik, encouraged him to offer his own brands. Liberty's most famous designer Archibald Knox (1864–1933), a Manxman of Scottish descent, drew on his Celtic roots to create Cymric silver (from 1899) and Tudric pewter (from 1901). From 1887 Liberty also retailed furniture made in their own workshops, which is best described as 'quaint'

Liberty & Co., 'Quaint and original decoration, furniture and fitments' from *The Studio*, Vol.13, No.59, Feb 15, 1898.

as it conflates Arts and Crafts and English rural traditions. However, Liberty's bestselling three-legged Thebes stool (1884), derived from an Egyptian prototype, turned up in the most unlikely places including the opening display at Bing's L'Art Nouveau. Copies were made for the Villa Karma, Vienna (1904–06) designed by Adolf Loos, the quarrelsome author of *Ornament and Crime* (1913), a polemic now seen to underpin Modernism.

By 1900 Liberty's was associated with both Arts and Crafts and New Art products. Following the company's success at the 1889 Paris Universal Exhibition, Maison Liberty was opened on the Avenue de l'Opera. Fashion conscious Parisian ladies flocked to purchase Liberty silks, dubbed *soie Liberty* and order aesthetic gowns; 'It was these silks, the product of the English Aesthetic movement, which so inspired the great Art Nouveau designer, Henry van de Velde. He first saw them in 1891 and described them as bringing "*une sorte de printemps*" new to the continental scene'[18]. *The British Warehouseman* claimed

that Liberty costumes had become the centre of a Parisian craze. Success allowed a move to grander premises at 3 Boulevard de Capucines, the spacious salons opulently decorated in the French Empire style. Scarves and shawls, cushions and bedcovers, alongside Oriental *objets d'art*, tempted the clientele. Liberty's success encouraged others: author and patron Edmond Picard (1836–1924) established the Maison d'Art, in his own home, 56 Gulden-Vlieslaan, Brussels, in 1894, while Bing opened L'Art Nouveau the following year.

Glasgow Style: The Four

In Britain the New Art was synonymous with the Glasgow Style or School as exemplified by Mackintosh and his compatriots the Glasgow Four: Herbert McNair (1868–1955), Margaret Macdonald Mackintosh (1864–1933) and Frances Macdonald McNair (1873–1921). Architect Edwin Lutyens (1869–1944)

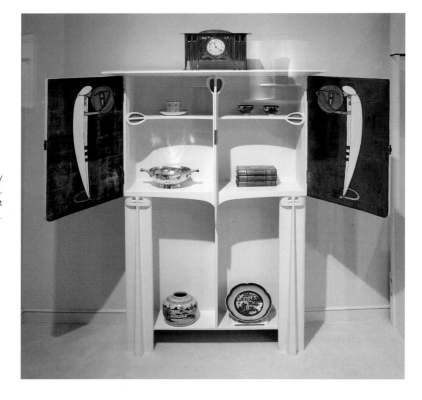

Mackintosh, 'kimono' cabinet, originally designed for 14 Kingsborough Gardens, Glasgow, house of Mrs Robert J. Rowat White, Royal Ontario Museum, Toronto.

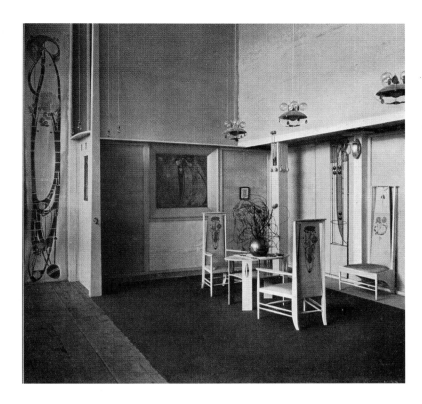

Mackintosh and Margaret Macdonald Mackintosh, 'The Rose Boudoir' at the Prima Esposizione Internazionale d'Arte Decorativa Moderna, Turin, 1902. *Deutsch Kunst und Dekoration*, Band X, April–Sept 1902, p.589.

found Miss Cranston's Buchanan Street Tea Rooms (1898), decorated by Mackintosh and George Walton (1867–1933), 'just a little *outré*'; apparently Miss Cranston had 'made a fortune by supplying cheap clean goods in surroundings prompted by the New Art Glasgow School'[19]. In all Mackintosh worked on five tea rooms for Miss Cranston: Argyll Street (1898/9), Buchanan Street (1898/9), Ingram Street (1900–12), the Willow Tea Rooms (1902–03) on Sauchiehall Street and the White Cockade (1911) a temporary installation for the Scottish Exhibition of National History, Art and Industry held in Kelvingrove Park.

Although the Glasgow School of Art (1896–1909) is revered, an exemplary Modernist building that allies function with beauty, Mackintosh's domestic projects take us into a fairy-tale realm thanks to the gesso plaster panels crafted by Margaret Macdonald. Husband and wife collaborated on many projects, Margaret's panels, featuring her signature 'spooky' ladies, enhancing her husband's interiors. The Mackintosh House (1908–13), reconstructed within the Hunterian Art Gallery, exemplifies Mackintosh's

design ethos: the spaces of the cool white, minimalist, Japanese-inspired drawing room/studio are augmented with dark furniture, a perfect balance of masculine and feminine, a 'yin and yang'. A cabinet, which opens like a Japanese kimono, is adorned with ethereal women holding pink 'cubist' roses, a symbolic motif now firmly associated with the Glasgow Style. As the Mackintosh's circle included the painter Jack Yates and Anna and Patrick Geddes who were attracted to Rosicrucianism, Theosophy and Spiritualism, this use of Symbolist imagery should not surprise us. That most feminine flower, the rose, being both symbolic of nature and the Virgin, was taken as the theme for the Rose Boudoir created for Turin 1902.

Mackintosh broke into the international scene in 1900 exhibiting at the eighth Vienna Secession Exhibition, which was devoted to the decorative arts. Attending in person, Mackintosh and Macdonald met many artists and designers associated with the Vienna Secession. Mackintosh's austere linear style influenced the direction taken by Josef Hoffmann and

Koloman Moser. Mackintosh and Hoffmann both favoured the square, which developed into the grid as seen at Hill House, Helensborough (1902) and his submission for 'A House for an Art Lover' (1901), a competition held by the German magazine *Zeitschrift für Innendekoration*. Using Mackintosh's portfolio, 'A House for an Art Lover' was constructed in Glasgow's Bellahouston Park. Begun in 1989, construction was halted by lack of funds; it was finally completed in 1996 after the Glasgow City Council and Glasgow School of Art revived the project.

Rather confusingly the Glasgow Four are also found in books on the Arts and Crafts movement; they participated in the fifth show organized by the Arts and Crafts Exhibition Society in 1896. Mackintosh was clearly influenced by Voysey, a leading exponent of rational architecture, who developed a distinctly English architectural idiom loosely based on vernacular precursors. Mackintosh's own style was shaped by Scottish vernacular forms, the towers, turrets and roughcast surfaces of the baronial castles of Aberdeenshire and Fife shaping his own nationalistic vision.

George Henry Walton

Recognizing the need for fashionable premises, Miss Cranston commissioned Mackintosh and Walton to revamp the interiors of her Argyll Street and Buchanan Street tea rooms. Walton ventured into almost every avenue of decorative art, helping to pioneer the distinctive Glasgow Style. With the family left in straightened circumstances after the death of his father, Walton worked as a bank clerk while attending evening classes at the Glasgow School of Art. Commissioned to redesign one of Miss Cranston's tea rooms at 114 Argyle Street, Glasgow, Walton was able to establish his own decorating company, George Walton & Co, Ecclesiastical and House Decorators in 1888. A pioneer in the use of domestic stained glass, Walton also promoted stencilling rather than the use of wallpaper.

Around 1896 he went into partnership with the Quaker architect Fred Rowntree (1860–1927), from a family better known for their confectionery; the Glasgow tea room style was brought to Scarborough with the commission to decorate Rowntree's West-borough Street tea rooms. Enough work followed to warrant opening showrooms in York in 1898. Elmbank, The Mount, York (1898), purchased by Sidney Leetham, was redecorated by Walton. Now operating as a hotel, its interiors have been carefully restored.

Through the photographer George Davison (1854–1930), who was a managing director of Kodak, Walton secured the contract to design their showrooms throughout Europe bringing him international fame as well as disseminating the Glasgow Style (London, Glasgow, Brussels, Milan, Vienna and Moscow). Relocating to London, Walton crossed over, becoming an architect. His first project was The Leys, Elstree (1901), an unpretentious design reflecting the influence of Mackintosh and Voysey.

Resigning from George Walton & Co. in 1903, Walton practised as an architect and designer, being admitted to the RIBA in 1911. After the war, the bulk of his income came from designing textiles for Morton Sundour Fabrics of Carlisle. Walton came from a talented family. His brother Edward Arthur was a leading 'Glasgow Boy', who practised *en plein air* painting, while his sisters Hannah (1863–1940) and Helen (1850–1921), 'Glasgow Girls', set up a decorating studio painting ceramics and glass.

James Salmon Junior and John Gaff Gillespie

Mackintosh was not the only young innovative architect working in Glasgow in the 1890s; James Salmon Junior (1873–1924), who followed his grandfather and father into the architectural profession, and John Gaff Gillespie (1870–1926) created their own distinctive architectural and decorative style along New Art lines. Working for James Salmon & Son, bank buildings were Salmon Junior and Gillespie's forte; more than ten were built between 1895 and 1906[20].

Salmon Jr and Gillespie, St Vincent Chambers, known as the The Hat Rack, Glasgow (1899–1902).

They are best known for creating one of Glasgow's first skyscraper or 'elevator buildings', the ten-storey The Hat Rack, officially St Vincent Chambers (1899–1902). This steel-framed, extensively windowed feat of engineering acquired its irreverent name due to its rooftop's spikey detailing, which resembles the pegs of a hat rack. The elegant front, the central recess sandwiched by two towers of bay windows, is mostly glass surrounded by a bare minimum of decorative sandstone. The sculptor Francis Derwent Wood (1871–1926) provided the detailing. The Old Oak Tea Rooms occupied the lower levels, utilizing the whole depth of the building. Opening in 1902, these elegant rooms rivalled those of Miss Cranston.

At Lion Chambers, Hope Street (1904), an eight-storey building, they pioneered the use of reinforced concrete as a building material using the Hennebique system patented in 1892. This innovative structural engineering permitted many windows. Nevertheless, the building's robust tower-like appearance was derived from Scottish roughcast castles, a source also exploited by Mackintosh, as seen at Hill House (1902). With the death of William Forrest Salmon, the partnership was dissolved in 1913.

Art Nouveau: Brussels

The emergence of Brussels as a cultural and artistic centre in the 1890s rests on the activities of a group of writers and painters who had contacts with the Parisian avant-garde. For ten years 'Les XX' or 'Les Vingt', a group of twenty Belgian painters, designers and sculptors, formed in 1883 by the lawyer, publisher, and entrepreneur Octave Maus, held an annual exhibition. Twenty international artists were also invited to participate. In 1893, 'Les XX' was transformed into 'La Libre Esthétique' or 'Free Aesthetics' (1893–1914), a collective dedicated to the unification of all the arts. The decorative and applied arts were presented on the same footing as the fine arts. Its first annual 'Salon de la Libre Esthétique' (1894) included a selection of English Arts and Crafts and New Art works. Morris's Kelmscott Press was represented by *The Defence of Guinevere*, *The History of Troy* and *A Dream of John Bull*. Writing in *The Studio*, the Belgian artist Fernand Khnopff observed 'the first appearance of these works… before the Brussels public, one can truly say has been a real triumph'[21]. Bookbinding by T. J. Cobden-Sanderson, furniture and metalwork by C. R. Ashbee and illustrations by Walter Crane, Laurence Housman, Charles Ricketts and Aubrey Beardsley, including his infamous illustrations for Wilde's *Salome* (1893–94), would have raised a few eyebrows. Such rich cultural exchanges fostered the emergence of the New Art.

Edmond Picard transformed his house, already a focal point of artistic life in Brussels, into the Maison d'Art (1894). In this home-turned-gallery, Picard exhibited objects in various media (ceramics, ironwork, glass, wallpaper, carpets, and bookbinding) in room settings establishing the concept of 'scenography'. Traditional distinctions between the arts were ignored in order to create living environments. Through staged interiors, the consumer could now imagine how an object would look in his own home, as well as gaining instruction on how to orchestrate decor. However, Picard did not commission objects for his room settings, as Bing would for L'Art Nouveau.

Gustave Serrurier-Bovy (1858–1910), the son of a Liège furniture maker, noted Picard's novel approach; at La Libre Esthetique's first exhibition (1894) he created an entire room rather than showing isolated pieces. His model installation, a *Cabinet de travail* (study) demonstrated the modern vision, the interior as a total artwork or gesamtkunstwerk. At the time of his marriage to Maria Bovy, Serrurier-Bovy had opened a gallery, Ameublement Serrurier-Bovy (1884) in Liège. Inspired by Liberty's, he imported fabrics and Japanese *objets d'art*. As his interest in interior décor developed, he began to make his own furniture. His linear forms and clarity of design were shaped by Arts and Crafts principles alongside rural furniture types and Japanese motifs: the structure of his suite of bedroom furniture echoes the torii of a Shinto shrine. With the architect Rene Dulong, Serrurier-Bovy established L'Art dans l'habitation (Art in the Home) in Paris just before the opening of the 1900 Universal Exhibition: 'the visitor enters a suite of rooms arranged entirely as private living-space, drawing-rooms, dining-rooms, bedrooms, complete with furniture and decoration'[22].

Urban Development

Leopold King of the Belgians desired a capital as imposing as Hausman's Paris. The river Senne was covered over allowing new boulevards to be created

Serrurier-Bovy, bedroom furniture (1899) Musée d'Orsay, Paris.

Blerot, Rue Vanderschrik, Saint-Gilles, Brussels (1900–02).

(Avenues Louise, de Tervuren and de Meise). These new roads called for grand apartment blocks. However, the local bourgeoisie preferred one-family houses and individualized façades leading to a rich eclecticism from neo-Gothic and neo-Northern Renaissance to Art Nouveau, as seen on the Avenue Palmerston. The Avenue Louise would be equally enriched; Horta added balconies and loggias to the four private mansions he constructed (Solvay, Max Hallet, Roger and Aubecq).

The so-called Squares District offers one of the best architectural walks in the city: Hotel van Eetvelde (Horta), Hotel Deprez-Van de Velde (Horta), Maison-Atelier Pierre Braecke (Horta); Hotel Defize (Leon Govaerts); Maison Saint-Cyr, Maison Van Dyck and Maison Strauven (Gustave Strauven) and Villa Elisa (Victor Taelemans). Tourists are offered architectural trails focusing on a specific architect or a well-preserved clutch of buildings. In this way Art Nouveau continues to be Art for the People.

Signifying urban renewal, whole areas of the city were transformed into Art Nouveau neighbourhoods. Clusters of buildings can be found in the communes of Ixelles, Saint-Gilles and Schaerbeek. Architect and property developer, Ernest Blerot (1870–1957), who was born in Ixelles, created an entire streetscape; Rue Vanderschrik, Saint-Gilles, numbering seventeen terraced houses (1900–02), is a complete sequence (1 to 13 and 15 to 25). While visually homogeneous, the

Strauven, Maison Saint-Cyr, Ambiorix Square, Brussels (1901–03).

houses were not standardized; every façade is different, the characteristic bow windows set at different levels. A diverse bestiary appears over windows and doors; a crowing rooster, swallows flying across the sky, owls, peacocks, dogs or cats. Every decorative element was customized; Blerot designed stained-glass windows, sgraffito work, decorative ironwork, mosaics and door handles with meticulous attention to detail.

Regulations set the widths and depths of the lots in the new residential neighbourhoods, the norm being a six-metre façade. However, the Saint-Cyr house (1901–03, Gustave Strauven) is only four metres wide, making for an extremely vertiginous façade. The verticality is made more overt through the metalwork, the superimposed wrought-iron balconies rising to a circular loggia and ornate gable. Gustave Strauven (1878–1919), Horta's protégé, took the *coup de fouet* or whiplash motif to extremes, as seen in the metalwork and the window fenestration.

Horta's Whiplash

The buildings of Horta, Hankar and van de Velde represent the first architectural expressions of the artistic movement. Horta's career climaxed in the 1890s and early 1900s with a succession of outstanding private residences all bearing the name of the patron; the Autrique (1893); the Tassel (1893); the Frison (1894); the Solvay (1894–95); the Van Eetvelde (1895 and 1899–1900); Deprez-Van de Velde (1896); the Aubecq (1899) and Max Hallet (1902). His own house and studio, on the Rue Americaine, dates to 1898–1901. Horta's network of private clients was built up through the Freemasons; he joined the Philanthropic Friends Lodge in 1887 meeting Eugène Autrique and Emile Tassel, both engineers, who commissioned his first houses. His Art Nouveau phase lasting little more than ten years, Horta likened himself to a blazing meteor whose fires quickly vanished into space. Later he would nostalgically recall this happy period, when his creative vision had so perfectly matched the taste of the times.

The basis of Horta's architectural language was the springing movement of a *coup de fouet* or whiplash curl. In his *Memoires*, Horta observed: 'It was considered that the curved lines which I introduced in my architecture were fantasy. I had been searching for them ever since I left school… the starting point was the curving of the column, an age-old curve'[23]. Nature, but not servilely imitated, was his inspiration; 'the initial line, the natural line, remains a principle,

Horta, winter garden, l'Hotel Frison, 37, Rue Lebeau, Sablon, Brussels (1894).

but an anonymous principle, and develops, through his adaptations, in strength, movement, expression, without losing any of its charm'[24]. From the plant, he only 'kept the stem, not the flower'[25]. Horta organically linked all aspects of a building using curves; his expressive line runs through all his materials, woodwork, metalwork, murals and stained glass. The result was a completely homogeneous, harmonious entity.

Paul Hankar: L'Art nouveau géométrique

While Horta epitomizes the *coup de fouet* style, Paul Hankar (1859–1901) is said to have initiated L'Art Nouveau Géométrique or Geometric Art Nouveau, a restrained, abstract, symmetrical use of line influenced by Japanese minimalism. Serrurier-Bovy and van de Velde also favoured this approach, their simplified curves creating flowing form. This linear brand of Art Nouveau is said to influence Jugendstil, as well as the geometric current within the Vienna Secession, ultimately leading to post-war Art Deco and Modernism.

Hankar was barely forty years old when he died unexpectedly of a chill. Studying alongside Horta at the Académie Royale des Beaux-Arts, he became interested in materials, particularly forged iron. From 1879 to 1892 Hankar worked in the offices of Henrik Beyaert (1823–94). He established his own practice in 1893, the same year in which he built his influential house on the Rue Defacqz. Hankar took a logical approach, based in part on Viollet-le-Duc's 'rational architecture', the façade expressing the building's structure. A third, containing the entrance and stairs (identified by the narrow-arched windows), is offset from the remaining two-thirds containing the public rooms. A three-storey projecting box-oriel window, supported on stone corbels, provides ample light to the second and third floor rooms with a balcony for the fourth. Its exposed iron frame is explicitly modern, while the asymmetrical arrangement clearly references Japonisme. The reworked Flemish-Renaissance elements (polychrome brick and stone) are

Hankar, Maison Hankar, Rue Defacqz 71, Saint-Gilles, Brussels (1893).

overlaid with Japonesque Art Nouveau detailing. The colouristic effect is striking, achieved using red brick, blue stone, white limestone and pink puddingstone. Sgraffito panels by Adolphe Crespin in an arcaded frieze below the eaves represent the times of the day. The two panels under the oriel windows are strikingly overlaid by the geometric wrought-iron balustrades.

Close to the Hankar House, the Ciamberlani House (1897) epitomizes the architect's approach. The façade is dominated by two horseshoe-arched windows. They are compartmentalized with narrow glazing bars in an extreme Japonist style. Following Viollet-le-Duc's rationalism, these large windows were designed to light the drawing room. The façade is asymmetric, the front door offset to one side. The glazing bars of the lower windows are arranged in a striking grid pattern that looks forward to Mackintosh and Hoffman.

Hankar, Chemiserie Niguet, 13 Rue Royale, Brussels (1896).

The Chemiserie Niguet, 13 Rue Royale, Brussels (1896), a rare surviving shop front designed for a purveyor of shirts, also expresses Hankar's use of line. The tripartite composition centres on the recessed entrance surmounted by a richly ornamented transom. The door's daring asymmetric linear forms are emphasized by a brass overlay. At first sight this exceptional frontage, made of mahogany, appears to echo Horta's *coup de fouet* style. But the lines do not curl back on themselves; rather they flow in the manner of van de Velde. The source of Hankar's expressive linear forms lies in the graphic style of eighteenth-century Japanese print makers.

Hankar's Legacy

Hankar's students Léon Sneyers and Paul Hamesse perpetuated his geometric-linear stylization. At Turin 1902, Sneyers collaborated with Crespin exhibiting a studio decorated and furnished in memory of Hankar. Here Sneyers discovered German Jugendstil (Olbrich and Behrens) and the Viennese Secession (Wagner and Hoffmann); this revelation encouraged the use of linear and geometric forms. His designs for the Belgian pavilions created for the international exhibitions held in Milan (1906) and Venice (1906–07) were based on the work of Wagner and Olbrich. Sneyers also promoted the Modernist ethos through his gallery L'Intérieur, later the Galerie Sneyers, in Brussels.

Hamesse also took Hankar's geometric style forward. Having transformed the shopfronts of the Grand Magasins Cohn, Donnay & Cie in Liège and Brussels, he was commissioned by Berthold Cohn-Donnay to refurbish the interior of the family's town house Maison Cohn-Donnay (1904). At first sight, you could be forgiven for thinking you are in an Art Deco milieu. But this is Jugendstil/Vienna Secession transplanted to Brussels with some Mackintosh touches seen in the white lacquered furniture of the Salon Blanc. Like Sneyers, Hamesse would have encountered Olbrich, Hoffmann and Mackintosh at Turin 1902. Geometric motifs and parallel lines predominate in the yellow-hued stained glass and glazed skylights. The square-headed gilded Trees of Life in the billiard/smoking room have come straight from Olbrich's Secession House (1898). The magnificent radiator covers, by Lucien Rion, are a metallic bestiary featuring a peacock, birds of paradise and a brace of pelicans. They are also adorned with Glasgow roses and Celtic motifs. This remarkable interior has been transformed into a brasserie-restaurant aptly named De Ultieme Hallucinatie (1981).

Henry van de Velde: Line and Form

Van de Velde's approach was shaped by Arts and Crafts simplicity resulting in a more restrained use of line. His role in disseminating the modernist ethos was vital. He introduced Parisians to the new style, designing room settings and furniture for Bing's L'Art Nouveau (1895–96) and Julius Meier-Graefe's La Maison Moderne (1899). He also took the New Art to Germany, exhibiting his furnished interiors at the Dresdner Kunstgewerbe Austellung (Dresden Craft Exhibition) in 1897. Commissions soon followed, from Meier-Graefe, Harry Graf Kessler and Baron Eberhard von Bodenhausen, one of the founders

of the influential magazine *Pan*. While based in Berlin, van de Velde was commissioned by Karl Ernst Osthaus to design the Folkwang Museum, Hagen (1900–02), deemed to be the first gallery devoted to contemporary art. In 1902 van de Velde took the post of artistic advisor to Wilhelm Ernst Grand Duke of Saxe-Weimar-Eisenach. He reorganized the Kunstgewerbeschule (Arts-and-Crafts School) and the Academy of Fine Art, laying the foundations for the amalgamation of the two bodies into the Bauhaus in 1919. Van de Velde, therefore, provides a tangible link between Jugendstil and the emergence of Modernism in the post-war era.

Van de Velde switched from a career as a painter to architecture after building his own home, Bloemenwerf, Uccle (1895), described in *Art Decoratif* as a cottage of sobriety and simplicity. An idealist who argued art had the power to shape a better society, he was influenced by the writings of Ruskin and the example of Morris, whose foray into the applied arts also resulted from building his own home. However, Japonisme was his key design source, first seen in his paintings with their blocks of colour and strong linear contours. Van de Velde developed line as an abstract medium of expression, in his view 'the time for ornamentation made of tendrils, flowers and

Rion, birds of paradise radiator cover, Maison Cohn-Donnay, 316 Rue Royale, Saint-Josse, Brussels (1904, Paul Hamesse). Currently De Ultieme Hallucinatie brasserie-restaurant (since 1981).

women was over. The art of the future should be abstract'[26]. Being based on pure line, the construction and ornamentation of his furniture are fused into one, an indivisible whole.

His flat patterns rely on the line creating form, especially the interplay of solid and void. His influential advert for Tropon (1896–98), an egg-based protein extract, exemplifies his pattern making. This uses abstract flowing lines to evoke cracking eggs, white and yellow forming an eye-catching motif. Companies looking to establish their brand realized the power of the New Art. It could offer them a cohesive identity through packaging and posters. In this way art was democratized, as Art Nouveau/ Jugendstil forms were used to market everyday commodities, such as coffee, chocolate and biscuits. Van de Velde was called on by the Havana Cigar Co., Berlin (1899–1900) to create new interiors; every element, from the door handles to chairs, assumed the same flowing linear forms. The shelves for the cigars, which extend into the arch, cleverly achieve a symbiosis of construction and ornament. Usefulness

van de Velde, chair designed for Bloemenwerf, Uccle, Brussels (1895).

van de Velde, Havana Cigar Company, Mohrenstraße, Berlin (1899), *Innen-Dekoration*, Vol.11, Oct 1900, p.28.

is also combined with pictorial Symbolism, as the frieze running along the top of the wall mimics the upward spiralling of cigar smoke.

Art Nouveau: Paris

By the 1890s Paris was the centre of the artistic universe. Every artist who could afford to do so enrolled into one of the famous ateliers to complete their education. The best known, the Académie Julian, founded by Pierre Louis Rodolphe Julian in 1867, nurtured Mucha. In the Fine Arts, Impressionism had now run its course to be succeeded by neo-Impressionism and Symbolism. Yet it was the opening of Bing's La Maison l'Art Nouveau on Rue de Provence

Trézel, 'Autumn', glass panel, Bouillon Julien, rue du Faubourg-Saint-Denis, 10th arrondissement, Paris (1901–02, Édouard Fournier).

in December 1895 that brought the New Art to the French capital. Once planted in new soil, Art Nouveau burgeoned, although the best French expressions are to be found in the decorative and graphic arts, the glass of Émile Gallé, the jewellery of Lalique and the posters of Mucha. Genuine interiors can be experienced by visiting one of several surviving restaurants; Le Montparnasse 1900; Vagenende, Boulevard Saint-Germain; Bouillon Racine, Rue Racine; Mollard, Rue Saint-Lazare or Bouillon Julien, Rue du Faubourg-Saint-Denis.

The Art of Shopping

Georges Chedanne's (1861–1940) Galeries Lafayette (1907–12) exemplifies the 'luxury bazaar'. His assistant Ferdinand Chanut called upon l'École de Nancy to decorate the interior. The banister of the magnificent sweeping staircase (now removed), inspired by the Paris Opera House, was designed by Louis Majorelle (1859–1926), who is also credited with the ironwork surrounding the balconies. The stained-glass dome, rising to a height of 43m, designed by Jacques Grüber (1870–1936) in a neo-Byzantine style, steals the show.

Architect Frantz Jourdain (1847–1935) was hired to undertake the remodelling and expansion of La Samaritaine, the ever-expanding retail enterprise founded by Ernest Cognacq and Marie-Louise Jaÿ in 1869. Belgian born, Jourdain was granted French citizenship in 1870. He is best known as an art critic and theorist publishing over 200 articles in some sixty magazines and newspapers. At the forefront of Art Nouveau, he was critical of academic training that sent architects to Rome to study antiquities. As a founding member of the Société du Nouveau Paris, he promoted the modernization of Paris. In 1903, he was also responsible for founding the Société du Salon d'Automne (Autumn Salon) as an alternative to the official Paris Salon. He was supported by Guimard, avant-garde painters Felix Vallotton and Edouard Vuillard, the sculptor Paul Berthoud and Maison

Chedanne,
Galeries Lafayette,
Boulevard
Haussmann, 9th
arrondissement,
Paris (1907–12).

Jourdain, La Samaritaine, Quai du Louvre/Rue de Rivoli, Paris (1899).

Jansen, founded in 1880 by Dutch-born Jean-Henri Jansen, an interior design company which served an international clientele. Open to paintings, sculptures, photographs (from 1904), drawings, engraving and the applied arts, the Salon d'Automne showcased modern art.

Beginning as a small clothing shop, La Samaritaine expanded into a number of buildings in the 1st arrondissement, between the Louvre and Notre Dame, with a total of ninety different departments. Jourdain constructed Magasin 2, before updating Magasin 1. The construction was undertaken in stages, as the store had to remain open in order to bring in revenue (1899, 1905–10). The exposed steel frame and use of glass are both radical and functional. The decoration of the façade with panels of enamelled stoneware in brightly coloured hues of yellow, white, green, and gold is attributed to Alexandre Bigot (1862–1927). In addition to proclaiming the name of the store, various commodities are also advertised using elaborate calligraphy attributed to the artist Eugène Grasset (1845–1917).

The interior décor was entrusted to the decorator Francis Jourdain (1876–1958), son of the architect; the ironworker Edouard Schenck; Grasset and Bigot. The central atrium is dominated by the monumental staircase, which rises through all the floors to a top-lit gallery (Jourdain Gallery) decorated with a stencilled frieze of peacocks and roses by Francis Jourdain. However, for visual impact, these cannot compete with the sculptural peacocks that adorn the Fouquet-Mucha jewellery boutique now installed in the Musée Carnavalet, Paris.

Fouquet-Mucha Jewellery Boutique

Georges Fouquet (1862–1957), who took control of the family business in 1895, commissioned Mucha to design all aspects of his new premises on the prestigious Rue Royale (1899–1901). Mucha was given carte blanche for both the exterior and interior, including the furniture, light fittings and display cases. Conceived as a gesamtkunstwerk, the interior was a showcase for Fouquet's equally opulent jewels; 'a jewel of a space which would create a magical ambience and act as a perfect backdrop to the spirit of the new jewellery'[27]. Pride of place is given to two spectacular bronze peacocks, back lit by a glowing stained glass window. Fouquet's audacity was warmly praised in the *Revue de la Bijouterie*:

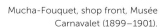
Mucha-Fouquet, shop front, Musée Carnavalet (1899–1901).

The creations of Art Nouveau require a new kind of framework, a framework which will set the artwork off effectively and which will thus create a harmony... And now, suddenly someone has been brave enough to make it a reality. He has opened a new kind of shop in the very heart of Paris. He has raised it to the level of his art, furnished it in accordance with the canon of his soul and he has done it so brilliantly that the jeweller and his products find themselves in a milieu which is so appropriate to its intended application that it almost seems to be a talking sign[28].

Devoted to female adornment, Art Nouveau style women are everywhere; archetypal Mucha heads in the ten stained-glass roundels of the shop-front windows or diaphanous in the bronze sculpture made by the Christofle workshop. Japonisant elements occur in the stained glass and wall murals: carp, water lilies and hogweed. In one original design, the shell or horseshoe-shaped fireplace was to carry *La Nature*, his most famous sculpture; she is wearing the most opulent Byzantine-style headdress, echoing the jewels Mucha designed for Fouquet. Opposite, an eye-popping fountain is topped with a water nymph. Snakeheads adorned the furniture; Mucha designed an outrageous serpent bracelet for the famous actress Sarah Bernhardt. The Parisian skyline, with the Eiffel tower dominating, is said to be represented in the mosaic floor. Mucha's fantasy remained in place until 1923 when it was removed in favour of Art Deco fittings. The ensemble was gifted to the Musée Carnavalet in 1941 but not fully displayed until 1989.

Mucha-Fouquet, shop design for a fireplace, Musée Carnavalet (1899–1901).

Style Guimard

The concentration of Art Nouveau residences in the 16th arrondissement, along the Rue Jean de La Fontaine and Rue Mozart, is due to Guimard. He developed a highly personal 'Style Guimard', a moniker promoted by the architect himself. Finding its full expression in the Paris Métro (1900–13), it is also known as Style Métro. Guimard's twisted forms, dubbed 'Abstract Naturalism', are easy to distinguish from other practitioners. His highly plastic shapes, which can verge on the bizarre, were based on vegetal forms. During a meeting with Horta, which took place in 1895, Guimard was advised to discard the leaf and flower, retaining only the stem. Abstract linearity was applied with fervour in the interiors of the capricious Castel Béranger apartment block (1895–98), Guimard's masterwork on the Rue de la Fontaine, Paris. Here the whiplash is seen at its most effective in the metalwork of the entrance lobby; the three-dimensional abstract tiles covering the walls recall molten lava or swirling water. This is organic decoration at its most extreme. The ideals of harmony and continuity led him to design all aspects of the interior: the furniture, ornamental ironwork, stained glass, carpets, wallpaper, door locks and doorknobs. His obsession with detail culminated in the creation of l'Hotel Guimard, his own perfect home, a wedding present to his American wife.

While no one else achieved the same level of decorative freedom as Guimard, there were other distinguished architects working in Paris. Jules Aimé Lavirotte (1864–1924) is best known for the buildings he created in the 7th arrondissement, Paris. Collaborating with the ceramist Bigot, he created highly imaginative and exuberantly decorated façades that defy description. He won the City of Paris prize for the most original façade three times; the Lavirotte Building (1901); the Ceramic Hotel, 34 Avenue de Wagram (1904), and the building at 23 Avenue de Messine (8th arrondissement) in 1907.

L'École de Nancy

L'École de Nancy, a consortium of architects, artists and designers based in the regional capital of Lorraine, was officially formed in 1901 following success

Guimard, entrance to Castel Béranger, Rue de la Fontaine, 16th arrondissement, Paris (1895–98).

at Paris 1900. While l'École de Nancy is sometimes considered a provincial phenomenon, it was the powerhouse of French Art Nouveau, second only to Paris in terms of manufacturing. Émile Gallé (1846–1904), the first president of l'École de Nancy, specialized in faience, glass and furniture; the Daum brothers, Auguste (1853–1909) and Antonin (1864–1930) concentrated on glass, working in collaboration with stained-glass designer Jacques Grüber; Louis Majorelle was the premier furniture maker and metalworker, while Lucien Weissenburger (1860–1929), Eugène Vallin (1856–1922), George Biet (1868–1955), Henry Gutton (1874–1963) and Émile André (1871–1933) forged their own distinctive floreale architectural style. Yet this Golden Age had only come about due to a disastrous war and mass-migration.

The city's destiny, and that of France, had been determined by the Franco-Prussian War (1870–71). A humiliating defeat led to the loss of France's eastern territories. Most of Alsace and approximately one-third of Lorraine, the Moselle department, was annexed by the German Reich following the Treaty of Frankfurt, which was signed on 10 May 1871. This became the Imperial territory of Alsace-Lorraine (Reichsland Elsaß-Lothringen). In 1872 French citizens in the annexed areas were given a stark choice; stay and take German nationality or leave. Many choose to leave; Nancy, now only a few miles from the border, was transformed into the regional capital, the premier city in the remaining French territories of Alsace-Lorraine. The flow of refugees more than doubled the city's population in four decades; 50,000 inhabitants in 1866 grew to 120,000 in 1911. This influx of labour and capital transformed the decorative art industries. Many of the refugees were highly skilled workers, previously employed in the glass and ceramics industries located in the Vosges mountains. To give just one example, Jean Daum (1825–85), a notary who migrated from Bitche in the Vosges, bought the Sainte-Catherine glassworks in Nancy. Taking his sons, Auguste and Antonin, into partnership, the fortunes of the company were turned around with the production of art glass. The Daum brothers were Gallé's natural successors in the field of decorative glass following his premature death in 1904.

Urban Development

Urbanization gathered pace; there was a building boom, as in addition to new housing, the city centre was soon adorned with new shops, banks, and cafés.

Weissenburger house-studio, Cours Leopold, Nancy (1904).

There would never be a better time to be an architect in Nancy. The Cours Leopold, on the edge of the old town, acquired new houses and apartments; the Weissenburger house and atelier (1904), the residence of the architect, promoted the new style. The classic model for a private mansion was updated with neo-Gothic and Art Nouveau naturalist forms. Incorporating ceramics, stained glass and metalwork, it offered a fresh approach but the result was not radical. The structure obeys the principle of bays and levels in a totally symmetrical façade. However, the seaweed decoration appears to grow out of the façade, looping over the balconies and rising to culminate in an impressive neo-Gothic chimney. The transoms and mullions of the side window also transform into seaweed, ingeniously forming a Cross of Lorraine. The

Pain, Maison de Lotissement, Rue Felix-Faure, Nancy (1900–07).

Sauvage, Villa Majorelle or Villa Jika, 1 Rue Louis Majorelle, Nancy (1901–02).

seaweed theme is continued in Majorelle's wrought iron and Grüber's stained glass. Tucked away at entablature level is a row of glazed tiles that bring colour and texture. Weissenburger's investment paid dividends; he constructed the Maison Chardot (1905–06) on the corner of the Cours Leopold.

The area around the Parc Sainte-Marie was developed as a new suburb. The Rue Pasteur, Rue Felix-Faure and the Avenue Foch, a new road that led directly to the railway station, offered a showcase for Art Nouveau apartments, houses and villas. One of Nancy's prettiest rows of houses, Maison de Lotissement, (1900–07) can be found on the Rue Felix-Faure (Nos. 24–28) built by César Pain (1872–1946). Each house bears a different painted motif on its stucco façade: Clementine (Villa Talliana), Clematis, Camelia. With their distinctive neo-Gothic wooden gables, they form an architectural ensemble of rare uniformity. Each house is distinguished by its detailing; different coloured glazed bricks (red, blue, green), wooden or wrought-iron balconies.

Although Pain was prolific, little is known about him; he built seventeen houses on the Rue Felix-Faure, including twelve between 1909 and 1912; the

Villa Hélène and adjoining house (1903) are in his rural-cottage style, coarse millstone grit with neo-Gothic gables, coloured bricks and wooden balconies. His name is associated with over fifty building projects in the city. His distinctive tile name plaque can also be found dotted around the Parc Saurupt, Nancy's garden suburb. He appears to have been a developer or speculator rather than a trained architect; he began his career as a *métier du bâtiment* (quantity surveyor) for private and industrial buildings. He left Nancy in 1925, moving to Nogent-sur-Marne, where he concentrated on the sale of buildings.

The most outstanding Art Nouveau residence in Nancy, the Villa Majorelle or Villa Jika (1901–02), was not by a local man; Majorelle gave the young Parisian architect Henri Sauvage (1873–1932) this important commission. The villa served as a showcase for Majorelle's furniture and light fittings, as well as Bigot's glazed stoneware and Grüber's stained glass. With Majorelle purchasing Bing's Maison l'Art Nouveau following his retirement in 1904, l'École de Nancy secured both national and international markets.

Weissenburger and Marjorelle, interior Brasserie Excelsior, 50 Rue Henri-Poincaré, Nancy (1911).

Style Florale

Weissenburger oversaw the building of the Villa Majorelle, implementing Sauvage's plans. Being a little older, he had dabbled in the eclecticism of the 1880s. Developing his own Art Nouveau idiom, he designed the Magasins Réunis (1890–1907; destroyed) for its proprietor Eugène Corbin and the Brasserie Excelsior and Hotel Angleterre in collaboration with Alexandre Mienville (1911). While the Magasins Réunis expressed all the exuberance of the Style Florale, the façade of the Excelsior is relatively sober, its verticality betraying the influence of the Viennese Secession. Such neo-Classical linearity looks ahead to Art Deco. However, the interior is a perfect expression of l'École de Nancy, with woodwork by Majorelle, stained glass by Grüber and light fittings a collaboration between Majorelle and Daum.

Weissenburger's domestic projects include the Villa Corbin, 38 Rue Sergent Blandan (1904–09) and the quirky aquarium in its grounds; the Maison Bergeret (1903–04) and the outlandish Villa Henri-Emmanuel Lang in the Parc Saurupt (1906). He was

Weissenburger, Aquarium, Villa Corbin, 38 Rue Sergent Blandan, Nancy (1904–09).

Weissenburger, Maison Bergeret, 24 Rue Lionnois, Nancy (1903–04).

also the architect of the Société Anonyme d'Habitations à Bon Marché (SAHBM), Nancy, which provided social housing. The Siegfried Law of 1894 encouraged the provision of low-rent social housing through tax exemption. Blocks were built on the Rue de Saverne and Rue de Solignac (1911–13).

Eugène Vallin

Vallin began his career as a cabinet maker, declaring his allegiance to Art Nouveau with the doors of Gallé's new manufactory (1897). They carry the pre-eminent glass-maker's motto, *'Ma racine est au fond des bois'* (My root is in the woods). He designed entire room ensembles for notable Nancéiens including Eugène Corbin, his business partner and brother-in-law Charles Masson and Albert Bergeret, a postcard manufacturer. Committed to the gesamtkunstwerk he inevitably wanted to direct the entire architectural project. However, the transition to self-taught architect was not an easy one and his buildings were not always successful. Based on the *ombelle* or umbel stem, the structural and

Weissenburger, Villa Henri-Emmanuel Lang, 1 Boulevard Georges-Clemenceau, Parc Saurupt, Nancy (1906).

Vallin, *ombelle* motif, Adam display cabinet (1903–04) Musée l'École de Nancy.

Biet and Vallin, Biet house, 22 Rue de la Commanderie, Nancy (1901–02).

Biet and Vallin, cat sliding down the roof of the Biet house, 22 Rue de la Commanderie, Nancy (1901–02).

decorative ribbed lines of his furniture were transferred to architectural forms. He developed a signature motif, the top of the rib resembling an unopened bud. Vallin is credited with the first Art Nouveau building in Nancy, his own house and workshop on the Boulevard Lobau (1895–96, with George Biet). Perhaps sensing his own deficiencies, he often collaborated with others. He designed 22 Rue de la Commanderie (1901–02) in collaboration with Biet; the project was for his partner who intended to use the *bel étage* for his own use. Tourists crane their necks in search of the cat sliding down the roof; those in the know immediately recall Théophile Steinlen's poster *Le Chat Noir* (The Black Cat) (1897), advertising the famous Parisian cabaret. The nocturnal habits and sexual promiscuity of cats ensured their popularity as an Art Nouveau motif. The ground level is dominated by its spikey metalwork, stylized hogweed, designed by Vallin. Although almost half the building was destroyed in the bombardment of 1917, Biet rebuilt it almost identically with the aid of Jean Prouvé (1901–84) in 1922. Vallin was prepared to experiment with new materials, adopting the use of concrete reinforced with steel for the construction of the pavilion of l'École de Nancy at the Exposition Internationale de L'Est de la France (1909), an event seen to mark the apogee of Style Florale.

Émile André

From an architectural background, André returned to Nancy in 1901 after an extensive European Grand Tour; he travelled through Tunisia, Egypt, India and Italy gaining knowledge of architectural history, styles and constructional materials. He collaborated with his father Charles André and Eugène Vallin in the construction of the Vaxelaire store (1901); using the *ombelle* stem, Vallin's signature, they created an eye-catching façade, a series of bays forming peacock eyes. The theme was carried through the store, as seen in the fitting-room screens. Here, the peacock eyes were filled with stained glass by Grüber; they can now be seen in the Musée d'Orsay, Paris.

André's Huot House (1903) is also dominated by a peacock-eye window framed with turquoise tiles; the entrance is surrounded with carved pinecones, a popular local motif referencing the forests of Lorraine. This façade certainly makes a statement; positioned directly beside the train line to Paris, it was not only an advert for André's Style Florale, it also proclaimed Nancy's commitment to modernity. This semi-detached house uses a multiplicity of materials: rocky limestone, cut stone, ceramics, wood, metal and

C. André, E. André and Vallin, Vaxelaire et Cie store, Rue Raugraff, Nancy (1901).

Émile André, Maison Huot, Quai Claude Le Lorrain, Nancy (1903).

stained glass. Yet the overall effect of the picturesque composition is unity.

André, alongside Henry Gutton, was also employed on Nancy's most ambitious architectural project, the Parc Saurupt, a private garden suburb inspired by English precursors. Twenty-eight villas were proposed, to be constructed on large plots of 800 to 2,000m^2 within 20 hectares of land. Privacy was guaranteed by gates, which closed off the park's roads where they intersected with public thoroughfares. A keeper's house flanked the main entrance. André's Villa Les Roches (1902–04), an interpretation of an Italian model with broad, overhanging eves, is built entirely of millstone grit. Perhaps influenced by Guimard's villas, the rustic flavour was intended to invoke the countryside. The entrance posts are decorated with beautiful blue-glazed water lilies supplied by Gentil and Bourdet of Boulogne. Opposite Villa Les Glycines (Wisteria) (1902–04), is quite different, its material dressed stone. This reprises the peacock-eye window of the Huot House. The gates for the Parc Saurupt (1903, André) have survived albeit relocated to the Square Jules-Dorget. By 1906, failure became obvious; only eight plots had sold. The project was restructured, the subdivisions drastically reduced allowing terraces to be constructed as well

Émile André, Villa Les Roche, corner of Rue des Brice and Rue du Colonel-Renard, Parc Saurupt, Nancy (1902–04).

Émile André, Villa Les Glycines, Rue des Brice, Parc Saurupt, Nancy (1902–04).

Émile André, Lombard Apartments, 69 Avenue Foch and France-Lanord Apartments, 71 Avenue Foch, Nancy (1902–04).

as individual villas.

On the Avenue Foch, two speculative apartment blocks (Nos. 69 and 71) show André's sensitive combination of neo-Gothic forms and naturalist ornament; No. 71 (1902–04) is distinguished by an abundance of sculptural decoration, ferns and flower heads, as well as its floral pinnacle. A signature of the Style Florale, this pinnacle extends the roofline upwards, like a Gothic spire. Often purely decorative, it normally takes a floral form suggesting the building is organically growing from the earth to the sky.

Metz

While Nancy's artists were busy expressing 'Frenchness,' Kaiser Wilhelm II was stamping German Imperial identity on Metz. At the centre of the new Imperial district, masterminded by Conrad Wahn (1851–1927), lay the Railway Station (1904–08) designed by Jürgen Kröger (1856–1928). Germanization was articulated through architectural forms that blended

Romanesque with Jugendstil, the pale grey stone of Niderviller, expressing the hardness of the north, in marked contrast to the other buildings of the city, which are mainly built in yellow limestone. In the station's Imperial Quarters, a stained-glass window depicting Charlemagne bears Wilhelm's features, while the legendary knight Roland looks down from the clock tower. German authority was legitimized through Charlemagne and the Holy Roman Empire; the German Reich had taken back territories that were rightfully theirs, both historically and culturally.

The newly created Kaiser-Wilhelm-Ring, now the Avenue Foch, became a showcase for cosmopolitan bourgeois architecture, historicist and modern forms lying side by side (1903–14). With identity expressed through architectural forms, there is an interesting melange of styles. No. 16, Villa Wildenberger (1903), is an outstanding expression of the modern idiom by Karl Griebel of Thionville; Mucha-style mascarons vie with sunflowers. For No. 22, the Villa Burger, also known as Villa Salomon (1904), Eduard Hermann Heppe, a local man, reverted to medievalism with

Kröger, Railway Station, Imperial Quarter, Metz (1904–08).

Griebel, Villa Wildenberger, Avenue Foch, Metz (1903).

Heppe, Villa Burger, also known as Villa Salomon, Avenue Foch, Metz (1904).

regional pseudo-timber-framing, including a picturesque turret, combined with neo-Renaissance sculptural details. A similar juxtaposition of historicist styles alongside Art Nouveau and Jugendstil can also be found in Strasbourg and Luxembourg.

Jugendstil: Youth-style

The term Jugendstil (Youth-style) is derived from the magazine, *Jugend: Illustrierte Wochenschrift für Kunst und Leben*, which showcased modern art, founded in Munich by Georg Hirth in 1896. Used in German-speaking regions as well as the Baltic States and Scandinavia, it is not simply the German translation of Art Nouveau. These countries developed their own distinctive architectural and design idioms that embody their national identity as well as responding to modernity.

Rather than copying foreign stylistic forms,

Germany needed to develop its own, independent, modern art. This dream would be realized at Turin 1902; Behrens' Hamburger Vorhalle des Deutschen Reiches (Hamburg Vestibule of the German Reich), the entrance hall of the Imperial Germania pavilion, expressed Germany's national identity through Jugendstil forms. Behrens' message proclaimed a new dawn; a cave-like structure, illuminated by a stained-glass sunburst in the central vault, framed a richly bound copy of Friedrich Nietzsche's *Thus Spoke Zarathustra* displayed in a shrine-like cabinet. The cover took as its leitmotiv *das Zeichen*, the crystal, symbol of 'Life as Art', echoing the last section of *Zarathustra-Das Zeichen*:

This my morning, my day begins
Rise up now, rise up, great noontide.
Thus spoke Zarathustra and left his cave, glowing
and strong, like a morning sun emerging behind
dark mountains.[29]

Prof. Peter Behrens—Darmstadt. Hamburger Vorhalle
des Deutschen Reiches. Ansicht vom Eingang nach rechts.

Behrens, Hamburger Vorhalle des Deutschen Reiches, at Turin, 1902. *Deutsch Kunst und Dekoration*, Band XI, Oct 1902–March 1903, p.21.

Behrens, skylight, Hamburger Vorhalle des Deutschen Reiches, at Turin, 1902. *Deutsch Kunst und Dekoration*, Band XI, Oct 1902– March 1903, coloured plate.

Stanford Anderson concludes, Behrens' Palace of Power and Beauty embodied the 'life of the citizens, the representational needs of the state and the whole expression of a culture'[30]. Behrens hoped his *Nietzschean Stil* (Great Style), a synthesis of Art and Life, could be disseminated throughout the German Empire. Expressing modern 'Germanness', the cultural and industrial order of the Reich, Jugendstil had evolved into a pan-German phenomenon.

The New Order, a quest for complete synthesis, would find full expression in Behrens' fully integrated branding for AEG (Allgemeine Elektricitäts-Gesellschaft); taking up his post as artistic adviser in 1907, he designed the turbine hall, innovative electrical products, including the first electric kettle and clock, as well as all promotional materials. A founder member of the Deutsche Werkbund (1907), a progressive German alliance of artists, architects, designers and manufacturers, Behrens considered industrial products to be the province of the artist. Behrens provides a link between Jugendstil and Modernism, as Walter Gropius, Mies van der Rohe and Le Corbusier all joined his office.

Munich, Darmstadt, Hagen and Weimar

Munich is regarded as the birthplace of Jugendstil, being the first German city to respond to the New Art. Some ninety-six artists 'seceded' or broke away from the Münchner Künstlergenossenschaft (Munich Artists' Association) in 1892. While there was no self-proclaimed leader many looked to the painter and sculptor Franz von Stuck (1863–1928) and painter and graphic designer Otto Eckmann (1865–1902), who developed a floriform Jugendstil. Eckmann switched to the graphic arts around

1894; his imaginative floral compositions were published in the magazines *Pan* and *Jugend.* Interested in calligraphy, Eckmann made his name by developing the typeface known as Eckmann. Alongside Eckmann, Behrens, Hermann Obrist (1862–1927), August Endell (1871–1925), Bruno Paul (1874–1968) and Richard Riemerschmid (1868–1957) were all core members of the Munich Secession. Nevertheless, Munich would forfeit its role as pacemaker to Darmstadt, Hagen and Weimar. Given the federal nature of Germany its city-states vied with each other in the race to modernize; Darmstadt, Weimar and Hagen all embraced Jugendstil. These cities enjoyed the patronage of a leading local figure who recognized the social and economic benefits of allying Art and Life.

Darmstadt

In Darmstadt, Grand Duke Ernst Ludwig led the way by example, commissioning Baillie Scott and Ashbee to redecorate the drawing room in the Neues Palais (1897). A year later the Erste Darmstädter Kunst- und Kunstgewerbe-Ausstellung (First Darmstadt Exhibition of Fine and Decorative Art) showcased the Art Nouveau glass and furniture of Émile Gallé. Innovative German applied arts were represented by tapestries from the Art Weaving School Scherrebek, ornamental glass by Karl Koepping, ceramics by Max Laeuger, Theo Schmuz-Baudiss and Max Heider, and metalwork by Riemerschmid. The Blaue Zimmer was dominated by the Munich school, with furniture by Wilhelm Michael and the decorative wall patterns of Eckmann. Rather than being arranged by materials, objects were presented within room settings. As Ulmer notes this presentation of 'modern, artistically fashioned dwelling rooms and high-quality craftsmanship... showed in an exemplary way the possibility of reviving old craft traditions and thereby gave impulses to the local small-scale industry'[31]. A pan-German emphasis was perhaps intended to spur local Hessian manufacturers into action.

This venture convinced Ernst Ludwig that the

Olbrich, Kleines Haus Glückert or Haus Rudolf Bosselt, Mathildenhöhe, Darmstadt (1900–01).

Olbrich, interior Großes Haus Glückert, Mathildenhöhe, Darmstadt (1900–01).

Behrens, dining room, Haus Behrens, Mathildenhöhe, Darmstadt (1900–01).

economic fortunes of his small principality, which boasted few natural resources, could be revived by rejuvenating local industries. The way forward was a freelance community of artists working alongside one another in a collegial relationship. Seven artists were invited to join the Künstlerkolonie; contracted for three years, their basic stipend was determined by their age, marital status and reputation. The Austrian Joseph Maria Olbrich, the most experienced architect, assumed the leadership of the colony. Fellow artists numbered Hans Christiansen (1866–1945), known for his designs for textiles and graphics; the architect and designer Patriz Huber (1878–1902) and artist-turned-architect Behrens. Ernst Ludwig's princely patronage, which extended to providing both land on the Mathildenhöhe and financial resources, was not an exercise in altruism. By forging a Darmstadt Jugendstil ethos, nationhood could be vested in cultural progress; Darmstadt would be at the cutting edge, a beacon of modernity.

Determined to put Darmstadt on the map, ahead of Munich, Karlsruhe, Dresden or Berlin, a major exhibition styled Ein Dokument Deutscher Kunst von bleibendem Wert (A Document of German Art with Lasting Value) was held in 1901[32]. A conventional exhibition with temporary structures was rejected in favour of permanent building prototypes[33]. In effect Olbrich laid out a small suburb; eight model homes were created on the Mathildenhöhe embodying a 'Celebration of Life'. Olbrich provided the architectural plans for all, apart from the Haus Behrens – Haus Olbrich, Haus Christiansen, Haus Ludwig Habich, Haus Keller, Haus Deiters, the Kleines Haus Glückert (Haus Rudolf Bosselt) and Großes Haus Glückert[34]. Drawing on both German vernacular traditions and Mediterranean classical prototypes, each house was individually conceived. The House Beautiful, in Olbrich's words a 'space for life', dominated, with every fitting, however humble, artistically conceived. The Haus Behrens was a model gesamtkunstwerk, with the architect designing the drinking glasses, porcelain and cutlery for his dining table.

At the centre lay the Ernst-Ludwig-Haus (1899–1901), the 'Temple of Work', intended as studios and workshops for the colony artists. This is now a museum dedicated to the Künstlerkolonie. The building is approached through a ceremonial arched recess inscribed with the slogan 'May the artist show his world that never was and never will be', attributed to Austrian poet Hermann Bahr[35]. This is flanked by Ludwig Habich's (1872–1949) gigantic figures of Man and Woman, embodying 'Strength and Beauty' and 'Youth and Creativity', the keystones of the New Art. Ernst Ludwig's dream of building an Acropolis on the Mathildenhöhe was realized.

Hagen

A nationalistic impulse also led Karl Ernst Osthaus (1874–1921), son of the Hagener banker Carl Ernst August Osthaus, to transform his hometown into a leading centre for the European avant-garde; he is credited with initiating the 'Hagener Impuls'. Collecting works by Cézanne, Gauguin, van Gogh, Hodler, and Matisse amongst others, Osthaus's ambitions were realized in the Folkwang Museum (1902, van de Velde). An architectural masterpiece, the Folkwang was hailed by Danish-German painter Emil Nolde as a 'Beacon for western Germany'. Osthaus also attempted to construct a garden suburb in Hohenhagen, Hagen-Eppenhausen. Although the First World War prevented the completion of this project, the focal point, the Villa Hohenhof (1906–08), an exemplary gesamtkunstwerk masterminded by van de Velde, was created as a residence for Osthaus. Riemerschmid was called to design the Walddorfstraße workers' housing complex (1907), eighty-seven dwellings with community facilities including a kindergarten, while the Dutch artist Jan Thorn Prikker was commissioned to design a stained-glass window for the Hauptbahnhof Hagen known as 'The Artist as Teacher of Commerce and Industry'. Enlightened patronage transformed Hagan into a symbol of national progress.

van de Velde, Kunstgewerbeschulbau (Arts and Crafts School), Weimar (1905–06).

Weimar

Wilhelm Ernst, Grand Duke of Saxe-Weimar-Eisenach (1876–1923) also acknowledged the economic and social benefits of embracing art as the 'Teacher of Commerce and Industry'. As early as 1860, Grand Duke Charles Alexander (1818–1901) founded the Weimar Saxon-Grand Ducal Art School, engaging the painters Arnold Böcklin and Franz von Lenbach and sculptor Reinhold Begas. His grandson and successor Wilhelm Ernst, the last Grand Duke, invited van de Velde to Weimar in 1902. The Grand-Ducal School of Arts and Crafts, established in 1905, would evolve into the Bauhaus under the leadership of Walter Gropius. Although indelibly associated with the emergence of functional-utilitarian Modernism, the Bauhaus program was initially rooted in the romantic Arts and Crafts tradition. Whether instigated by artists, entrepreneurs or even princes the zeal for reform was undoubtedly pan-German.

Secession

Georg Hirth is said to have coined the expression 'Sezessionismus' (Secession) to characterize dissent; forward-looking artists, designers and architects, inevitably a disgruntled younger generation, elected to break with tradition or 'secede' from conservative art institutions. The dissenters in Munich had their eye on exhibiting at the upcoming World's Columbian Exposition, Chicago (1893). They promoted artistic freedom, even calling into question what constitutes art: 'One should see, in our exhibitions, every form of art, whether old or new, which will redound to the glory of Munich, whose art will be allowed to develop to its full flowering'[36]. The Munich Secession adopted a multidisciplinary approach. The founding members numbered some 100 painters, sculptors, lithographers, architects and draughtsmen, including painter, architect, designer and city planner Richard Riemerschmid. Although Riemerschmid, a founder member of both the Vereinigte Werkstätte für Kunst im Handwerk (United Workshops for Art in

Riemerschmid, *Room for an Art Lover*, Paris 1900. *Deutsch Kunst und Dekoration*, Band VII, Oct 1900–March 1901, p.24.

Handcrafts) and the Deutscher Werkbund (German Association of Craftsmen), prized craftsmanship, he also advocated machine production for artist-designed commodities. Riemerschmid typifies the 'universal artist' designing furniture, wallpapers, textiles, ceramics and glass. Initially a Symbolist painter and graphic designer, he widened his artistic practice designing his own home, down to the smallest individual component, in Pasing, Munich (1897–98). He created the 'Room for an Art Lover', an iconic interior, for the German section of Paris 1900.

Vienna Secession

In Vienna, a group led by the painter Gustav Klimt (1862–1918) resigned from the Gesellschaft bildender Künstler Österreichs (Association of Austrian Artists), based at the Künstlerhaus, in 1897. The Secession's premier architect Otto Wagner was,

Wagner, Kassenhalle (banking hall), Österreichische Postsparkasse (Austrian Postal Savings Bank), Vienna (1904–06 and 1910–12).

like Klimt, already well established. One can trace his development from Historicism through Secession style to Nutzstil or Use-Style, modern functionalism, based on the caveat 'the sole mistress of art is necessity'. Like many of his generation, he believed 'art and artists should and must represent their times.

Our future salvation cannot consist in mimicking all the stylistic tendencies that occurred during the last decades . . . Art in its nascence must be imbued by the realism of our times'[37].

His schooling was conventional and thorough; the Vienna Polytechnic Institute from 1857–59, Berlin

Wagner, Majolica House, Weinzeile 40, Vienna (1898).

Royal School of Architecture from 1860–61 and the Vienna Academy from 1861–63. Finally, he worked for a year in the studio of Ludwig von Förster (1797–1863), who contributed to the planning and architecture of the famous Viennese Ringstrasse, the grand boulevard that serves as a ring road around the historic Innere Stadt (Old Town). Nevertheless, Wagner was open to the use of new materials as seen in the construction of the Majolica Haus (1898), which has a ceramic façade and the Österreichische Postsparkasse (1904–06 and 1910–12), which uses reinforced concrete.

Wagner's masterpiece, Kirche am Steinhof, also known as the Church of St Leopold, Penzig (1903–07) combines beauty with practicality. Built for the Steinhof Psychiatric Hospital, Wagner was sensitive to its function as a chapel for mentally ill patients. With mosaics and stained glass by Moser and sculptural angels by Othmar Schimkowitz (1864–1947), Kirche am Steinhof vies with Gaudí's Sagrada Familia for its originality and splendour. Unfortunately, Kirche am Steinhof did not win the approval of Archduke Franz Ferdinand, who inaugurated the building; he preferred the mid-eighteenth century Imperial 'Maria-Theresian' Rococo style exemplified by Schönbrunn Palace. Without official support, and thwarted by his adversaries, several ambitious projects remained unfulfilled, such as the New Academy of Arts (c.1898), the City Museum (c.1901–14), and the University Library (c.1914).

Wagner was as much an engineer as an architect, working on all aspects of the Wiener Stadtbahn (1894–1900), designing bridges and viaducts as well as stations. His remit covered elevators, signage, lighting, and decoration. Wagner's Karlsplatz stations, one of which has been transformed into a museum dedicated to the architect, utilized industrial materials. A visible skeletal iron framework, clad with white marble slabs, is crowned with a barrel-shaped roof made of corrugated sheet iron. While such utilitarianism struck a modern chord, standing close to St Karl Borromäus or Karlskirche (Charles Church), Josef Fischer von Erlach's Baroque masterpiece, it also provoked indignation.

Olbrich

Wagner hired seventy artists and designers to cope with the Wiener Stadtbahn project including two young designers who later became very prominent in the birth of modern architecture, Olbrich and Hoffman. The exuberant decoration of the Karlsplatz Stadtbahn station, notably the distinctive golden sunflowers, has been attributed to Olbrich. The Hofpavillon, the royal station at Schönbrunn (1898), created

Wagner, Wiener Karlsplatz Stadtbahn Station, Karlsplatz, Vienna (1898).

Wagner, Olbrich, Fischl and Bauer, interior Hofpavillon, Schönbrunn, Vienna (1898).

for the opening ceremony of the municipal railway, was also a collaboration involving Olbrich, Carl Fischl and Leopold Bauer. A perfect gesamtkunstwerk, the Imperial waiting room is a harmonious whole from its etched glass to the spectacular carpet. The dominant motif of both the carpet and silk wall covering is the *Monstera deliciosa* (ceriman) or cheese plant.

A 'decorator of rare taste', Olbrich was tasked with creating the Secession exhibition building[38]. Constructed in just six months, it was completed in time for the Secession's second exhibition in 1898. The entrance is guarded by three Medusa heads or Gorgoneion, representing Painting, Architecture and Sculpture; taken up by other architects, this triumvirate symbolized the New Art's struggle against convention and prejudice. Despite becoming a popular target of ridicule, the 'Golden Cabbage' secured Olbrich's reputation; he was hailed as the leader of a younger generation of architects. However, although commissioned to build an exclusive development of houses on the Hohe Warte, a hillside on the edge of the Vienna woods, Olbrich accepted Ernst Ludwig's

Olbrich, Secession exhibition building, Vienna (1898).

offer and transferred his talents to Darmstadt. Leaving
in August 1899, Olbrich contributed to both the Austrian and German sections of Paris 1900.

Wiener Werkstätte

In 1903 Hoffmann and Moser with financial backing
from the industrialist Fritz Waerndorfer founded
the Wiener Werkstätte (Vienna Workshops). The
concept, bringing together architects, artists and
designers working in ceramics, fashion, silver, furniture and the graphic arts, was inspired by the Arts
and Crafts ethos. In addition to unifying functionality with beauty, the Viennese workshops produced
furniture and metalwork of outstanding craftsmanship. With many pieces bespoke, designed for specific interiors, their clients had to be both wealthy
and enlightened.

Hoffmann was committed to the gesamtkunstwerk
as seen in the villas he designed on the Hohe Warte
(1900–02), a project inherited from Olbrich. The
houses created for Moser and fellow artist Carl
Moll also reveal a stylistic shift. While the exteriors
exhibit Arts and Crafts preferences, the roughcast and

Hoffmann, Sitzmaschine Chair with adjustable back (c.1905).
Leopold Museum, Vienna.

half-timbering drawn from rural precursors, the interiors betray the influence of Mackintosh. Hoffmann, who met Mackintosh at the 8th Secession exhibition (1900), developed a stylistic vocabulary based on linear forms, notably the grid. With the departure of Olbrich, the so-called Golden phase of the Secession, characterized by the floral décor of the Hofpavillon and the Karlsplatz Stadtbahn station buildings, was over. Hoffmann's linear restraint looked forward to post-war Art Deco and Modernism.

Plečnik: Ljubljana

Teaching at the Academy from 1884–1913, a Wagner school was moulded: Olbrich, Hoffmann, Jan Kotera (1871–1923), Jože Plečnik (1872–1957), Otto Schönthal (1878–1961), Ernest Lichtblau (1883–1963) and Max Fabiani (1865–1962). Another student Rudolph Schindler (1887–1953), who took Modernism to Los Angeles, claimed 'Modern Architecture began with Mackintosh in Scotland, Otto Wagner in Vienna, and Louis Sullivan in Chicago'[39].

Plečnik's Zacherlhaus, Wildpretmarkt (1903–05), in the heart of historic Vienna, makes a modern statement. Commissioned by Johann Evangelist Zacherl, whose fortune came from insecticide, the façade is faced with polished grey granite plates. The cornice is supported by *atlantes*, their heads bent forward to carry the weight of the structure across their shoulders, designed by Franz Metzer (1870–1919). The Archangel Michael, poised to spear the dragon, was conceived by Ferdinand Andri (1871–1956), best known for his 1906 Secession poster.

Eventually returning to his native land, Slovenia, Plečnik transformed the capital Ljubljana. His landmarks include the iconic Triple Bridge (1932) and the Slovene National and University Library (1930–31), as well as the embankments along the Ljubljanica River. His architectural imprint on the city has been compared to the impact of Gaudí on Barcelona. As a teacher, like Wagner, he established a school of followers.

Plečnik, Zacherlhaus, Wildpretmarkt, Vienna (1903–05).

Gesellius, Lindgren and Saarinen, Pohjola Insurance building, Aleksanterinkatu 44 and Mikonkatu 3, Helsinki (1899–1900).

Nationalism

Secession is now used more broadly; you may come across its use in Prague (Czech *Secese*), Budapest (Hungarian *Szecesszió*), Kraków (Polish *Secesja*), Ljubljana (Slovene *Secessija*) and Bratislava (Slovak *Secesia*). These breakaway groups are often linked to emerging nationalism, as in the case of Młoda Polska ('Young Poland', 1895–1914) or Jaunlatvieši ('Young Latvians'), a term applied to the intellectuals of the First Latvian National Awakening (c.1850s–1880s). Artistic, literary and political activism coalesced as nations, who considered themselves both culturally and politically oppressed, sought to establish their unique identity. National Romanticism arose in reaction to dynastic or imperial hegemony; self-determination was the driving goal. A National Romantic style arose in Scandinavia (Norway, Finland, Denmark and Sweden) and the Baltic (Latvia and Estonia).

Architects and designers turned to early medieval architecture, seen as expressing the Northern spirit, in their attempt to construct a style appropriate to the perceived character of a people. Folk art also played its part in expressing regional or national identity.

Magyar Szecesszió

Ödön Lechner (1845–1914), the 'Hungarian Gaudí', strove to assert national identity in the socio-political climate that followed the crushing of the Hungarian revolution in 1848–49. Following this national calamity, the country sank into 'passive resistance'. Hungarian nationalists struggled to promote the Magyar language and culture, as well as their goal to achieve greater independence from German Austria. The Hungarian language, the 'mother tongue', is so distinctive, so different to other European languages, that it was the obvious way to assert national identity. Orally transmitted folk legends, fairy tales, ballads and songs were collected and published, creating a national canon. They were absorbed into high culture through the music of Béla Bartók and Zoltán Kodály.

Hungarian separatists were appeased by the Austro-Hungarian Compromise (1867), which established the dual Monarchy of Austria–Hungary. The two realms were governed separately by two parliaments from two capitals, with a common monarch and common foreign and military policies. Emperor Franz Joseph was crowned King of Hungary with much pomp and ceremony in Matthias Church, a splendid neo-Gothic confection that crowns the Buda hill (1833–96, Frigyes Schulek). Although dedicated to the Virgin, its popular name Matthias Temple references Hungary's golden age under King Matthias Corvinus (1443–90); its architectural forms implanted 'national and individual spirit into the majestic style of the Middle Ages'[40].

The old capital Buda and Óbuda (Ancient Buda) were officially merged with the third city, Pest, thus creating the new metropolis of Budapest in 1873. Seven years later it was decided to construct a

parliament building that expressed the sovereignty of the nation. Following a competition Imre Steindl (1839–1902) emerged the victor. Still the largest building in Hungary, the neo-Gothic structure (1885–1904) sits on the Pest bank of the Danube like a beautiful wedding cake. Based on a grid pattern, Pest was remodelled along the lines of Hausmann's Paris. The memory of Hungary's first Prime Minister, Count Gyula Andrássy, is enshrined in the famous Andrássy Avenue, which leads to Heroes Square. The palaces and villas that sprung up along Pest's new thoroughfares range in style from historicist to Secession.

The Hungarian Millennium

The creation of Austria-Hungary, the largest country in Europe after Russia, ushered in an era of unprecedented prosperity; the population of Budapest tripled, while the number of its buildings doubled. Budapest Metro Line 1, which runs along Andrássy Avenue, the oldest electrified underground railway system in continental Europe, was completed in time for the Hungarian Millennium celebrations of 1896. Patriotic sentiments rose to a crescendo with these festivities, the anniversary of the Magyar's arrival in the Carpathian Basin. This moment was marked with many ambitious projects. The Millennium Column, crowned with the Archangel Gabriel and surrounded at its base by statues of the chieftains of the seven Magyar tribes who entered the Carpathian Basin in 896, rose to its height of 96m above Hősök Tere (Heroes Square). Buildings were set at this obligatory height (marking 896), including the dome of the new Parliament, which was inaugurated on the 1,000th anniversary. Heroes Square is now framed by the neo-Classical Museum of Fine Arts (1906, Albert Schickedanz and Fülöp Herczog) and the Műcsarnok (Palace of Arts) (1896, Albert Schickedanz and Fülöp Herczog) built for the celebrations.

Behind Heroes Square, Városliget (City Park) was laid out, with Vajdahunyad Castle (Ignác Alpár) recreating the kingdom's historic buildings, notably the Hunyad Castle in Transylvania. A wonderful medley of Western architectural styles, Romanesque, Gothic,

Sterk, Hegedűs and Sebestyén, Gellért Hotel and Thermal Baths and Swimming Pool, Kelenhegyi út 4, Buda (1912–18).

Renaissance and Baroque, it was originally made from wood and plaster. But it proved so popular that is was rebuilt in stone and brick (1904–08). Finally, the Szabadság Hid (Liberty Bridge), originally named in honour of Franz Joseph (1894–96, János Feketeházy) provided a new link between Pest and Buda; it leads to the famous Gellért Hotel and Thermal Baths and Swimming Pool (1912–18, Izidor Sterk, Ármin Hegedűs, and Artúr Sebestyén), one of the capital's most distinctive neo-Baroque Secession buildings.

Looking East: Ödön Lechner

The Millennium marks the moment when Budapest became a modern metropolis. It was in this context that Lechner was given the responsibility of designing the Museum of Applied Arts (1893–96). As a repository of international art and design, the third oldest after the V&A and the MAK, Vienna, ironically Lechner wanted to create a national icon that broke with Western architectural forms which were seen by many to embody Austrian oppression. As the

new building was to be completed for the Millennial celebrations, Lechner looked back to the Magyar, the founders of the Hungarian nation. As an ethnic group, the Magyar were identified with Finno-ugric nomads who arrived in Pannonia, geographically the Carpathian Basin, under the leadership of Prince Arpad. His kinsman Istvan (St Stephen) converted to

Lechner and Partos, Museum of Applied Arts, Üllői út 33–37, Pest (1893–96).

Stevens, Chhatrapati Shivaji Terminus, Mumbai (1878–87).

Lechner, atrium, Museum of Applied Arts, Pest (1893–96).

Christianity and was crowned King of the Magyar in either 1000 or 1001.

Looking for a mythic past, Lechner concluded the roots of Hungarian visual culture lay in western Asia and the Indian subcontinent. His thinking would have been shaped by Turanism, which linked the Turks, Finns, Magyars and Mongols largely through language and race; the common root was ancient Sanskrit, one of three languages that originated from what is now referred to as Proto-Indo-European. Turanism was a counter measure, by smaller ethnic groups, to Pan-Germanism and Pan-Slavism.

In *Magyarische Ornamentik* (1898), the ethnographer Josef Huszka (1854–1934) stressed the Asian origins of the Hungarian nation. He found direct analogies between traditional Hungarian patterns seen on regional costumes and woodwork; and Indian and Sassanid stone carvings[41]. Formulating a Hungarian language of form, Lechner daringly combined old Magyar and Turkic folk art with Hindu, Mogul and Islamic forms; his weird exotic designs recall Eastern carpet patterns.

As Gavin Stamp observes, 'Lechner was not the only architect to subscribe to this engaging nationalist fantasy, but what is extraordinary is that he became interested in contemporary British colonial architecture designed in the so-called Indo-Saracenic style'[42]. This mishmash, also known as Indo-Gothic, Mughal-Gothic, and even Hindoo Style, drew from Mughal architecture, which the British regarded as the classic Indian style. Mughal architecture reached its zenith during the reign of Shah Jahan (1592–1666), whose legacy includes the Taj Mahal, the Jama Masjid and the Red Fort. 'Saracenic' added Moorish and Arabic elements, from North Africa and Spain, such as horseshoe-shaped arches. Indo-Saracenic blended onion-shaped domes, towers and minarets, pointed and cusped arches and contrasting voussoirs round an arch, especially red and white. According to Lechner, 'The English, a highly cultured people, were not ashamed of researching into the relatively lower culture of a colony, adopting part of it and blending it with their own. Was it not at least as much the duty of us Hungarians to study the culture of our own people (Magyar) and weld it together with our general culture?'[43] Lechner's Museum of Applied Arts is modelled on the Victoria Terminus, now the Chhatrapati Shivaji Terminus, Mumbai (1878–87, Frederick William Stevens), which blends the Venetian Gothic Revival with Mughal domes and turrets. Lechner adopted the engrailed arch, a cusped or scalloped arch, sometimes called a Peacock arch for the atrium of the museum.

Folk Art

Lechner added Hungarian folk art motifs to his decorative repertoire, such as the convex palmette or tulip found in embroidery. The urban intelligentsia discovered folk art, now romantically redefined as 'The Works of our People', at the Budapest National Exhibition (1885). This included an ethnographic village recreating characteristic buildings and furnishings from the Carpathian Basin. From then on folk motifs acquired symbolic significance and could be referenced as a 'source of regeneration… conveying national values'[44]. Hungary had a rich textile tradition, both embroidery and weaving, with bold floral motifs, tulips and roses, stitched in very bright colours, especially red. Lechner took these tiny motifs and enlarged them. They were transformed into sculptural forms becoming architectural components, such as railings, banisters, parapets and roof-ridges. Above all he

Lechner, etched glass with tulip motif, Hungarian National Geological Institute, Stefánia út 14, Pest (1896–99).

Lechner, façade, Hungarian National Geological Institute, Stefánia út 14, Pest (1896–99).

pervaded his buildings with a nationalistic spirit; he created a language of forms, a vehicle for his patriotic message. His aim was to create a style that spoke to all classes, that was a democratic 'Art for the People'. Yet his forms and decoration still relate to function, the cave-like corridors of the Geological Institute (1896–99) resembling the galleries of mines[45]. The façade is distinguished by Lechner's characteristic bands of brick, which surround the windows. The façade ends in a rippling cornice, edged in brick; a feature that will be developed on his iconic Postal Savings Bank.

Lechner's Postal Savings Bank

Lechner's Szecesszió achieved a unique and original synthesis. As his style evolved, he moved away from Indian motifs towards vernacular folk-art forms, as seen in the Postatakarékpénztár (Postal Savings Bank) (1900–01, with Sándor Baumgarten). This form of banking, which originated in England, was to encourage rural labourers to save small sums; it was argued

Lechner with Baumgarten, detail bees and beehives, Postal Savings Bank, Hold u.4, Pest (1900–01).

Lechner with Baumgarten, Postal Savings Bank, Hold u.4, Pest (1900–01).

people were more likely to save if local post offices offered banking services. The grandiose buildings of private banks were intimidating and likely to deter the humble saver from entering. Hence, the building had to be relatively modest.

By decorating the vertical, flat façade with Hungarian folk-art motifs, Lechner was certainly trying to create a 'people's bank'. The vast façade is broken up with brick pilaster strips, each topped with a Zsolnay yellow-glazed ceramic beehive, symbolizing industry. Bees march towards the hives up the pilaster

Treasure of Nagyszentmiklós, in present-day Romania, Kunsthistorisches Museum, Vienna.

strips. The façade is crowned with a pierced, lace-like cornice, inspired by Upper-Hungarian Renaissance forms; undulating winged serpents form the ridge. Are they guarding the treasure or attempting to steal it? This prepares you for the extravagant roof of Zsolnay glazed tiles in bright green and yellow. The central tower is curved like a nomad's tent paying homage to the nation's Hun ancestors. Its crowning bullheads are derived from the drinking cups in the Treasure of Nagyszentmiklós (Kunsthistorisches Museum, Vienna), discovered in 1799. The origins of this important hoard of twenty-three early medieval gold vessels is still contested but in Lechner's day they were romantically said to have belonged to Atilla the Hun. As motifs referencing the treasure of Atilla, the bullheads were much more than symbols of wealth and power; they embodied the nation's great past.

A Hun-Hungarian Secession Style

The Hun myth played an important role in Hungarian identity; Atilla (c.406–53), leader of a tribal empire consisting of Huns, Ostrogoths, and Alans, invaded Roman Gaul and even attempted to take Rome. Linked to the Scythians, Atilla's supposed

Töry, Pogány and Györgyi, Hungarian Pavilion, Esposizione internazionale dell'industria e del lavoro, Turin (1911).

The most overt manifestation of Hun-Hungarian Romanticism came in 1911, with the Hungarian Pavilion for the Turin Esposizione internazionale dell'industria e del lavoro (International Exhibition of Industry and Labour) which coincided with the fiftieth anniversary of the unification of Italy. The 42m-high pavilion, topped with a distinctive pyramidal roof, was designed by Emil Töry, Maurice Pogány and Dénes Györgyi. The monumental entrance was guarded by six helmeted sentinels, bearing swords that recalled the original Magyar chieftains; it certainly made a statement. Hungary's architectural fantasy was voted the best national pavilion.

Lechner's Followers

Lechner's three most important buildings, the Museum of Applied Arts, the Geological Museum and the Postal Savings Bank aroused opposition. The conservative Hungarian establishment favoured neo-Baroque, which ticked the Imperialist box. Gyula Wlassics, the Minister of Culture declared, 'I do not like the Secessionist style, and... it is not uncommon to meet the Secessionist style under the name of the Hungarian style... Official Hungary wants none of the Lechner style'[47]. 'Too Hungarian and too Secessionist', Lechner received no more public commissions in the capital[48]. The government 'refused to accept the romantic myths of the nation's origins'[49].

However, Lechner continued to gain commissions in the provinces, for example the so-called Deutsch Mansion (1900–01, with Milhály Erdélyi) in Szeged, southern Hungary. Moreover, by this stage Lechner had influenced a younger generation who perpetuated his Secession style. Believing children needed to grow up in the nationalistic spirit, Ármin Hegedűs (1867–1936), a faithful follower of the Lechner school, created an exemplary Elementary School (1905–06). Hegedűs considered every aspect, the children's health and comfort as well as their aesthetic and educational development. Characteristic Lechner brick ribbons frame the windows; the mosaics were

ethnicity also supported the Hun's Eastern origins. Drawing on a mythic past, a Hun-Hungarian Secession promised a cultural regeneration.

The purest Hungarian folk art was said to come from Transylvania and the Carpathians, the Hungarian homelands. Aladár Körösfői-Kriesch, Sándor Nagy and Ede Toroczkai Wigand, members of the Gödöllő artists' colony (1901–20) drew on Hun-Hungarian legends and Székely folk tales in their quest for national identity. An ethnic group in Transylvania who claim descent from Attila's Huns, Székely traditions played a decisive role in underpinning Hungarian National Romanticism. The Cultural Palace of Marosvásárhely (Târgu Mures, Romania) (1911–13, Marcell Komor and Dezso Jakab) fully expresses this desire for an indigenous architecture. As building commenced, mayor György Bernády declared, 'it must be a treasury of visual and applied art that draws subjects from Hungarian history and Székely folk tales'[46].

Hegedűs, Elementary School, Dob utca 85, Pest (1905–06).

Lajta, Rozsavolgi, former Leitersdorfer (tailor's shop), Szervita ter 5, Pest (1912).

designed by the painter Zsigmond Vajda and executed by Miksa Róth. In the middle, boys and girls are playing 'Blind Man's Bluff'. Folksy motifs include giant tulips, seen as the national flower.

Béla Lajta (1875–1920) adopted Lechner as his role model until c.1906 when he went his own way[50]. From then on, his geometrical patterns, as seen on the Rozsavolgi (formerly Leitersdorfer tailor's shop) shops and apartments (1912), echo the Wiener Werkstätte school. In fact, Lajta took these patterns from the folk motifs of the southern Alföld, the great Hungarian plain. The façade of the upper residential floors is broken horizontally, with colourful ledges of bronze, copper and Zsolnay pyrogranite tiles. Lajta's Parisiana Night Club (1908) departs even further from Lechner. Its stylized geometrical frieze of bronze caryatids, each holding a letter of the theatre's name, could be forerunners of Art Deco. Yet the ziggurat

Lajta, Parisiana Night Club, Paulay Ede utca 35, Pest (1908).

Hegedűs and Böhm, former Török Bank House, Szervita ter 3, Pest (1905–06).

Róth, mosaic *Patrona Hungariae*, former Török Bank House, Szervita ter 3, Pest (1905–06).

motif, running along the ridge, can still be deemed Hungarian. Destroyed in the 1960s, the distinctive façade was reconstructed between 1987–90.

The former Török Bank House (1905–06, Ármin Hegedűs and Henrik Böhm) is crowned with a patriotic mosaic, the most splendid of its kind in Budapest, honouring Patrona Hungariae. Designed and executed by Miksa Róth, it depicts the triumphant arrival of the Hungarians. An enthroned Virgin Mary is surrounded by Hungarian heroes: Lajos Kossuth, Istvan Szechenyi and Ferenc II Rákóczi, leader of the Hungarian uprising against the Habsburgs in 1703–11. The Medusa heads, above the glazed enclosed balconies, recall Olbrich's Viennese Secession Building. While the mosaic looks back to a heroic past, the façade uses the latest materials; glass cladding on a reinforced concrete framework.

The Fiatalok or the 'Youngs'

In 1906 a small circle of architectural students coalesced into a group known as the 'Youngs' or 'Younger Group'; their ages ranged from twenty-one to twenty-three. Their principles were formulated by Károly Kós (1883–1977), who emerged as their

Neuschloss-Knusli with Kós and Zrumeczky, main entrance, Budapest Zoo (1910–12).

leading figure: Béla Lajta, Ede Toroczkai Wigand, Dénes Györgyi, Dezső Zrumeczky, Valér Mende, Béla Jánszky, Tibor Szivessy and Lajos Kozma fall into this

Neuschloss-Knusli with Kós and Zrumeczky, Elephant House, Budapest Zoo (1910–12).

Zsolnay elephant mascaron, Elephant House, Budapest Zoo (1910–12).

group. Rejecting Lechner's Secession idiom, Kós was inspired by Hungarian folk architecture, especially by Székely/Transylvanian rural buildings. Taking a more archaeological approach, surveying traditional housing and churches, the 'Youngs' developed native architectural forms; a new national style could be based on a continuation of 'the architecture of the Middle Ages as mediated by the vernacular architecture'[51]. They would have looked to English Arts and Crafts precedents and Finnish Jugend Suomessa or Kansallisromantiikka examples (Romantic Nationalism).

The main entrance to the Budapest Zoo (1910–1912, Kornel Neuschloss-Knusli, Károly Kós and

Kós and Zrumeczky, Wekerletelep, Kispest (1909–29).

Árkay, Reformed Church of Fasori, Városligeti fasor 5–7, Pest (1912–13).

Dezso Zrumeczky) introduces you to the beasts within: polar bears, elephants and allegedly mice, who live in the little castle on top. The domes and minarets of the Neuschloss-Knusli (Elephant House) were intended to evoke their homeland. The mascarons are not enticing maidens but Zsolnay hippos and rhinos!

Kós and Zrumeczky worked on the Wekerletelep, Kispest (1909–29), a state initiative designed to house the city's workers in a garden suburb. Named for Sándor Wekerle, then Hungarian prime minister, the Wekerletelep was inspired by Ebenezer Howard's Garden City concept. The properties, two- or three-roomed apartments, were built in Kós' favoured Transylvanian style: high roofs, turrets and plenty of timberwork. It retains its rural character, the cottage-inspired houses framed by gardens and tree-lined avenues. A 'village in the city', the inhabitants enjoy a sense of community.

Aladár Árkay (1868–1932) is best known for the Reformed Church of Fasori (1912–13), a Hun-Hungarian Secession masterpiece. The monumental

doorway is tiled with brown, black and gold Zsolnay ceramics with Hungarian folk-art motifs arranged in a Wiener Werkstätte grid. The parabolic or catenary arches reference Finnish forms.

Looking West: Vienna Secession, Jugendstil and Art Nouveau

While Lechner looked to the East, many preferred to ally Hungary to the modernizing West, to pan-German identity, favouring traditional European styles or Vienna Secession, German Jugendstil and even French Art Nouveau. The façade of Liszt Ferenc Academy of Music (1904–07, Floris Korb and Kalman Giergl) returns to an eclectic, essentially Baroque, formula. Yet the interior is an outstanding Secession masterpiece, with paintings by Körösfői-Kriesch; *Art as the Source of Life* dominates the upper floor. The interior is clad with iridescent eosin-glazed Zsolnay tiles (*see* Chapter 4).

A good example of this Western outlook is the

Körösfői-Kriesch, *Art as the Source of Life*, Liszt Ferenc Academy of Music, Liszt Ferenc ter 8, Pest (c.1907).

Gresham Palace (1905–07, Zsigmond Quittner and József Vágó), the former London Gresham Insurance Company, named in honour of Sir Thomas Gresham, the founder of the London Stock Exchange. Like the Gellért Hotel and Baths, this could be dubbed Baroque-Secession.

Modernisme: Barcelona and Valencia

Catalan Modernisme acquired its unique spirit through the architecture of Antoni Gaudí i Cornet (1852–1926), Josep Maria Jujol i Gibert (1876–1949), who worked alongside Gaudí, Lluís Domènech i

Quittner and Vágó, Gresham Palace, Széchenyi István tér 5–6, Pest (1905–07).

Montaner (1850–1923), Josep Puig i Cadafalch (1867–1956), and Enric Sagnier i Villavecchia (1858–1931).

A cultural revolution that encompassed painting, literature and music, as well as architecture and design, Catalan Modernisme can also be read as a form of National Romanticism, an attempt to assert Catalonian identity in the face of perceived 'oppression'. As Catalonia grew in wealth and power, the region strove to re-establish its national identity, separate to Castilian Spain, firstly by restoring its language after 150 years of repression, a cultural renaissance known as the *Renaixença,* but equally by a conscious injection of modern ideas intended to reinvigorate Catalan society. The impact of Spain's defeat in the 1898 Cuban War, and the ensuing loss of its last overseas colonies, played a psychological and emotional role: Spain seemed mired in nostalgia, unable to grapple with the loss of imperial status. Against the image of an isolated, decadent Spain, arose the vision of a modern European Catalonia, driven by industry and commerce. Barcelona's civil society was underpinned by numerous local associations: the Orfeo Catala, choral society; the Caixa, the largest savings bank; the Cercle del Liceu, a private members club; the Reial Automobil Club and even the Futbol Club Barcelona founded in 1899. According

to Vicenc Villatoro, Catalonia devised a 'coherent cultural ideology' based on Modernisme, nationalism and mercantilism[52]. Catalonians demanded transformation and regeneration.

Urban Development

The city expanded exponentially, from the medieval Old Town outwards to amalgamate the neighbouring villages of Gracia, Sants, Sant Marti and Sant Andreu into one huge metropolis. This new, vast zone of Barcelona based on the plans of Ildefons Cerda (1815–76) was dubbed the Eixample (Catalan for 'The Addition'); it is based on a grid pattern with chamfered corners. The Eixample became the showcase for the Modernista architects. Industrial materials, metal, glass and tile, were combined with fabulous ornamentation inspired by Hispano-Arabic and Gothic architecture. Wealthy aristocrats and industrialists commissioned show-stealing mansions in the new style, notably on the district's central boulevard, the Passeig de Gracia; the façades of Domènech's Casa Lleó Morera (1906), Puig's Casa Amatller (1898–1900) and Gaudí's Casa Batlló (1906) vie with each other on the so-called 'Manzana de la Discordia'

Puig i Cadafalch, Casa Amatller (1898–1900) and Gaudí i Cornet, Casa Batlló (1906) Manzana de la Discordia (Block of Discord), Passeig de Gracia, Barcelona.

Rigalt i Blanch, stained glass, dining room, Casa Lleó Morera, Passeig de Gracia, Barcelona (1906, Lluís Domènech i Montaner).

(Block of Discord). The Casa Lleó Morera, with furniture and joinery by Gaspar Homar i Mezquida and Josep Pey i Farriol, as well as sculptures by Eusebi Arnau i Mascort and stained glass by Antoni Rigalt i Blanch, is a tour de force, a perfect expression of the gesamtkunstwerk that draws on the talents of several leading artists. Casa Amatller celebrates the fortune made by Antoni Amatller i Costa from cocoa and chocolate. Close by Gaudí's Casa Mila (1905), known as La Pedrera, as it resembles a stone quarry, flouts the rules of conventional style with its undulating rough-hewn façade.

Gaudí, Casa Mila (La Pedrera), Passeig de Gracia, Barcelona (1905).

Antoni Gaudí i Cornet

Gaudí took the tenets of Modernisme to daring extremes and developed a style unmistakably his own, from the serpentine curves of the bench of the Parc Güell (1911–13) to the impossibly grandiose Roman Catholic Temple Expiatori de la Sagrada Familia (1882–), where nature is referenced in virtually every form. The Nativity façade is smothered with animals, from the cow and donkey framing the holy family to the ducks, geese and turkeys that are served during the Christmas festivities. Motifs from the natural world are chosen intentionally to reinforce the symbolic meaning. Facing east, the façade marks a new beginning, the birth of Christ; the central portal, Charity, represents the Three Wise Men and the Shepherds. White lilies and irises symbolize the Virgin's purity. La Sagrada Familia came to dominate Gaudí's life, as the intensely pious architect lived out his final years in the church's crypt working on the project, which is still unfinished. Many criticized Gaudí for his ostentatious bad taste but when he was struck down by a tram aged seventy-four, the whole of Barcelona attended his funeral. Eusebi Güell i Bacigalupi, 1st Count of Güell (1846–1918) was his most loyal patron, the Güell Palace and Parc Güell lasting tributes to their partnership.

Domènech i Montaner

Gaudí can be counted amongst Domènech's pupils at the Escola d'Arquitectura, where he held a forty-five-year tenure as a professor and director. Domènech launched his Modernista career with the Castell dels Tres Dragons (1888), situated in the Parc de la Ciutadella. Serving as a restaurant during the 1888 Universal Exhibition, this marks the moment Barcelona asserted its identity both as the capital of Catalonia and a modern city. The son of a

Gaudí, Nativity Portal, La Sagrada Familia, Barcelona (1882–).

Gaudí, Güell Palace, Carrer Nou de la Rambla, Barcelona (1886–88).

Domènech, Castell de Tres Dragons, Parc de la Ciutadella, built to house the café and restaurant for the Barcelona Universal Exposition 1888.

Domènech, Hospital de Santa Creu i Sant Pau, Barcelona (1902–30).

bookbinder, Domènech was a multi-talented intellectual, who engaged in politics, journalism, botany and heraldry amongst other interests. In search of a national architecture, he blended Gothic forms with Moorish elements alongside the organic naturalism of Art Nouveau. Local traditions were also expressed using brick, tiles and mosaics. He orchestrated the mammoth project of the Hospital de Santa Creu i Sant Pau, Barcelona (1902–30) and the Institut Pere Mata, Reus (1897–1919) for the mentally ill. His private residences include the opulent Casa Lleó Morera and Casa Thomas in Barcelona, Casa Navàs in Reus and the Casa Solà Morales in Olot. His Hotel España (1903) in the Raval district has been beautifully restored; the Saló de les Sirenes (Mermaids' Room), with paintings attributed to Ramon Casas, now serves as the breakfast room. Nevertheless, his most stunning contribution to Modernisme is the Palau de la Música Catalana (1905–08).

Puig i Cadafalch

Another fearsome intellectual and patriot, Puig took up the presidency of the Institute of Catalan Studies from 1942 to his death in 1956. A generation younger than Domènech and Gaudí, Puig drew from both in creating his own decidedly neo-Gothic masterpieces.

Highlights include the Casa Amatller and the Fabrica Casaramona, a textile factory at the foot of Montjuïc, which has been repurposed to house the Caixa Forum. He also designed La Casa Marti (1896), which houses on its ground floor the legendary Els Quatre Gats café, where intellectuals and bohemians of the day (including the painters Ramon Casas and Pablo Picasso) met for many a drink and a discussion. The Avinguda Diagonal is dominated by Puig's castle-like Casa Terrades, popularly known as the Casa de les Punxes or 'House of Spikes' in honour of its pointed turrets. The façade is topped with ceramic murals; one depicting the patron saint of Barcelona St Jorgi (St George) slaying the dragon reads 'Patron Saint of Catalonia give us back our freedom'. Modernista architects harnessed architectural forms and decoration

Puig, La Casa Marti, Els Quatre Gats café, Carrer Montsió, Barcelona (1896).

Puig, Casa Terrades or Casa de les Punxes ('House of Spikes'), Avinguda Diagonal, Barcelona (1905–06).

Valeri, Casa Comalat, Avinguda Diagonal, Barcelona (1906–11).

to express Catalan nationalism.

Coming towards the close of the Modernista era, the Casa Comalat (1906–11, Salvador Valeri i Pupurull) bankrupted its would-be owner. Joan Comalat was forced to cede the property to Damia Mateu. Judging by the abundance of decoration in the lobby, the project overran its cost. The best craftsmen in Barcelona worked on the project: Antoni Rigalt and Jeroni Granell designed and fabricated the windows, while the polychrome ceramics, used as bosses within the plasterwork, were created by Lluís Bru. The awesome two-dimensional whirling patterns recall Baroque opulence.

Modernisme Valencià

Barcelona was not the only Catalan city to respond to modernity and nationalism. Modernisme Valencià is the name given to the New Art and literature associated with the Valencian community: Alcoy, Novelda (Alicante) and Sueca are all members of the Art Nouveau European Route. The architects Demetrio Ribes Marco (1875–1921) and Francisco

Ribes, North Station, Valencia (1906–17).

Mora, Mercado de Colón, Carrer de Jorge Juan, Valencia (1914–16).

Mora Berenguer (1875–1961), who was appointed the municipal architect, transformed the regional capital, Valencia. Ribe's North Station, opened in 1917, is Valencia's most famous Modernista building. The influence of Domènech is clear; the mosaics reflect the Valencian countryside, specifically the Albufera, a cherished area. Known as the 'small sea', the area's unique ecosystem attracts many migratory birds. The local houses are distinguished by their thatched roofs and adobe walls covered with white limewash. Mosaic panels welcome or bid farewell to travellers in different languages. Mora's Mercado de Colón (Christopher Columbus Market) (1914–16) is equally indicative, like the North Station making use of brick, tiles and mosaics; charming vignettes of grape-picking and flower-arranging can be seen in the spandrels of the main entrance arch.

Stile Floreale or Stile Liberty: Milan and Turin

In Italy Stile Floreale or Stile Liberty, taking its name from Liberty's of Regent Street, offers a wonderfully eclectic mix, with quintessential floral ornamentation cascading over buildings that often reference the Baroque or neo-Classicism. Stile Liberty quickly acquired a new sense, creative freedom transformed into an expression of Italian liberation. However, Liberty was primarily motivated by prosperity and fashion rather than nationalistic fervour. Following the Triple Alliance (1882), an agreement between Germany, Austria-Hungary and Italy against France, an injection of capital boosted the economy. Liberty was favoured by the nouveau riche and seen as the style of the bourgeoisie. In addition to lavishing a great deal of money on their town houses, villas were built around the Italian lakes and especially at the seaside. Often holiday homes, their architectural forms are light-hearted and playful.

While residential properties abound, Liberty was deemed too frivolous for civic or ecclesiastical buildings, although the church of Sant'Elisabetta (1907, Pietro Fenoglio), servicing the Leumann Village, a model workers' village in Collegno on the outskirts of Turin, is a notable exception. This originally housed around a thousand residents, employees and their families. Of Swiss origin, Napoleon Leumann, founder of Cotonificio Leumann (Leumann Cotton Mill), was one of several entrepreneurs who resettled in Turin. Augusto Abegg and Emilio Wild, also Swiss, founded the textile company Wild & Abegg, later

Brega, Villino Ruggeri, Pesaro (1902–07).

the Cotonificio Vallesusa. These incomers helped to transform Turin into a 'capital of industry', the Turin Industrial League being founded in 1906.

In Italy individualism prevailed, apparently leading to 'aesthetic anarchism'. Fahr-Becker considers the 'floral sumptuousness… waxed into a wedding-cake building style of totalitarian pomp'[53]. Perhaps she had in mind Villino Ruggeri (1902–1907), Giovanni Brega's seaside villa in Pesaro for Oreste Ruggeri, a pharmaceutical industrialist. The ultimate expression of Stile Floreale, its four façades are covered with the most amazing abstract-floral decorations that swirl in all directions. On the first floor are four themed rooms, the horse chestnut room, the wisteria room, the narcissus room, and the sunflower room.

The obvious historical sources for such extremes can be found in Italian Mannerism, in the paintings of Giuseppe Arcimboldo (1526–93), who constructed faces out of vegetables and flowers, and the spectacular Boboli Gardens, created by the Medici family in Florence. A heady alliance of architecture and nature, the Mannerist garden set out to entertain and surprise, to astonish and scare. The most extreme is the Sacro Bosco (Sacred Wood), also known as the Park of the Monsters, at Bomarzo, created for Vicino Orsini (c.1552–84), the design attributed to Pirro Ligorio. Fantasy clearly motivated Giuseppe Sommaruga (1867–1917) whose buildings certainly defy architectural conventions.

Regione Lombardia

Although Stile Liberty can be found all over Italy, the best expressions are concentrated in Turin, Milan and the Regione Lombardia around Lake Como. The former's proximity to Milan resulted in the development of hotels and villas along the lake shore. The building boom resulted in a heady mixture of architectural styles, from neo-Classical public buildings to mountain chalets as well as Liberty-style villas.

The silk magnate Davide Bernasconi positioned his new villa close to his factory in Cernobbio, Lake

Como. Designed by Alfredo Campanini (1873–1926) the Villa Bernasconi (1904–06) celebrates the source of its owner's wealth; the principal leitmotiv is the silkworm among mulberry leaves. All the decorative elements were orchestrated by Campanini, harmoniously integrating many materials from cement to ceramic tiles. The wrought iron was a collaboration between Campanini and Alessandro Mazzucoteilli (1865–1938), known as the 'magician of iron'. Campanini also worked with Eugenio Quarti (1867–1926) a leading decorator and cabinet maker who favoured unusual materials and lavish ornamentation. His use of inlays of silver, copper, bronze, pewter and nacre resulted in his nickname 'goldsmith of furniture makers'. He designed furniture for Palazzo Castiglioni, Milan and Villa Carosio, Stresa on Lake Maggiore, for Sommaruga.

Milan

The National Exhibition of 1881, twenty years after the unification of the nation, saw Milan establish itself as an industrial centre. Wealthy entrepreneurs, industrialists and bankers, who joined the city's aristocratic elite, required sumptuous palazzos and villas, expressing their wealth and status. They initially favoured Milanese Eclecticism: Luca Beltrami (1854–1933), best known for his restoration work and Camillo Boito (1836–1914), whose 'Stile Boito' is the Italian equivalent of High Victorian architecture, won many commissions. However, the best example of Milanese Eclecticism is the famed Galleria Vittorio Emanuele II, built by architect Giuseppe Mengoni (1829–77) between 1865 and 1867; its glass and iron roof is a testament to technological innovation.

Although many preferred to stick to the tried and tested styles, Liberty was given a boost by the 1906 International Exhibition of Milan celebrating the opening of the Simplon Tunnel. Of the 225 buildings constructed, those designed by the young Tuscan architect Orsino Bongi were largely in the Liberty style. Milan's Civic Aquarium is the only one to

Locati, Civic Aquarium, Viale Gadio, Milan (1906).

survive, designed by Sebastiano Locati. Originally dedicated to fish farming, it serves its new purpose admirably being decorated with aquatic-themed tiles. A fountain forms the centrepiece, water streaming from a hippo's head.

Giuseppe Sommaruga

Sommaruga's breakthrough came with the Palazzo Castiglioni (1901–04) said to be the first expression of Liberty style in the city. Built for the fabulously wealthy entrepreneur Ermenegildo Castiglioni, it has been dubbed the 'manifesto' for Liberty in Milan, a challenge to the Milanese conservative élite. Nevertheless, the building still echoes the great *palazzi* of the Renaissance. The façade is a tour de force, dominated by Sommaruga's preferred motif, putti and Mazzucotelli's twisted ironwork. Although much of the décor has been restored, notably the magnificent gilded peacocks, the original furniture was destroyed

Sommaruga,
Palazzo Castiglioni,
Corso Venezia,
Milan (1901–04).

Bazzaro, *Peace and Industry*, Villa Romeo-Faccanoni, Via
Michelangelo Buonarroti, 48, Milan (1911–13).

at the end of the Second World War.

The rather louche figures by Ernesto Bazzaro (*Peace and Industry*) surrounding the entrance portal earned the building the epithet 'Ca' di ciapp', or House of the Buttocks. They were removed and placed on the Villa Luigi Faccanoni (1911–13). Following its purchase in 1919 by the famous businessman Nicola Romeo, creator of Alfa Romeo, it became the Villa Romeo-Faccanoni. Now functioning as a medical clinic, little survives of the original interior. However, the exterior is a riot of different materials, a base of rough ashlar, bands of coloured stone, moulded tiles and an abundance of putti in litho-cement.

Urban Development

During the opening years of the new century, Milan's ruling class embraced Stile Liberty, commissioning town houses and apartments from Sommaruga, Campanini, Giulio Ulisse Arata (1881–1962), Giovanni Battista Bossi (1864–1924), Ulisse Stacchini

Sommaruga, Villa Romeo-Faccanoni, Via Michelangelo Buonarroti, 48, Milan (1911–13).

(1871–1947) and Andrea Fermini. However, what really distinguishes Milanese Liberty is the metalwork of Mazzucotelli, seen at its best on the Casa Ferrario (1902), by Ernesto Pirovano (1866–1934).

Campanini, whose reputation rests on the Villa Bernasconi (1904–06) and Casa Campanini (1904–06), was both architect and speculative builder. The Casa Campanini stands next to the Palazzo Castiglioni in exemplifying Milanese Liberty. Following Sommaruga in favouring sculptural decoration

Mazzucotelli, Casa Ferrario, Via Spadari 3, Milan (1902, Ernesto Pirovano).

Campanini, Casa Campanini, Via Bellini 11, Milan (1904–06).

Bossi, Casa Guazzoni, Via Malpighi 12, Milan (1904–06).

in litho-cement, his forms are generally lighter. However, the entrance doorway is flanked by two monumental sculptures by Michele Vedani, these demur *femmes-fleurs* representing the arts of painting and architecture.

A clutch of Liberty apartment blocks can be found along Via Marcello Malpighi due to the redevelopment of the area; with the replacement of horse-drawn trams by electric trams, the depot in Via Sirtori, which housed 280 horses, was no longer needed. Bossi's Casa Guazzoni (1904–06), built for the speculator and master builder Cav. Giacomo Guazzoni, was influenced by Sommaruga. The façade is covered in litho-cement sculpture, Sommaruga-style putti and Mucha-style female mascarons in a tangle of foliage. On the corner, two superimposed and conjoined balconies are supported by putti cavorting in all directions. The balconies are linked with iron columns and railings, whose expressive style exemplifies Mazzucotelli's work.

However, Bossi's Casa Galimberti (1902–05), named for the entrepreneurial brothers who financed the project, is completely different. The most photographed example of Milanese Liberty, the façade stands out due to its figural and floral tiles. Designed by Bossi, the tiles were fabricated by the Società ceramica Lombarda, Ing. A. Bertoni & C. The figures were painted by Ferdinando Brambilla, the naturalistic flowers and foliage by Pio Pinzauti. Both elements celebrate rural life, male and female figures picking grapes, plums and figs, an evocative *rus in urbie* or 'country in the city'. The wrought ironwork, also designed by Bossi, was executed by the company Arcari and Bellomi.

The Casa Laugier (1905–06, Antonio Tagliaferri), built for the Baron Laugier, is also distinguished by its ceramics attributed to Galileo Chini (1873–1956). Painter, designer and potter, Chini was a prominent member of the Liberty movement. In 1897, with his partner Vittoria Giunta, he founded a workshop

Bossi, Casa Galimberti Via Malpighi 3, Milan (1902–05).

Santa Teresa pharmacy (1910, Botticelli Company), Casa Laugier, Corso Magenta 96, Milan.

Tagliaferri with tiles by Chini, Casa Laugier, Corso Magenta 96, Milan (1905–06).

L'Arte della Ceramica in Florence. Chini specialized in stoneware with richly coloured lustre glazes. However, most tourists are enraptured by the Santa Teresa pharmacy, which retains its original fixtures and fittings (1910, Botticelli Company).

Despite war damage, one side of the Via Carlo Pisacane retains a complete streetscape of Liberty apartments; it also provides a Who's Who of Milanese Liberty architects. Casa Battaini (1903), distinguished by its painted frieze and rich organic forms, is attributed to Campanini. Casa Balzarini (1902), with horse chestnut leaves providing the motif and Casa Cambiaghi (1902) dominated by peacocks, are by Andrea Fermini. Best known for creating Milan's iconic Stazione di Milano Centrale (1906–31), its style fancifully dubbed Assyrian-Lombard, Ulisse Stacchini was responsible for Casa Via Carlo Pisacane 22 (1903).

In the Porto Venezia area, Giulio Ulisse Arata created several residential buildings for the

Liberty-style buildings along the Via Carlo Pisacane, Milan.

Berri-Meregalli family. Born in 1881, Arata belongs to a younger generation. Beginning his career in his hometown, Piacenza, he trained at the Brera Academy, Milan, before graduating from the Academy of Fine Arts, Rome, in 1906. While at the Brera he was influenced by Luca Beltrami, known for his restoration of Milan's famous Castello Sforzesco, absorbing a thorough knowledge of medieval architectural traditions. Combining historical sources with the Liberty ethos, Arata developed a language of his

Campanini, Casa Battaini, Via Pisacane 12, Milan (1903).

Fermini, Casa Balzarini, Via Pisacane 16, Milan (1902).

Fermini, Casa Cambiaghi, Via Pisacane 18/20 (1902).

Arata, Palazzo Berri Meregalli, Via Cappuccini, Milan (1911–12).

own that spoke to the nationalist aspirations of the early twentieth century. Alongside his friend Antonio Sant' Elia (1888–1916), a key member of the Futurist movement, he was a co-founder of the group New Trends (1914).

His best-known work, the monumental Palazzo Berri Meregalli (1911–15) resembles a castle[54]. No expense was spared, with artists Pietro Adamo Rimoldi (1869–1939) and Angiolo d'Andrea (1880–1942) supplying paintings and mosaics and Mazzucotelli the wrought iron. At the top of the façade, huge putti stand out in the round clinging to the downspouts. The massive walls and low arches recall Roman architecture, while the colourful geometric mosaics add a Byzantine note. The dark and mysterious atrium leads to a remarkable sculpture *Victory* (1919) by Adolfo Wildt (1868–1931), commemorating the end of the war. Wildt was also responsible for the expressive ear-shaped intercom (c.1930) on the Palazzo Sola Busca, Via Serbelloni 10 (1927, Aldo Andreani), inevitably renamed the Ca 'dell'ureggia

Arata, atrium with *Victory* (1919) by Adolfo Wildt, Palazzo Berri Meregalli, Via Cappuccini, Milan.

(House of the Ear). According to the legend, if you wish into the ear, your dreams will come true.

Turin

Turin, the first capital of the kingdom of King Victor Emmanuel II (ruled 1861–78) following the unification of Italy (*Risorgimento*) in 1861, was exalted as Italy's shining beacon of modernity: FIAT, Fabbrica Italiana di Automobili Torino, was founded in 1899, the first plant opening the following year. Their factory, Primera sede FIAT, via Carlo Marochetti (1906) was built in a restrained Liberty style by Alfredo Premoli, the most striking feature being the gates. The Fréjus Tunnel (1871) also made Turin an important communication node between Italy and France. The city was chosen to host the Prima Esposizione Internazionale d'Arte Decorativa Moderna (1902), a high point in the evolution of Modernism[55]. Trained in Austria, Raimondo D'Aronco (1857–1932) was responsible for designing the pavilions; the Triple Alliance encouraged cultural links with Germany and Austria. The Byzantine flavour of the main pavilion can surely be attributed to Aronco's recent return from Istanbul. Modernist tendencies were also promoted by new magazines; *L'Arte decorativa moderna*, published in Turin from 1902 and *L'Architettura italiana* (1905–34). One of the major contributors to the latter was Turin's most famous Liberty architect, Pietro Fenoglio (1865–1927).

Pietro Fenoglio

Born in Turin, Fenoglio trained as an engineer graduating in 1889. His architectural mentor was Carlo Ceppi (1821–1929), known for the neo-Gothic Palazzo Bellia (1898). Fenoglio's first projects were also in a neo-Gothic style but participating in Turin 1902, he was converted to the New Art. Over the course of roughly thirteen years, from his studio on Via XX Settembre, he devised over 300 projects, apartments, villas and palaces. Several can be found in the affluent area around the Corso Francia. He developed a distinctive style, his stucco façades combining pastel colours and with inscribed linear elements and floral subjects. The sculptural details are usually in litho-cement rather than stone. Cement plays an important role in Turin's Liberty architecture both as structure and decoration. Thanks to

D'Aronco, Prima Esposizione Internazionale d'Arte Decorativa Moderna, Turin (1902).

Ceppi, Palazzo Bellia, Via Pietro Micca, Turin (1898).

Fenoglio, atrium, Fenoglio-Lafleur house, Corso Francia, Cit Turin (1902–03).

Fenoglio, Fenoglio-Lafleur house, Corso Francia corner with Via Principi d'Acaja, Cit Turin (1902–03).

the initiative of its owner, Giovanni Porcheddu, the Porcheddu Company was the first Italian construction company to gain the rights to the reinforced-concrete Système Hennebique.

Fenoglio's most indicative building is his own residence, now known as the Fenoglio-Lafleur house (1902–03). In a commanding position on the corner of Corso Francia and Via Principi d'Acaja, Cit Turin, his studio-home was intended to be a stylistic manifesto. This three-storey building boasts a striking façade, the corner dominated by a box-shaped oriel window with coloured glass windows. Fenoglio opted for purely abstract curvilinear and linear forms that continue the inscribed and moulded decorative motifs of the façade. An unusual glass canopy, reminiscent of those created by Guimard for the Paris Métro, crowns the corner. The decorative forms, compass-inscribed lines, show a clear debt to the Vienna Secession; the combination of interlocking circles and flowing lines is seen at its

Fenoglio, staircase, Fenoglio-Lafleur house, Corso Francia, Cit Turin (1902–03).

best in the gate. Despite these borrowings, the overall effect is original and distinctive. Inside, the compass-inscribed lines continue in an imposing atrium door, while the staircase echoes Horta's whiplash. The wooden handrail becomes an abstract

three-dimensional sculpture. Casa Fenoglio was sold to a wealthy Frenchman named Lafleur and from then became Casa Fenoglio-Lafleur.

Nearby the Villino Raby (1901), a collaboration with Gottardo Gussoni, was commissioned by Michele Raby. The asymmetrical plan is dominated by a large, square oriel window, which projects over a corner. This is lavishly decorated, its female mascaron a tribute to Mucha. The coloured glass windows are attributed to the master glassmaker Ciravegna. Although the interiors have been remodelled, much of the decoration by Domenico Smeriglio from Poirino remains. Also of note is the scrolling wrought-iron railing of the staircase leading to the first floor, which extends over three ramps, by Mazzucotelli. He was also responsible for the lampost at the base of the staircase and the hall lantern.

Fenoglio collaborated with Gottardo Gussoni (1869–1952) on several projects. However, Gussoni

Fenoglio, Villino Raby, Corso Francia, Cit Turin (1901).

Fenoglio, staircase, ironwork by Alessandro Mazzuccotelli and painted decoration by Domenico Smeriglio, Villino Raby, Corso Francia, Cit Turin (1901).

Gussoni, Casa della Vittoria or the House of Dragons, Corso Francia, Cit Turin (1918–20).

is best known for Casa della Vittoria, known locally as the House of Dragons (1918–20) on Corso Francia, which returns, on a massive scale, to the castle theme for an appartment block. The building celebrated Italy's victory in the war; it also marks the end of Liberty style.

Urban Development: San Donato and Cit Turin

As one might expect, there are few Liberty buildings in the city centre. However, the experimental Palazzo Bellia (1898), on the new Via Diagonale (now via Pietro Micca) by Carlo Ceppi is said to be Turin's first building in the Liberty style. It was also the first to apply the Système Hennebique for reinforced

Bellini, Casa Florio, Via San Francesco d'Assisi, Turin (1902).

Bellini, Casa Florio, Via Cibrario, Cit Turin (1902).

Bernazzo, Casa Tasca, Via Beaumont, Cit Turin (1902–03).

concrete. Still Gothic in terms of its forms, with four slender towers, the detailing anticipates Liberty's floral motifs. Much of the decoration is in lithocement. The Palazzo Bellia fits harmoniously into the urban context, the new central artery continuing the arcades that are such a distinctive feature of the city. Contributing to this new urban landscape, the Casa Florio (1902), with its commanding corner oriel window, could be mistaken for the work of Fenoglio. Its architect Giuseppe Velati Bellini (1867–1926)

Besozzi, Edificio di civile abitazione, Corso Rodolfo Montevecchio 58 San Donato, Turin (1904).

Battista Alloati, sculptural relief, Casa Maffei, Corso Rodolfo Montevecchio, 50, San Donato, Turin (1904–06, Antonio Vandone).

confusingly created several Casa Florios, the apartment block on via Cibrario (1902), Cit Turin, being equally well known for its sgraffito decoration in the Viennese style.

Cit Turin or Little Turin, northwest of the historic centre, boasts many Liberty buildings. Some have yet to be attributed but the work of Giovan Battista Bernazzo (1872–1949) stands out. His Casa Tasca, via Beaumont (1902–03), dominates a corner plot, the box-shaped oriel window rising to an open loggia echoing the Fenoglio-Lafleur house.

San Donato boasts two remarkable residences on Corso Rodolfo Montevecchio; Giuseppe Besozzi's Edificio di civile abitazione (1904), its reliefs transplanting a rural idyll to the city and Antonio Vandone's (1862–1937) Casa Maffei (1904–06), with metalwork by Mazzucotelli and sculpture by Giovanni Battista Alloati. The iconograpy of the latter is perplexing; on one side a woman riding an eagle (Zeus?) is framed by a Greek harpist and a dancer. In the centre we have an idealized father and mother. This is followed by a male rider mounted on a horse, framed by a violinist and a dancer! The atrium is decorated with a riot of linear forms, flowers and Greco-Roman motifs.

Vandone, atrium Casa Maffei, Corso Rodolfo Montevecchio, 50, San Donato, Turin (1904–06).

de Pinho, Vila Africana, Rua Vasco da Gama, 135, Ílhavo (1907–08).

Arte Nova: Portugal

Portugal's Arte Nova followed architectural developments in Europe rather than leading them. Nevertheless, Arte Nova is a very distinctive blending of regional preferences, notably the use of *azulejos*, painted tiles, with New Art forms. Arte Nova's exuberance is particularly associated with the seaside town of Aveiro, which enjoyed unprecedented prosperity at the turn of the century. Emigrants, known as returnees, who had become rich in Brazil or Portugal's African colonies began to come back to Aveiro and the surrounding area. Vila Africana, Ílhavo (1907–08, José de Pinho) was built for Dr José Vaz, who had served in the African Maritime Partnership, Cape Verde.

Wealth and status demanded opulent residences; money appears to have been thrown at the façades in an act of bravado, expressing the social standing and economic power of the owner. The dominant factor is ostentation. While exteriors are laden with decoration, tiles, metalwork and sculpture, the interiors followed a normal plan as befitting the requirements of conventional bourgeoise living. Casa Mário Pessoa (1906–09), the most extreme example in Aveiro, is a good case in point. Attributed to Francisco Augusto da Silva Rocha (1864–1957), and the Swiss-born Ernesto Korrodi (1870–1944), the façade is an ornamental

da Silva Rocha and Korrodi, Casa Mário Pessoa, Rua Doutor Barbosa de Magalhães 10, Aveiro (1906–09).

tour de force. The building rises through four floors culminating in an arched window resembling a turret, crowned with a large, sculpted sea-eagle grasping a fish in its talons. The decoration runs around doors

da Silva Rocha and Korrodi, entrance, Casa Mário Pessoa, Aveiro (1906–09).

da Silva Rocha and Korrodi, rear courtyard, Casa Mário Pessoa, Aveiro (1906–09).

and frames the windows; the central window is topped with an eagle holding a sunflower in its beak, perhaps an allusion to the New World. Behind a wrought-iron grill of sunflowers, the entrance stretches its curvilinear forms across the width of the façade.

The rear façade is equally extravagant; a Portuguese

lion at is zenith completing the ensemble. However, this façade is also marked by a large expanse of windows, letting in more light than was usual; an arched window takes up the whole of the ground floor, while an arcade on the second floor encloses a loggia reached by an external staircase. A local paper, *Campeão das Províncias*, praised Silva Rocha's architectural achievements:

> [Aveiro] is taking on a more civilized garb, because, lately, houses have been built of beautiful appearance such as those of Mr. Francisco Augusto da Silva Rocha, distinguished director of the School of Industrial Design. The new building that the capitalist, Mr. Mário Belmonte Pessoa, has built in Rossio, is the most modern and distinctive that has so far been completed.

In Porto, Arte Nova buildings cluster around the Mercado do Bolhão (1893), which means 'big bubble', alluding to the marshy land on which the market was built. Another group can be found around the famous Livraria Lello & Irmão bookstore (1906, Francisco Xavier Esteves). In a neo-Gothic style, the shop front's sgraffito decoration, signed Bielman, appropriately alludes to the Arts and Sciences. Thousands visit the bookshop, as the quirky staircase, which rather alarmingly hangs in the centre, is said to have inspired the moving staircases of Harry Potter's Hogwarts. The prettiest Arte Nova house in Porto can be found on Rua Cândido dos Reis, 75–79; its floral forms decidedly Art Nouveau, the central tripartite window references Horta (c.1903). On the parallel Rua da Galeria de Paris, another Horta-inspired façade is dominated by a large ocular window, surrounded by whiplash detailing (c.1903).

Conclusion

Despite this confusing array of names, the mission of Art Nouveau/Jugendstil remained broadly the same. The New Art sought to address the needs of

Esteves, Livraria Lello & Irmão bookstore, Rua das Carmelitas, Porto (1906).

Rua da Galeria de Paris, Porto (c.1903).

Rua Cândido dos Reis, 75–79, Porto (c.1903).

modern life, to utilize the latest technologies and to bring beauty and originality to the urban landscape. A 'Life lived in Art' also demanded 'beautiful objects of everyday use'. Forging an alliance between art and industry, the decorative or applied arts were brought closer to the fine arts. This encouraged painters and sculptors to work in many different media – stained glass, metalworking, ceramics and textiles as well as the graphic arts. Manufacturers, who recognized the economic potential, were encouraged to found art industries employing artists as designers. Increasingly sophisticated consumers appreciated these high-quality commodities. Women were encouraged to fashion a House Beautiful with stunning glass and ceramic *objets d'art* and bronze figurines. Happiness appeared to lie in surrounding oneself with beauty. While many could not afford such luxuries, beauty did reach the people as the New Art transformed the city: banks, department stores, shops, restaurants and even railways stations were transformed into Palaces of Art.

However, while 'batch production', the repetition of certain components and inter-changeable parts, and cheaper materials made the New Art forms more accessible, mass-production led to a plethora of inferior Art Nouveau/Jugendstil commodities. The style, seen everywhere and on everything, from a building to a biscuit tin, literally played itself out. The avant-garde, always trying to stay one step ahead, moved on.

Notes

1. Morris, William, 'The Beauty of Life', *Hopes and Fears for Art*, London: Ellis and White, 1882, p.75.
2. Morris, p.110.
3. von Falke, Jacob, *Art in the House, Historical, Critical and Aesthetical Studies on the Decoration and Furnishing of the Dwelling*, translated from the third German edition by Charles C. Perkins, Boston: L. Prang and Company, 1878, pp.311–16.
4. Baillie Scott, Mackay Hugh, *Houses and Gardens* (1906), reprinted Woodbridge: Antique Collectors' Club, 1995, p.302.
5. The two other leading members were Herbert Percy Horne (1864–1916) and Selwyn Image (1849–1930).
6. Preface to *The Hobby Horse*, January 1886; Naylor, Gillian, *The Arts and Crafts Movement*, London: Studio Vista, 1980, p.117.
7. Sharp, Dennis, 'Mackintosh and Muthesius', Patrick Nuttgens (ed.), *Mackintosh and his Contemporaries*, London: John Murray, 1988, p.15.
8. Breuer, Gerda (ed.), *Haus eines Kunstfreundes, Mackay Hugh Baillie Scott, Charles Rennie Mackintosh and Leopold Bauer*, Stuttgart: Axel Menges, 2002, p.15.
9. Baillie Scott, M.H., 'Some Furniture for the New Palace, Darmstadt', *The Studio*, 14, 1898, pp.91–96.
10. Ulmer, p.22.
11. They did not divorce until 1901.
12. Baillie Scott, 1906, pp.302 and 307.
13. Naylor, Gillian, 'Domesticity and Design Reform: The European Context', Michael Snodin and Elisabet Stavennow-Hidemark, *Carl and Karin Larsson Creators of Swedish Style*, exhibition catalogue, London: V&A, 1997, p.81.
14. Aslin, Elizabeth, *The Aesthetic Movement; Prelude to Art Nouveau*, London: Elek, 1969.
15. Hitchings, Glenys, *George John Skipper (1856–1948). The Man who created Cromer's Skyline*, Norwich: Iceni Print and Products, 2015.
16. Hallam, J. W., *Souvenir of the Royal Arcade, Norwich*, Jarrold and Sons, 1889; Salt, Rosemary, *Plans for a Fine City*, Victorian Society East Anglian Group, Norwich, 1988.
17. Archer, John H. G., *Edgar Wood, architect*, Middleton: Edgar Wood Community Centre, 1987, manchesterhistory.net/edgarwood/bio.html, accessed July 2019.
18. Aslin, p.158.
19. Percy, Clayre and Ridley, Jane (eds), *The Letters of Edwin Lutyens to his Wife Lady Emily*, London: Collins Ltd, 1985, 1st June 1898, p.56, following.
20. Although Salmon Junior became a partner in the firm in 1898, neither his name nor that of Gillespie was acknowledged in the practice title until November 1903 when the firm became Salmon Son & Gillespie.
21. Khnopff, Fernand, 'Some English Art Works at the "Libre Esthetique" at Brussels', *The Studio*, Vol.3, No.13, April 1894, p.32.
22. Watelet, Jacques-Gregoire, *Serrurier-Bovy*, London: Lund Humphries, 1987, p.35.
23. Horta, *Memoires*, p.16; Dierkens-Aubry 1990, p.35.
24. Sedeyn, E., 'Victor Horta', *L'Art decorative*, March 1902, p.238; Dierkens-Aubry 1990, p.37.
25. Boileau, L. C., *Architecture*, 15 April 1899 quoted in Berger, p.238.
26. Julius Posener quoted in Fahr-Becker, p.152.
27. Mucha, Sarah, *Alphonse Mucha*, Prague: Mucha Ltd. and Malcolm Saunders Publishing, 2013, p.82.
28. Mucha, p.82.
29. Anderson, Anne, '"My Hesse should flourish, and

the art in Hesse too", Ernst-Ludwig's Darmstädter Künstlerkolonie: building nationhood through the Arts and Crafts', in Milinda Banerjee, Charlotte Backerra and Cathleen Sarti (eds), *Transnational Histories of the Royal Nation*, London: Palgrave Macmillan, 2017, p.33.

30. Anderson, Stanford, *Peter Behrens and a New Architecture for the Twentieth Century*, Cambridge and London: MIT, 2000, p.33.

31. Ulmer, p.56.

32. Bahr, Herman, *Ein Dokument deutscher Kunst: die Ausstellung der Künstler-Kolonie in Darmstadt, 1901*, Munich: Festschrift (Ernst Ludwig, dem Großherzog von Hessen und bei Rhein) p.6.

33. Some of the buildings were temporary: the ticket booths, flower house, theatre, restaurant and the art gallery were swept away. But the eight houses and the studio complex remained permanent fixtures.

34. Olbrich's dominance caused some resentment; three founding members left after their contracts expired in 1902 – Bürck, Huber and Christiansen. Behrens withdrew the following year. Appointed director of the Applied Art School in Düsseldorf, he also secured a position for Bosselt. Johann Vincenz Cissarz, Paul Haustein and Daniel Greiner were appointed in their place. It was this team who staged the second exhibition on the Mathildenhöhe in 1904. Despite economic ups and downs, alongside the comings and goings of the artists, more exhibitions followed in 1908, 1914 and even 1918.

35. Ulmer, p.89.

36. Segieth, Clelia, 'Memorandum des Vereins Bildender Kunstler Munchens', Michael Buhrs and Bettina Best, *Secession 1892–1914*, exhibition catalogue, Munich: Edition Minerva, 2008, pp.20–24.

37. Sarnitz, August, *Otto Wagner: Forerunner of Modern Architecture*, Köln: Taschen, 2005, p.7.

38. Latham, Ian, *Joseph Maria Olbrich*, London: Academy Editions, 1980, p.18.

39. Sarnitz, p.14.

40. Moravanszky, Akos, *Competing Visions: Aesthetic Invention and Social Imagination in Central European Architecture, 1867–1918*, Cambridge: MIT Press, 1998, p.68.

41. Gerle, Janos, *Art Nouveau in Hungarian Architecture for Connoisseurs*, Budapest: 6BT. Kiado, 2013, p.6.

42. Stamp, Gavin, 'Creating a new architecture: Ödön Lechner in Hungary', *Apollo*, 13 Nov 2015. https://www.apollo-magazine.com › Architecture, accessed July 2019.

43. Stamp, 'Ödön Lechner'.

44. Gerle, p.5.

45. Gerle, p.9.

46. Bede, Béla, *225 Highlights Hungarian Art Nouveau Architecture*, Budapest: Corvina, 2015, p.290.

47. Bede, p.39.

48. Alofsin, Antony, *When Buildings Speak: Architecture as Language in the Habsburg Empire and its Aftermath*, Chicago: University of Chicago Press, 2006, p.149.

49. Stamp, 'Ödön Lechner'.

50. Lajta also worked briefly in Richard Norman Shaw's London office. *See* Edward Heathcote, 'The modern architect who gave Budapest a taste of the future', *Apollo*, 21st May 2018, online version.

51. Gerle, p.56.

52. Villatoro, Vicenc, 'Catalan Modernisme as a Social Movement', *The Sant Pau Modernista Precinct*, Barcelona: Fundacio Privada Hospital de la Santa Crue I Sant Pau, 2014, p.32.

53. Fahr-Becker, p.179.

54. He was also responsible for the Casa Berri Meregalli Via Settembrini/Via Mozart 21 (1911).

55. The site of the exhibition was Valentino Park.

Chapter Three

Art Nouveau/Jugendstil Symbolism

ART NOUVEAU AND JUGENDSTIL WERE much more than architectural or decorative styles; they expressed the zeitgeist, the spirit of the age, being driven by intellectual concerns. Through interconnecting circles, shared friendships and allegiance to the avant-garde, architects and designers were aware of contemporary developments in the fine arts, painting and sculpture, literature and music. The Vienna Secession and Jung-Wien (Young Vienna) exemplify this collective outlook: the painter Gustav Klimt, the architect Josef Hoffmann, the designer Koloman Moser, the composer Gustav Mahler (1860–1911) and the playwright Arthur Schnitzler (1862–1931) moved in the same circles. They were bound by the desire to address the complexitiy of modern life, especially social issues. Artists and writers challenged the 'moralistic stance of nineteenth century literature in favour of sociological truth and psychological – especially sexual – openness'[1]. By challenging the moralistic stance, artists and writers would be accused of immorality and depravity.

Evolution and Degeneration

Pulled in different directions by competing and contradictory ideologies, the era has been described as 'febrile'; 'the new confidence in science and rationalism fought with doubt and pessimism about the direction of civilization'[2]. At the heart of this uncertainty was Darwin's theory of evolution and the notion of the 'survival of the fittest'. Apparently, life was directed by accidental mutations, which through competition either survived or became extinct. Life was either a deterministic mechanism or totally insecure, with things just as likely to go badly as well.

Degeneration (1892), as conceived by the writer Max Nordeau (1849–1923), was the flipside of progressive evolution; the *fin de siècle* was really the *fin de race*, with the leading class, 'the rich inhabitants of great cities', suffering from 'feverish restlessness… the prevalent feeling is that of imminent perdition and extinction'[3]. This mood of pessimism and despair had led to a breakdown of discipline; 'to unbridled lewdness, the unchaining of the beast in man; to the withered heart of the egoist, disdain of all consideration for his fellow man, the trampling under foot of all barriers which enclose brutal greed of lucre and lust of pleasure… it means the end of an established order'[4]. *Fin de siècle* artistic movements, which challenged existing ideals, were singled out linking degeneration to Aestheticism and the cult of Art for Art's Sake.

Emerging in the 1860s, Aestheticism privileged the senses over any other faculty. A work of art was to appeal directly to the eye through its forms, colours and textures. It was to engage the senses – sight, touch, smell, taste and sound. Many works of art strove to link the visual arts with music. In the case of James McNeil Whistler (1834–1903), musicality was directly alluded to in the painting's title, being a nocturn, symphony or harmony. Above all, in order to combat the ugliness of life, a work of art was to be 'beautiful', remembering that beauty was in the 'eye of the beholder'. According to the philosopher Walter Pater (1839–94) a work of art was relevant if it spoke to you, provoked a reaction or, by forging a connection, had meaning.

Pater argued, in his influential 'Conclusion' to *Studies in the History of the Renaissance* (1873) that 'experience itself, is the end'[5]. As life was short, we should live in the moment, constantly seeking new impressions and sensations, to grasp any 'exquisite passion' that would 'set the spirit free for a moment'; 'any stirring of the sense, strange dyes, strange colours, and curious odours, or work of the artist's hands'[6]. A full life meant 'getting as many pulsations as possible' into our allotted time on earth. Art promised a quickening of the senses, offering us 'the highest quality to your moments as they pass, and simply for those moments' sake'[7]. The detractors of Art for Art's Sake were alarmed by this emotionalism, which was seen to erode masculinity; with no narrative, didactic or moral purpose, art was now solely for pleasure and self-gratification. According to Nordau, aesthetes felt 'the bliss of the Beautiful possessing them to the tips of their fingers'[8]. Egotistical and snobbish, the aesthete preferred to lock himself away in a beautiful Palace of Art or dream world. He had no wish to engage in the problems of the day, nor did he care about his fellow man. Encouraging a self-indulgent lifestyle, the New Art was condemned as perverse and unhealthy.

Symbolism

This emphasis on feelings and emotions led artists and writers to explore the inner man. Spirituality and mysticism rather than daily life, the humble and the ordinary, now took precedence. Painters abandoned 'rural-realism', scenes of country life reliant on working directly from nature out of doors. Artists now wished to express ideas; the imagination was given free rein, even on the façade of a building. This reaction against naturalism and realism was dubbed Symbolism. Poets and painters preferred suggestion to plain meaning, using metaphors; 'For a work to be considered Symbolist, its purpose must be to suggest something other than what is actually represented'[9].

Inspired by the new sciences of Neurology and Psychology, taboo subjects featured in novels as well as appearing on stage and canvas. Psychoanalysis, developed by Sigmund Freud (1856–1939), sought to release repressed emotions and experiences, making us aware of our unconscious thoughts. Delving into dreams and childhood memories was a means of revealing repression and conflicts. This insight was considered cathartic. Sexuality looms large, with the femme fatale, a mysterious, seductive woman whose charms ensnare men, taken as a popular leitmotiv. One of the most threatening aspects of the promiscuous 'maneater' was her rejection of motherhood, since denying future generations led to the ultimate destruction of the species. As with Art for Art's Sake, Symbolists were accused of amorality, sickness and decadence; 'their vision has always been somewhat feverish, with the diseased sharpness of over excited nerves'[10].

Symbolic Metaphors

Drawing on ancient myths and legends, Hindu mythology as well as the Bible, natural things were imbued with meaning. The intellectual rigour associated with the high arts of painting and sculpture was now readily applied to functional objects: even a wallpaper could carry a symbolic resonance, as seen in Walter Crane's *Peacock Garden* (1888, V&A). A perennial symbol, the peacock carried both Christian and pagan meaning. As the bird sheds its tail and grows a new one every year, it was taken to embody ever-lasting life and resurrection; it can be seen in many Nativity scenes. In Greek mythology, the peacock was created by Juno, its many eyes keeping a watch on unfaithful Zeus. For some its 'all-seeing eye' was an omen of ill fortune. For the aesthetes, who also venerated lilies and sunflowers, the peacock feather was central to the Cult of Beauty; 'Ars Longa, Vita Brevis' (Life is short, but Art endures). They abound in Riga, ornamenting the façades of Konstantīns Pēkšēns (1859–1928) and Mikhail Eisenstein (1867–1920). Everything in the Art

Quittner and Vágó, Gresham Palace, Széchenyi István tér 5–6, Pest (1905–07).

Nouveau or Jugendstil idiom speaks to you, whether it is a wallpaper, glass vase or a building.

Many symbols are universal, relating to numerous belief systems – the cockerel (dawn), the owl (night), snake (rebirth/healing) and tortoise (longevity/wisdom). The latter is often seen at the foot of Venus, acting as the support of the deity. In Hindu myths the world was created on the turtle's back. On the Nativity portal of Gaudí's Sagrada Familia, two massive columns are supported by a tortoise (land) and turtle (sea), symbolizing the permanence or stability of the cosmos. However, the tortoise is also a symbol of ideal female domesticity, as it is silent and never leaves its house! Artists, attracted to such contrary meanings, played with ambiguity.

The Language of Flowers gave every bloom a meaning; the lily of the Annunciation defined purity, while the rose, drawing on Greek myth as well as

Gaudí, Turtle, Nativity façade, La Sagrada Familia, Barcelona (1882–completed after his death).

Bossi, female mascaron, Casa Guazzoni, Via Malpighi 12, Milan (1904–06).

Monet's series of water lily paintings, begun in 1899, must have contributed to their popularity.

Art Nouveau architects developed a sophisticated floral language based on plants and flowers. The seasons of the year could also express the ages of man, from youth to maturity and ultimately death. Decay and mortality became potent symbols of the *fin de siècle*, the dying century. Yet the New Art, on the cusp of the twentieth century, always looked ahead to renewal and regeneration.

Architecture as Language

Early nineteenth-century Romanticism sparked an interest in myths and ancient rituals. Friedrich Creuzer's encyclopaedic four-volume *Symbolism and Mythology of the Ancient Peoples* (1810–12), translated into English in 1829, linked Greek myth to Indian sources. Creuzer argued fertility symbols, pre-dating language, were the first expressions of man's understanding of the world. Richard Payne Knight's *Inquiry into the Symbolical Language of Ancient Art and Mythology* (1818) revealed the similarity between all ancient religions; the wheat of Demeter and the grapes of Dionysus lay behind the bread and wine of the sacrament. All the gods were personifications of nature, with oppositions of male and female, Heaven and Earth. He argued the lotus, pomegranate and barleycorn were emblems of female 'passive generative power', while their counterpart, the 'male or active generative attribute', was the pinecone[11]. German-born philologist and founder of Indian studies, Max Müller's (1823–1900) *Comparative Mythology* (1856) argued pagan religions shared a common root, hence the Indo-European father-god appears under various names: Zeus, Jupiter, Dyaus Pita (Sky Father). His lectures on 'natural religion' (pantheism) led to accusations of blasphemy.

Scholarship and antiquarianism encouraged the use of Symbolism in architecture, as seen in Sarah Losh's (1785–1853) remarkable church St Mary's, Wreay, Cumbria (1840–42). This is festooned with

Biblical associations, was emblematic of love. The lotus was one of the earliest symbols of creation; according to Egyptian mythology, before the universe existed there was only an infinite ocean, a primeval entity, Nun. A lotus flower arose out of Nun and as the blossom opened a child stepped out, the self-created sun god Ra. Hence, the lotus was the womb of the Earth. It also represented light, its petals the rays of the sun. Closing at sunset and opening at dawn, it embodied continuing life. In Eastern religions the lotus represented unworldliness. Related to the lotus, the water lily means much the same. Buddhists regard the water lily as a symbol of enlightenment, as the bloom emerges from the mud. It simultaneously represents purity, spontaneous generation and divine birth. The blooms on Wagner's Majolica House, Vienna (1898–99) seem to float on water. Claude

lotus flowers, pinecones and palms. Losh's church was known to Rossetti, who wrote to his mother 'She must have been really a great genius and should be better known. She built a church in the Byzantine style, which is full of beauty and imaginative detail' (1869)[12]. Rossetti wanted his friend Philip Webb to see the church; perhaps the Arts and Crafts architect William Lethaby (1857–1931) knew of this remarkable building. It might have encouraged him to write his own treatise on architectural Symbolism.

Architecture, Mysticism and Myth

Lethaby argued, 'if we would have architecture excite an interest, real and general, we must have symbolism, immediately comprehensible by the great majority of spectators'[13]. In his highly influential treatise *Architecture, Mysticism and Myth* (1892), Lethaby

Lethaby, frontispiece, *Architecture, Mysticism and Myth* (1892).

ARCHITECTVRE
MYSTICISM AND
MYTH. *By W. R. Lethaby*
with illustrations by the Author

'*Are there symbols which may be called constant; proper to all races, all societies, and all countries?*' CÉSAR DALY.

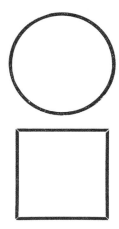

Lethaby, title page, *Architecture, Mysticism and Myth* (1892).

claimed architecture utilized a system of symbols with identifiable philosophical meanings. Looking at diverse ancient traditions he collated the 'esoteric principles of architecture'[14]. He was thereby able to reveal the interconnected myths that underlie all built structures:

> *The perfect temple should stand at the centre of the world, a microcosm of the universe fabric, its walls built four square with the walls of heaven. And thus they stand the world over, be they Egyptian, Buddhist, Mexican, Greek,*

Watts, angel holding the labyrinth or maze, Compton Memorial Chapel, Compton, Surrey (1898).

Lethaby, Eagle Insurance offices, Colmore Row, Birmingham (1900).

or Christian, with the greatest uniformity and exactitude.[15]

According to Lethaby, there were 'global' symbols that could be called constant; proper to all races, all societies, and all countries. The frontispiece carried a circle and a square, the square equalling Earth: 'God created the earth square… and from the top of Mount Sinai, which is the centre of the world, traced a great circle whose circumference touched the four sides of the square'[16]. The circle of God signified infinity, while vaults and domes expressed the sky or heaven, a transcendental realm. The Babylonian terraced pyramid, composed of seven stages, rose to paradise. The labyrinth, numbering seven circles, was the path of life, while the egg was the symbol of creation.

Lethaby put his theories into practice. His Eagle Insurance building on Colmore Row, Birmingham

(1900) is topped by a frieze featuring an eagle flying through a sequence of squares and circles below a continuous wavy line. This could be construed as the firmament or sky. These motifs might also allude to the elements (squares/earth; circles/air; wavy line/water; eagle/fire). The entrance portals recall the Gates of the East and the Gates of the West: 'Through the one the sun enters in the morning… to pass out at the other in the evening, and thence pursue its way back by the dark path to the underworld'[17].

Lethaby's 'comprehensible symbolism' led to the abundant use of heart-shapes ('Home is where the heart is'); birds (harmony); trees (Tree of Life) and peacocks (beauty). Orchard House, Great Smith Street, London (1898) aptly features two Doulton terracotta plaques over its doorways by Neatby, one bearing three stylized fruit trees (apples or pomegranates) and the other confronting peacocks. Everlasting life and the regenerative cycle of nature were classic

Neatby, Orchard House, Great Smith Street, London (1898).

fin de siècle themes. The building also bears some charming female corbels, two representing day and night, another, swathed in greenery, alluding to the dryad, the spirit within the tree.

Trees of Life

Charles Harrison Townsend favoured the Tree of Life as the decorative motif for the Bishopsgate Institute (1895), the Whitechapel Art Gallery (1901), and the Horniman Museum (1898–1901, extended, 1911). The distinctive clock tower of the Horniman appears to pay homage to Lethaby's theories; four turrets,

Townsend, Horniman Museum, Forest Hill, London (1898–1901, extended, 1911).

Wagner, Tree of Life, 'Golden House' or 'House of the Medallions', 38, Linke Wienzeile, Vienna (1898–99).

piercing a circular halo cut with squares, are ornamented with the Tree of Life. Sacred trees abound in world mythology: Yggdrasil, an immense sacred ash tree found in the middle of Asgard, played a central role in Norse cosmology. It had at its roots the spring of knowledge guarded by the Norns, the northern Fates. The Biblical Tree of Life and Tree of Knowledge, the latter invariably conjoined with the serpent of temptation, were fixed in the Christian psyche. Townsend could also draw on Lethaby's examples; at the top of the world mountain sprang a heaven tree on which perched the solar bird. A perennial fountain flowed from its roots – the waters of life, the four rivers and the celestial sea[18]. While Mackintosh's weathervane for the top of the Glasgow School of Art recalls the heaven tree with its solar bird, its meaning for Glaswegians was more obvious. As the bird and the tree were symbols of St Mungo, the patron saint of the city, the message was patriotic[19].

Golden laurel trees grow up Wagner's so-called Golden House or House of the Medallions. Since antiquity, laurels (*Laurus nobilis*) have signified triumph, peace and being an attribute of Apollo, god of artistic creation, the poetic muse. The remarkable decoration on the Golden House includes nine

Moser, Medallions, 'Golden House' or 'House of the Medallions', 38, Linke Wienzeile (1898–99, Otto Wagner).

medallions, designed by Moser, featuring the muses flanked by laurels. They represent human character and aspiration. From left to right these are: Knowledge, Cheerfulness, Thought, Dignity, Seriousness, Love of Truth, Modesty, Conviction and Power. Golden palm branches, also emblematic of victory, peace and everlasting life, emerge from the medallions. At the building's corners, a tree emerges from a planter recalling the Tree of Life; this embodies the life-force, birth, growth and fruition[20]. The gilded laurel dome of Olbrich's Secession House, which has earnt the building its dubious nickname, the Goldenes Krauthappel (Golden Cabbage), bears the same message. Rising from four pillars, symbolic of the Earth (four seasons; four rivers; four continents), this temple dedicated to painting, sculpture and architecture asserted art had transcendent, life-changing power.

The Word in the Pattern

One can read such symbolic motifs as 'the word in the pattern', an expression coined by Mary Seton Watts (1849–1938), the wife of the artist George Frederick Watts (1817–1904). Interested in comparative religions and universal Symbolism, Mary Watts experimented on the ceiling of her home, Limerslease (1891,

Ernest George), before undertaking the challenge of building the extraordinary Compton Memorial Chapel, Surrey (1898). An exemplary Arts and Crafts project, constructed from local materials and hand-crafted by the villagers under Mary Watts' supervision, the Chapel has also been classed New Art through its use of organic curvilinear patterning and symbolic decoration. All the ornamentation carries a profound meaning, from the 'Seraphs clothed in crimson colour' surrounded by inscribed discs (inspiration, aspiration, meditation, mercy, sacrifice, balance) to the peacocked-winged angels that greet you at the portal, alternatively looking down on Earth or up to Heaven. Embracing all creeds, the Chapel celebrates Life, Death and Hope for Immortality.

Such complex iconography required an explanation; in *The Word in the Pattern* (c.1905), Mary declared 'a symbol may well be compared to a magic key… it unlocks a door into a world of enchantment'[21]. She did not intend proscriptive meanings, rather the old symbols were to be suggestive, 'as a song without words'[22]. Given Mary's Scottish roots, she reworked Celtic patterns inscribed on ancient crosses or decorating the borders of illuminated Bibles. The ground plan of the chapel was based on the Circle of Eternity bisected with the Cross of Faith. This divided the building into four quarters (North, South, East,

Watts, 'The Spirit of Truth' (Owl), terracotta panel, Compton Memorial Chapel, Compton, Surrey (1898).

Watts, Seraph, Compton Memorial Chapel, Compton, Surrey (1898).

West). Each quadrant bears a frieze – the Spirit of Hope (Peacocks), the Spirit of Truth (Owls), the Spirit of Love (Pelican) and the Spirit of Light (Eagle). In each quadrant the frieze rests on three corbels: The Labyrinth or Maze (The Way), The Boat of the Sun (The Truth) and The Vine (The Life). The interior is dominated by the Tree of Life, spreading its branches against the blue of Heaven and rising towards 'the Eternal relation of man with God'. Its curvilinear branches bind all the decorative elements together into one cohesive whole; the New Art's defining symbolic motif was the line.

The Infinite Line

Art Nouveau took as its basic premise movement with the flow of human life, a continuum, expressed in a curved, tensile line. The reflexive line that curves back on itself is referred to as whiplash or *coup de fouet*. These undulating, intertwining lines, which can have a hallucinatory effect, were to express the essence of life, its ebb and flow, birth and death (alpha and omega). Natural forms were abstracted into linear patterns; Horta and Guimard utilized plant stalks, stems and sepals rather than flower heads. The sepal is part of the reproductive system, expressing renewed life. The stalk, which provides the plant's structure, is constantly straining upwards, towards the light, a source of energy; organic growth was equated with human life.

Moving beyond metaphor to metamorphosis, plant forms appear to take over and subsume the entire structure of Horta's Hotel Tassel (1893). The vital impulse in life, growth takes control. Peter Kellow argues Art Nouveau's vitalism 'invents a new modern architectural style, the elements of which suggest a metamorphosis of inert, architectural form into living, growing plant form'. Metamorphosis 'implies a surrender to nature'; as this could easily slide into pantheism or paganism and eroticism, Art Nouveau challenged cultural norms. Like Symbolist paintings, it was dangerously subversive.

The sinuous line found expression in the ebb and flow of waves, the serpentine tresses of the femme fatale and as well the meanderings of climbing plants like the clematis. Cascading over wallpapers and even enveloping entire buildings, the whiplash was potently erotic; it sexualized architectural forms. The line is tense, expressing the anxieties of the modern mind caught between the spiritual and the material. The *fin de siècle* appears to live on its nerves, terrified by the speed of change and an uncertain future; the whiplash encapsulates the era's insecurity.

The Reflexive Line: First of its Kind?

Mackmurdo's designs from the 1880s are said to predict Art Nouveau's infinite line; they were known, through exhibitions and publications, to the Belgian

Mackmurdo, frontispiece for *Wren's City Churches*, Orpington: George Allen (1883).

However, the frontispiece was more than a simple rhythmical abstraction based on plant motifs. Closer inspection reveals a subtly encoded message. From the base of the design a phoenix's flame-like wings rise; the phoenix was the emblem of St Paul's Cathedral, which rose from the ashes of the Great Fire of London (1666). These tendrils metamorphosize into flowers, blooms that spring to life from the flames of destruction. It is tempting to equate these blooms with Protean flowers which symbolize change or transformation. Standing heraldically to either side are two elongated peacocks, emblems of eternal beauty. Although the pattern within the chairback is reduced to curvilinear asymmetric plant-based forms, the meaning remains the same – the flow of life.

The premise that an object could be useful, beautiful and meaningful had profound implications for Art Nouveau/Jugendstil designers. A magnificent silver candelabra (1898–99) designed by van de Velde was not only 'the final conquest of the third dimension by the line', it also expressed its function through its form – melting wax pooling at its base and eddies of smoke wafting from its sconces[25].

van de Velde, candelabra (1898–99), Musée du Cinquantenaire, Brussels.

avant-garde group Les XX. Pevsner claimed Mackmurdo's frontispiece for *Wren's City Churches* (1883) was 'the first work of art nouveau which can be traced', identifying its main sources as Rossetti and Burne-Jones, and ultimately, through them, the painter-poet William Blake (1757–1827)[23]. The design is dominated by sinuous lines. Timothy Rogers observes, 'by contorting the stalks into unnatural, whiplashed forms, Mackmurdo fuses the white, negative space between the dark forms into active components of the picture plane'[24]. This juxtaposition of solids and voids, as well as the balanced asymmetry, clearly shows awareness of Japanese compositions. Mackmurdo had already experimented with such sinuous forms; his chair with fretted back is dated 1881. It created a sensation when shown at the International Inventions Exhibition held in London in 1885.

·LINES· OF· MOVEMENT·

Crane, *Line and Form*, London: George Bell & Sons, 1900, p.15.

LINE·ARRANGE·
MENT·IN·RIBBED
SEA·SAND·

Crane, *Line and Form*, London: George Bell & Sons, 1900, p.17.

Walter Crane: Line and Form

The origin of Horta's trademark *coup de fouet* or whip-lash lies partly in Japanese graphics, Morris' textiles and Crane's *Flora's Feast A Masque of Flowers* (1889). The illustration 'That, reddening on the Triton's spear, Foretells the waning of the year', features a human-ized flower, its male body emerging from undulating curvilinear forms. In his influential treatise *Line and Form* (1900), Crane declared 'Outline… is the Alpha and Omega of Art… the ultimate test of draughts-manship'[26]. The Japanese, who drew with a brush, had accustomed themselves to draw in a direct manner without preliminary sketching and 'the charm of their work is largely owing to that crisp freshness of touch'[27]. Line had the power to express move-ment; broken curves suggested 'action and unrest, or the resistance to force'. A series of lines in the same direction, 'a kind of crescendo or wave-line movement', implied continuous force. The wave-line, seen in nature as flowing water and in the streams that channel the sands when the tide recedes, was 'the line of movement'[28]. Crane's wave-line evokes Hogarth's *Line of Beauty* (1753), the S-shaped curve or serpentine line, which also underpinned Rococo design. In 1891, the magazine *L'Art Moderne* carried an appreciation of Crane's work by the painter and designer Georges Lemmen (1865–1916). In the same year Lemmen lent Crane's illustrated books to the Les XX exhibition. Lemmen's cover for the Les XX

catalogue (1891), dominated by a rising sun emerging from swirling waves, pre-figures Horta's whiplash. The rhythmic 'undulating, spiral, serpentine, dancing line' became a common ideal[29].

Jugendstil Line

The Munich-based sculptor Hermann Obrist (1862–1927) utilized the whole plant, the roots, intertwining stems, buds, flowers and stamens, for his highly influ-ential embroidered wall-hanging *Cyclamen* (1895). A series of elegant, looping curves described at the time as *Peitschenhiebe* (whiplash curves), recall Horta and Guimard. Like so many of his generation, Obrist had studied botany, including aquatic flora and fauna. His design for the Krupp fountain in the courtyard of the Kunstgewerbehaus, Munich (c.1912) shows a debt to the research of naturalist and marine biologist Ernst Haeckel (1834–1919). His *Kunstformen der Natur*

Obrist, *Cyclamen*, also known as *The Whiplash*, silk and wool wall-hanging (1895), illustrated *Pan*, Heft III, IV und V, 1895–96, p.327.

Endell, Hofatelier Elvira, Munich (1896–97).

(Art Forms of Nature) (1895–99 and 1904) influenced many contemporary designers, particularly his *Sea Anemones* (Plate 49), *Octopus* (Plate 54) and *Discomedusae Jellyfish* (Plate 8). *Desmonema annasethe* was named in honour of his late wife, Anna Sethe, as the tentacles recalled her long, flowing hair.

Obrist's close friend August Endell (1871–1925), abstracted natural forms on the façade of Munich's most infamous Jugendstil building, the Hofatelier Elvira or Elvira photographic studio (1896–97; destroyed in WW2). The owners, Anita Augspurg and Sophia Goudstikker, were as audacious as their

building; staunch feminists, they were the first German women to set up their own company. A splendid asymmetrical stucco 'dragon' appears to rise out of a foam-topped wave on the otherwise flat surface; it was ridiculed as the 'Dragon's Castle', 'Octopus Rococo' or the 'Chinese Embassy'. Endell was probably influenced by Hokusai's *The Great Wave off Kanagawa* (c.1829–33), his most famous image, as well as Horta's reflexive lines. Apparently, while the façade remained green, the dragon motif changed colour, red, yellow, purple, according to contemporary tinted photographs. The aquatic/underwater fantasy continued inside, spreading over the ceiling and up the staircase. Endell's curvilinear fantasy may have informed fellow Munich architect Riemerschmid's *Room for an Art Lover* displayed at Paris 1900. Here Jugendstil tendrils are at their most extreme; the installation also included a fantastic Obrist wall-fountain. However, Paris 1900 also marked the demise of curvilinear excess. As the new century opened, architects and designers moved towards linear and geometric forms.

The Apotheosis of Line

Loie Fuller's (1862–1928) famous Serpentine dance appeared to bring Art Nouveau's ambiguous curves to life. Fuller's dance was based on swirling veils of diaphanous material held out on batons; these folds were echoed in the temporary theatre created for her by the architect Henri Sauvage (1873–1932) in collaboration with fellow architect Francis Jourdain, the sculptor Pierre Roche and the ceramist Alexandre Bigot, at Paris 1900. Dubbed the 'the Electricity Fairy', using lighting and mirrors, Fuller swirled around the stage transforming herself into a rose, a butterfly or a serpent. Seen as the 'apotheosis of Art Nouveau', Fuller inspired the sculptors François- Rupert Carabin and François-Raoul Larche as well as the jewellery of René Lalique. Franz von Stuck's (1863–1928) *Serpentinentänzerinnen* (Serpentine Dancers) (1896, Darmstadt) was used as the front cover for *Jugend* (1897). The 'Serpentine dance' encapsulated the sensual movement and sexual innuendo which many artists sought to capture in their work, be it a painting, a vase or a piece of jewellery.

Woman: *Femme Fragile, Femme Fatale* and Metamorphosis

Embodying the cycle of life, the New Art took woman as the leitmotiv of modernity. As silent as the mysterious sphinx, Mucha's sculpture *La Nature* also signifies

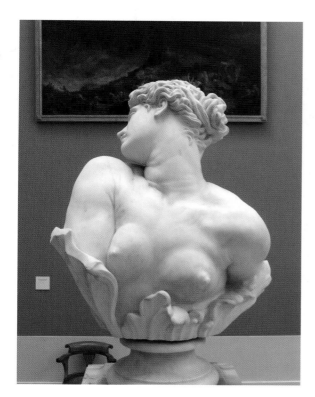

Watts, *Clytie,* marble (c. 1867–68) Harris Museum and Art Gallery, Preston.

date, in the British Museum. Transformed into a sunflower, Watts' *Clytie* strains to follow Helios, the sun god, as he crosses the sky. Drawing its meaning from Clytie, the sunflower came to signify 'hopeless longing and unfulfilled desire'. Alongside the lily and the peacock feather, it became a totem of the aesthetes; as a terracotta panel it can be found adorning many 'Queen Anne-style' buildings. It also features in Morris's wallpapers and textile designs. Significantly, sunflowers adorn the entrance to Bing's L'Art Nouveau, not only a homage to English Aestheticism but also a metaphor for desire.

Femme Fragile: Femme Fleur

The flower fairy or *femme fleur* was popularized by Crane's *Flora's Feast* (1889). Considered a precursor of Art Nouveau, Crane's masque of humanized flowers continues the tradition of Jean-Jacques Grandville's (1803–47) *Les Fleurs Animées* (The Flowers Personified) published in 1847. The *femme fleur* was perfected by Mucha, Eugène Grasset and Paul Berthon (1872–1909). The type can be equated with the *femme fragile*, a frail, child-like maiden in need of help and protection. Although lovely, they are superficial and vacuous. In a literary context, they often have a terminal illness that leads them to an early yet beautiful death.

The female mask, or mascaron, is ubiquitous, seen in Paris, Nancy, Milan, Prague, Budapest and Valencia. In Riga she adorns Eisenstein's lavish façades. His apartment block at Elizabetes iela 10b (1903) is dominated by two gigantic female mascarons that frame a peacock, its tail arched into a magnificent fan. Eisenstein's artistic development remains sketchy. He studied in Saint Petersburg and graduated as a civil engineer in 1893, soon after moving to Riga where he was responsible for many notable apartment blocks. The majority are grouped on Alberta iela (Alberta Street) and Elizabetes iela (Elizabeth Street). Several of these blocks were commissioned by his wealthy client, State Counsellor A. Lebedinsky. Known to

'universal wisdom'. As the female body was deemed to be unstable due to its childbearing capabilities, woman came to embody changefulness. Metamorphosis, which caught the female body on the cusp of a physical transformation, expressed this instability. Ovid's *Metamorphosis* provided plenty of actual examples; Daphne eludes Apollo by transforming into a laurel tree; abandoned by Demophon, Phyllis becomes an almond tree, while the water nymph Clytie, spurred by Helios, is transfixed as a heliotrope (sunflower). Burne-Jones was particularly fond of these themes; *Phyllis and Demophon* (1871, BMAG) was reprised as *The Tree of Forgiveness* (1882, Lady Lever Art Gallery). Upon returning, Demophon remorsefully embraces the tree, which blooms; Phyllis emerges to forgive and reclaim her faithless lover.

G. F. Watts' *Clytie* (1868–78, Watts Gallery), a sculpture produced in marble and bronze, was based on the so-called Townley Clytie, possibly Roman in

Eisenstein, apartment block, Elizabetes iela 10b, Riga (1903).

have visited Paris, Olbrich's Secession House (1898) also seems to have influenced Eisenstein. Female and male mascarons, peacocks and lions also imply a strong attachment to Symbolism. Jeremy Howard observes, 'the tenements create a distinctively stylized and energized ensemble, yet at the same time each building appears to compete with its neighbours in terms of modern decorative extravagance'[30].

An Ornamental Bestiary

Art Nouveau woman is constantly reverting into a flower or a 'beast': a butterfly, dragonfly, snake or, alluding to the Sphinx, even a cat. The concept of reversion or atavism was obviously disturbing, adding to the piquancy of the motif. Due to their short life cycle, butterflies symbolize life and transience. Emerging from a chrysalis they also embody transformation and resurrection. In Christian iconography they denote the soul. The most dramatic use of the butterfly can be found in Barcelona; the huge butterfly arch that tops the Casa Fajol, commonly known as the Casa de la Papallona (1912, Joseph Graner i Prat 1844–1930) is made from *trencadís* or

Graner, Casa Fajol, commonly known as the Casa de la Papallona, Carrer de Llança, 20, Barcelona (1912).

Arndt and Kutzner, 9, Avenue Foch, Metz (1906).

broken coloured tiles, a favoured Modernista technique. Butterflies were also the favoured motif of the Milanese metalworker Mazzucotelli; they were used to spectacular effect on the balconies of the Casa Ferrario (1902, Ernesto Pirovano) and the butterfly gate of the Casa Moneta, Milan (1904, Giuseppe Borioli).

The dragonfly is encoded with a similar message, its iridescence adding to its changefulness; it often appears in jewellery and glass but rarely in architecture. A notable exception occurs in Metz; 9, Avenue Foch (1903–14, Karl Arndt and Albert Kutzner) offers us a complete bestiary, both real and imaginary: a

Körössy, Walkó-ház (Walkó House), Aulich u. 3., Pest (1901).

Sommaruga, Villa Romeo-Faccanoni, Via Michelangelo Buonarroti, 48, Milan (1911–13).

Lavirotte, Lavirotte building, 29 Avenue Rapp, Paris (1901).

monkey, a cat and a frog about to consume a dragonfly rub shoulders with an impish demon. The motif of the frog and the dragonfly also occurs in Budapest on the Walkó-ház (Walkó House) (1901, architect Albert Kálmán Kőrössy, sculptor, Maróti Géza). In addition to frogs, on Sommaruga's Villa Romeo-Faccanoni (1911–13), one finds an improbable walrus!

The serpent, one of the most ancient symbols, is a complex duality of good and evil. In Christian iconography the serpent is associated with the Tree of Knowledge and Eve's temptation. Adam and Eve crown the entrance of the Lavirotte building, Paris (1901), named in honour of its architect. As snakes shed their skin through sloughing, they stand for rebirth, transformation, immortality, and healing. Serpents and the Rod of Asclepius, a serpent-entwined rod wielded by the Greek god of healing and medicine, were an obvious choice for pharmacies. The Engel Apotheke (White Angel Pharmacy), Vienna (1901–02), designed by Oskar Laske (1874–1951) is

Laske, Engel Apotheke (White Angel Pharmacy), Bognergasse 9, Vienna (1901–02).

Berend Broekma, Centraal Apotheek, Voorstreek 58, Leeuwarden, Friesland (1905).

particularly beautiful, being executed in mosaic. To either side of the façade, a winged angel, with a snake coiling round her arm, holds aloft a gilded bowl. She could be Hygieia, the goddess of health and daughter of Asclepius. A mystical vapour emanating from the bowl meanders up the building to frame a frieze of sunflowers harbouring a pair of serpents slithering round two beautiful pots. The Centraal Apotheek (1905, Gerhardus Berend Broekema, 1866–1946), Leeuwarden, Friesland, Holland, bears a similar motif, a tile panel with a snake coiling up Hygieia's arm to a chalice.

The head of Medusa, framed by her snake-like tresses, plays a central role in the iconography of the Vienna Secession. From the outset, Pallas Athena, goddess of wisdom as well as war, was taken as their totem, as seen on Villa Wagner II (1912–13). Athena's symbols include owls, olive trees, snakes and the Gorgoneion, the head of Medusa, worn for protection. The Gorgoneion, which has the power to turn men to stone, appears on Athena's shield, terrifying those who confront her in battle. Three Gorgoneion,

Wagner, Villa Wagner II, Hüttelbergstraße 28, Vienna (1912–13).

Olbrich, Gorgoneion, Painting, Architecture and Sculpture, Secession exhibition building, Vienna (1898).

Eisenstein, Gorgoneion, Lyebedinskiy apartment building, Alberta iela 4, Riga (1904).

symbolizing painting, architecture and sculpture, guard the portal of Olbrich's Secession House (1898). The snakes appear to detach themselves, running immediately below the building's golden dome. Eisenstein reprised the three Gorgoneion on his apartment block on Alberta iela 4, Riga (1904). They also appear in Budapest, most notably on the Török Bank (1905–06).

Athena's owls, designed by Moser, also feature on the Secession building. They were popular New Art emblems simply signifying night, as seen on the Maison Les Hiboux (1899, Edward Pelseneer 1870–1947) on the Avenue Brugmann, Brussels. Built for the Symbolist painter Fernand Khnopff, the house owes its name to the night birds settled on the crown of the façade. They can also be seen in the sgraffito above the front door.

Bats, also associated with the night, were given a fillip with the publication of Bram Stoker's *Dracula* (1897). Bats look down on you from the fourth-floor loggia of the apartment block on the Rue d'Abbeville (1901) by father and son architects Albert and

Albert and Edouart Autant, apartment block, Rue d'Abbeville, Paris (1901).

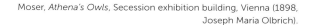

Moser, *Athena's Owls*, Secession exhibition building, Vienna (1898, Joseph Maria Olbrich).

Pelseneer, Maison Les Hiboux, avenue Brugmann, Brussels (1899).

Edouart Autant. The façade is richly decorated with lush vegetation and creepers, attributed to the ceramist Alexandre Bigot.

Romantic Nationalism

The New Art, although fostered through internationalism, was nevertheless often inward-looking. This was in part a reaction to globalization, technological innovations, industrialization and urbanization threatening to erode nationhood. This resulted in regional and national differences that were often shaped by patriotic sentiments. Identity lies at the heart of understanding all the manifestations of Art Nouveau, Jugendstil and Secession. In countries that felt oppressed (Norway, Hungary and Finland), recovering national identity inevitably led to a revival of folk art and crafts as well as indigenous, rural architectural forms. This could extend to a revival of the native tongue and the gathering of folk tales and sagas. Mackintosh, seen as an exemplary modern architect, was inspired by Celtic ornamentation and looked to Scottish baronial castles for his architectural forms. In Nancy, Frenchness was rooted in reviving mid-eighteenth century Rococo grandeur

rather than folk art. Nevertheless, l'École de Nancy was another attempt at asserting national identity in the face of German aggression. For the Darmstadt artist's colony, Jugendstil was a heady mix of modernity and nationalism, the desire to express a progressive ethos clothed in German forms. It was a means of bringing a fragmented nation together to create a 'Motherland'. Yet this search for a collective identity, Glaswegian/Scottish, Darmstadt/German or Barcelona/Catalonia, also encouraged individualism, with architects and designers creating their own distinctive language of forms.

In Barcelona, nationalism was expressed through symbolic emblems, notably those associated with St George, the patron saint of the city. The Christian knight is seen fighting the dragon by the entrance to Pugi's Casa Amatller (1898–1900), while next door the façade of Gaudí's Casa Batlló (1906) expresses the eternal battle between good and evil. The skeletal base is said to represent the bones of the dragon's victims, the mask-like balconies, with their empty eye-sockets, could be skulls or masks. The broken fragments of tile, trencadís, that glisten over the façade could be the scales of the dragon or tickertape thrown at a Mardi Gras, celebrating the death of the monster. However, this surface has also been interpreted as

Arnau, *St George and the Dragon*, Casa Amatller, Passeig de Gracia, Barcelona (1898–1900, Puig i Cadafalch).

Gaudí, staircase, Casa Batlló, Passeig de Gracia, Barcelona (1906).

Gaudí, Casa Batlló on St George's Day, Passeig de Gracia, Barcelona (1906).

Gaudí, roof line and four-armed cross, Casa Batlló, Passeig de Gracia, Barcelona (1906).

water strewn with water lilies. The dragon's back forms the staircase to the *piano nobile,* where the principal rooms are found. However, the tour de force is the roofline; a tower bearing a four-armed cross represents St George locked in battle with the dragon, whose scaly back is fashioned from roof tiles below the undulating ridge. This is architecture transformed into storytelling, the 'word in pattern'; a vivid imagination envisions the dragon roaring fire from the top of the building. On St George's Day (23rd April) the Casa Batllo is smothered with roses; according to the legend, a red rose grows from the spilt blood of the dragon.

National Romanticism was especially strong in countries seeking autonomy. Norway did not achieve independence from Sweden until 1905, while Finland remained a Russian Grand Duchy until 1917. Norway had a rich tradition to draw on. Artist and designer Gerard Munthe (1849–1929) turned to the Viking sagas; he created a fairy-tale interior for the Tourist

Schytte-Berg, entrance Svaneapoteket (Swan Pharmacy), now the Jugendstilsenteret, Ålesund (1905–07).

Schytte-Berg, Svaneapoteket (Swan Pharmacy), now the Jugendstilsenteret, Ålesund (1905–07).

Schytte-Berg, staircase, Svaneapoteket (Swan Pharmacy), now the Jugendstilsenteret, Ålesund (1905–07).

Flodin, *Trolls*, Pohjola Insurance building, Aleksanterinkatu 44 and Mikonkatu 3, Helsinki (1899–1900, Gesellius, Lindgren and Saarinen).

Gesellius, Lindgren and Saarinen, entrance, Pohjola Insurance building, Aleksanterinkatu 44 and Mikonkatu 3, Helsinki (1899–1901).

Hotel in Oslo that retold the story of Sigurd. Northern folklore provided plenty of tales involving wizards, witches, ogres and trolls: Edvard Greig's (1844–1907) musical setting for Ibsen's *Peer Gynt* features the 'March of the Trolls' (1875). When the coastal town Ålesund was destroyed by fire in 1904 the city was rebuilt in a distinctive Jugendstil style that draws on local traditions. Gaping-mouthed cod peer at you, much like gargoyles, from warehouses, while the prow of a Viking ship is transformed into a capitol. Helmeted Vikings become menacing face-masks. Celtic interlace and Viking back-biting animals wind their way across façades and around doorways. The preference for granite also speaks to the desire to express nationalism through local materials. The Swan Pharmacy, which now functions as a museum commemorating the fire and the rebuilding of Ålesund, features many of these distinctive devices as well as a plethora of owls.

A similar nationalist fervour swept Finland.

Painter Akseli Gallen-Kallela (1865–1931), who changed his name to the Finnish form as an act of patriotism, drew on the *Kalevala*, the national epic, while Jean Sibelius (1865–1957) immortalized his homeland in the 'tone poem' *Finlandia* (1899). In Helsinki the Pohjola Insurance building (1899–1901, Herman Gesellius, Armas Lindgren and Eliel Saarinen) plays with Finnish cultural identity, its façade highlighting the dangers you need to insure against; bears, wolves, trolls and devils, inspired by the *Kalevala*, look down on you[31]. The bear was also the company's symbol. The sculptures are attributed to Hilda Flodin (1877–1958), a pupil of Auguste Rodin (1840–1917). The chunky materials, rough-hewn soapstone, serpentine and red granite also allude to the harsh conditions of the North. However, behind the façades the building is brick with structural steel. The deeply recessed entrance shields an impressive door, its metalwork echoing Finnish folk-art motifs.

Saarinen, Central Station, Helsinki (1909–19).

by a huge, arched window, in Richardson Romanesque style, flanked by two pairs of monolithic male statues holding spherical lamps. The toothed and linear patterns surrounding the window echo Vienna Secession forms, as do the segmented gable ends. The station's architectural and decorative forms stand on the threshold of Art Deco. Jonathan Glancey rightly considers Saarinen 'a bridge between the architectural concerns of the nineteenth and twentieth centuries'[33].

Nancy's Style Florale

National Romanticism as expressed in Nancy is directly related to the annexation of the whole of Alsace and one-third of Lorraine by the German Reich, following the Franco-Prussian War (1870–71). Gallé, who fought in the Franco-Prussian war, used a rich array of symbolic motifs. He deployed the flora of the Vosges, pine trees, ferns, hogweed, as well as thistles, to express regional identity, alongside the cockerel and the rose, the traditional emblems of France.

As the name suggests, Style Florale relied on carefully selected plants and flowers, as well as other natural motifs; many were already well-established patriotic symbols. Gallé's emblematic *The Rhine* or *Grand Table Lorraine* created for Paris 1889 stands as his political manifesto. The marquetry top expresses the hope that the German Empire would be pushed back beyond the Rhine, which was deemed the natural border between France and Germany. The heavily carved legs feature the double-barred Cross of Lorraine, while the *entretoise* (stretcher) is transformed into a mass of impenetrable thistles. The *chardon* (thistle), complete with its roots, was incorporated into the city's coat of arms granted in 1575. Its prickles visualize the city's motto, *Nul ne s'y frotte* (No one attacks it) or *Non inultus premor* (No one attacks me with impunity). This warning refers to the Battle of Nancy in 1477, when René II, against the odds, defeated the much larger forces of Charles the Bold of Burgundy[34]. The moral of the motto was obvious; it was dangerous to underestimate the

Finnish architect Bertel Jung criticized the romantic elements as embodying 'primitive, partially crude and untamed force'[32]. This 'Finnish-naturalistic' was also informed by contemporary American buildings: Richardson's Cheney Building, Hartford (1875–76) was originally topped by a pyramidal tower. The tower on the Pohjola building has been likened to a pine-cone. The arched windows at ground level also echo Richardson's signature Romanesque. The interior is equally quirky, folklore themes conjoined with rustic woodwork, the doorways by Erik O. W. Ehrström and iron wheel chandeliers by G. W. Sohlberg. The cast-iron stair banister is based on pine-tree motifs, while the newel posts terminate in trolls or lanterns.

Helsinki's famous railway station conceived by Eliel Saarinen offers a unique blend of Romantic Nationalism and modernity (1909–19). Clad in Finnish pink granite, the entrance façade is dominated strength of Lorraine. The thistle can often be seen entwined round the double-barred cross of Lorraine; in this stained glass window, appropriately on the Rue Jeanne-d'Arc, the patron saint of France is flanked by the coat-of-arms of her birth place, Domrémy-la-Pucelle in the Vosges and the cross of Lorraine.

As well as thistles, the forests of the Vosges supplied many other meaningful emblems. Sacred since antiquity, the pinecone was a symbol of reproduction in Assyria, while in Babylon it was carried by the creator-god Marduk. It topped the staff of the Greek god Dionysus and the Roman Bacchus. Pinecones embody 'spiritual enlightenment', being associated with the pinecone-shaped pineal gland which the French philosopher René Descartes speculated was the 'abode of the spirit of man'; 'The soul has its seat in the little gland which exists in the middle of the brain'[35]. Pinecones are often allied with serpents, an allusion to the Tree of Knowledge. However, as evergreens they are also related to the Tree of Life, symbolizing everlasting or eternal life. For this reason, a pinecone crowns the Pope's sacred staff. Imbued with so many meanings, the pinecone has acquired totemic power. They frame the doorway of André's

Gallé, *The Rhine* or *Grand Table Lorraine*, shown at the Paris Exposition Universelle 1889 (Musée l'École de Nancy).

André and Charbonnier, Joan of Arc stained glass window, Ducret apartments, 66, Rue Jeanne-d'Arc, Nancy (1908).

André, Maison Huot, Quai Claude Le Lorrain, Nancy (1903).

Charbonnier and Majorelle, Ginkgo Pharmacy, Rue des Dominicains, Nancy (1915).

Huot House (1903). Pine fronds and ferns feature in Grüber's windows for the Excelsior café. Unfurling ferns implied rejuvenation, as seen on the Ginkgo Pharmacy (1915, Paul Charbonnier).

Style Florale favoured *ombelles* for both structural and ornamental forms: *berce des prés* (hogweed), *patte d'ours* (bear paw), *herbe du diable* (devil's herb). Hogweed (*Heracleum sphondylium*), a relative of cow parsley, grows abundantly in the forest of Lorraine. An 'umbellifer', it displays large, umbrella-like clusters of creamy-white flowers between May and August. Giant hogweed (*Heracleum mantegazzianum*) as the name suggests is a larger variety, which can grow to over 5m. The sap of the giant hogweed being toxic, causing blisters on the skin, means it is regarded as a noxious weed. Vallin, Grüber, Majorelle and Gallé exploited the structure of *ombelles*. Gallé's chaise *Berce des prés*

Gallé, chaise *Berce des prés* (1902) Musée l'École de Nancy.

(1902) uses the umbrella-like flowers to form the back of a sofa, as well as the tubular stalk for its structure. Vallin exploited the grooved stalk in both his furniture and architectural forms. The Kronberg desk and chair (1902, Musée l'École de Nancy), made for Jules Kronberg, a coal merchant; *Banquette-bibliothèque au mineur* (1902, Musée l'École de Nancy) and the Masson dining room (1903–06, Musée l'École de Nancy) for Charles Masson, all rely on the *berce des prés.* The most dramatic use of the *ombelle* motif can be found on Biet and Vallin's 22 Rue de la Commanderie (1901–02); the spikey forms of the wrought-iron entrance gate and railings are rather menacing.

Honesty, moonwort or satinpod (*Lunaria annua*) was a favourite motif of Majorelle; it decorates the entrance of his villa. Its attraction was its translucent seedpods, which gave rise to its name. But in South East Asia, it is known as the 'money plant' and in France *monnaie du pape* (the Pope's money). Its use in the Banque Renauld (1907–10, Émile André and Paul Charbonnier) was intended to signal the prosperity of the city. The motif appears on the mahogany counters, Majorelle's cast-iron and bronze stair banister and Grüber's imposts over the doors on the first floor.

The Ginkgo Pharmacy lives up to its name; a giant ginkgo leaf in mosaic dominates the floor. Given its

Vallin, cabinet, Maison Bergeret, 24, rue Lionnois, Nancy (1903–04, Lucien Weissenburger).

Biet building, 22 Rue de la Commanderie, Nancy (1901–02, George Biet and Eugène Vallin).

Marjorelle, entrance Villa Majorelle or Villa Jika, 1 Rue Louis Majorelle, Nancy (1901–02, Henri Sauvage).

Majorelle, staircase banister, Banque Renauld, Rue Saint Georges, Nancy (1907–10, Émile André and Paul Charbonnier).

Charbonnier and Majorelle, mosaic, Ginkgo Pharmacy, Rue des Dominicains, Nancy (1915).

Japanese origins, *Ginkgo biloba*, also known as the Maidenhair tree, was bound to be popular. A 'living fossil', the leaves are unique among seed plants, being fan-shaped with veins radiating out, sometimes splitting but never forming a network.

The 'Glasgow Rose'

Given the many emblems the Glasgow Four could have chosen why did the group favour the rose? Jesse Newberry (1864–1948), the wife of Francis Newberry, the Head of the Glasgow School of Art, is credited as the inventor of the angular Glasgow rose, which has been likened to a cabbage. Favouring embroidery, Newberry was keen to raise its status as an art form. She established an Embroidery Department within the Glasgow School of Art in 1894. The two Macdonald sisters, Margaret and Frances, who had enrolled at the School of Art by 1891, would have been familiar with Newberry's style. By 1894 the sisters were collaborating with Mackintosh and McNair, forming a collaborative partnership known as The Four.

Mackintosh based his enigmatic mural for Miss Cranston's Buchanan Street tea rooms (1897) on the rose. A likeness of Margaret, dressed in a white kimono, is either emerging from or being transformed into a rose tree, her head framed by a gilded moon-like disk or nimbus. The striking design was based on an earlier watercolour *Part Seen, Part Imagined* (1896). Was this a pun on the tea rose, the original tea-scented Chinas, a large Asian climbing rose with pale-yellow blossoms? Tea roses were named for their fragrance being reminiscent of Chinese black tea. With its central motif of a stylized tree, Mackintosh imagines a classic '*Rus in urbe*', an idyllic retreat within the grimy 'Second City of Empire' in which to take tea. Although still representational, Mackintosh's arabesques verge on the abstract. While he would have been familiar with Burne-Jones's monumental *The Legend of the Briar Rose* series (1885–90, Buscot Park), we can only speculate that he was aware of Horta or Guimard. However, there is no doubt that he was sympathetic to the Celtic revival; linear motifs based on the Celtic Triquetra (Trinity Knot), which interweaves one continuous line, the Triskele or Triskelion, another triad motif and the Celtic Tree

of Life were popularized by Archibald Knox, Liberty's chief designer.

French Connections: The Briar Rose

The rose has become indelibly associated with the Glasgow school, but it is also an important emblem for France. *Rosa La France* is a cultivar created by the rosarian Jean-Baptiste André Guillot in 1867. It is generally accepted to be the first hybrid tea rose, recognized as a class in the 1890s. It therefore marks the birth of the modern rose. The rose features in several French fairy tales. Charles Perrault (1628–1703) *Histoires ou contes du temps passé avec des moralités* (Histories or Tales from Past Times, with Morals) (1697) includes *Sleeping Beauty* or *The Story of the Briar Rose*. *La Belle et la Bête* (Beauty and the Beast), written by Gabrielle-Suzanne Barbot de Villeneuve (1740), hinges on a white rose. While her sisters demand expensive gifts, Beauty asks her father for a rose. He plucks one from the Beast's garden, who demands a terrible price, Beauty must take her father's place. Only by finding true love will the Beast revert into human form.

As an emblem of love, the rose has a long pagan and Christian history. Fair Rosamund or the 'Rose of the World' (*rosa mundi*), Rosamund Clifford, the mistress of Henry II of England famed for her beauty, was concealed from Queen Eleanor of Aquitaine in a complicated maze or bower. The story does not end well; discovered by Eleanor, Rosamund must choose between taking her own life or being killed. The immensely popular French medieval poem *Le Roman de la Rose* (The Romance of the Rose) was a treatise on chivalric courtly love; in the quest to pick the Rose (the conquest of love), the flower represents the lady and her wooing. The rose symbolizes female sexuality. Retold by Chaucer and Morris, in his epic poem *The Earthly Paradise* (1868), it was a favourite theme of Burne-Jones who envisaged a triptych. The Pilgrim of Love goes in search of true love. He is tempted by the Garden of Idleness, where various vices try to lead him astray (avarice, hate, envy). But Love leads the Pilgrim to *The Heart of the Rose* (1889, private collection), where true love awaits.

The expression 'sub rosa' (in secret) goes back to the Romans. Five-petalled roses were often carved on confessionals, indicating that the conversations would remain secret. The Tudor rose also has five petals; a large rose decorated the ceiling of the privy chamber where decisions of state were made in secret.

Mackintosh, mural, Buchanan Street Tea Rooms, Glasgow (1897). Gleeson White, 'Some Glasgow Designers and Their Work Part I', *The Studio*, Vol.11, No.152, July 15 1897, pp.96–7.

The Ancient and Mystical Order Rosæ Crucis (Rosicrucianism) naturally took the rose as an emblem of their order, whose secrets were 'concealed from the average man'. These secrets provided insight into nature, the physical universe, and the spiritual realm. Joséphin Péladan's (1858–1918) Salon de la Rose + Croix, six art and music salons hosted by the novelist and mystic, grew out of Péladan's Mystic Order of the Rose + Croix, a cultic religious movement he established in Paris. These salons attracted many prominent avant-garde Symbolist painters, writers, and composers including Fernand Khnopff, Jan Toorop, Jean Delville and Carlos Schwabe, who designed a poster for the first salon (1892).

Conclusion

Lethaby's argument appears to hold true, that an architectural language based on universal symbols was viable. Whether these symbols were intelligible to all is open to debate. The viewer needed to have read the Bible, be conversant with Greek legends and mythology as well as medieval sources and to be aware of popular culture such as the Language of Flowers. While some metaphors were obvious – peacocks (beauty), lilies (purity) and sunflowers (desire) – others were esoteric. However, by making us read or analyse a building through its decorative forms, as we would a painting, pushed the applied arts closer to the intellectually rigorous fine arts. Moreover, imbuing motifs with patriotic fervour enabled an empathetic connection between the citizen and the built environment. However, Horta moved beyond metaphor to metamorphosis, thoroughly embracing 'the vital impulse in nature'. By transforming inert materials into organic forms his buildings are living, growing, plant forms; the building becomes 'nature before our eyes'[36].

Notes

1.   Schorske, Carl E., *Fin-De-Siecle Vienna: Politics and Culture*, New York: Random House, 1981, p.212.
2.   Kellow, Peter, 'Vitalism and the Meaning of Art Nouveau', *American Arts Quarterly*, Vol.30, No.2, Spring 2013. www.nccsc.net › Archives › Painting › Essay, accessed January 2020.
3.   Nordau, Max, *Degeneration*, London: William Heineman, 1895, p.2.
4.   Nordau, p.5.
5.   Pater, Walter, *The Renaissance Studies in Art and Poetry*, Oxford: OUP, 1986, p.152.
6.   Pater, p.152.
7.   Pater, p.153.
8.   Nordau, p.19.

9. Facos, Michelle, *Symbolist Art in Context*, Berkeley: University of California Press, 2000, p.15.

10. Symons, Arthur, 'The Decadent Movement in Literature', *Harper's New Monthly Magazine*, Vol.87, November 1893, pp.858–68.

11. Knight, Richard Payne, *Inquiry into the Symbolical Language of Ancient Art and Mythology*, reprinted, 1836, London: Black and Armstrong, pp.32, 39–40, 124, 160.

12. Uglow, Jenny, *The Pinecone. The Story of Sarah Losh, Romantic Heroine, Architect and Visionary*, London: Faber and Faber, 2012, p.278.

13. Lethaby, William, *Architecture, Mysticism and Myth*, London: Percival & Co., 1892, p.7.

14. Lethaby, 'Preface'.

15. Lethaby, p.51.

16. Lethaby, p.73.

17. Lethaby, p.174.

18. Lethaby, pp.74–75.

19. The Bird: Mungo restored life to a robin that had been killed by some of his classmates. The Tree: Mungo had been left in charge of a fire in Saint Serf's monastery. He fell asleep and the fire went out. Taking a hazel branch, he restarted the fire.

20. Alofsin, Anthony, *Architecture as Language in the Habsburg Empire and Its Aftermath, 1867–1933*, Chicago: University of Chicago Press, 2006, p.65.

21. Watts, Mary, *The Word in the Pattern: A key to the Symbols of the walls of the chapel at Compton*, London: William H. Ward & Co., pp.30–31.

22. Watts, p.31.

23. Pevsner, Nikolaus, *Pioneers of Modern Design*, Harmondsworth: Penguin Books, 1975, p.90. Mackmurdo bravely came to the defence of Sir Christopher Wren's London churches; calls were being made for their demolition.

24. Arthur Heygate Mackmurdo, www.victorianweb.org/art/design/mackmurdo/21.html

25. Fahr-Becker, p.159.

26. Crane, Walter, *Line and Form*, London: George Bell & Sons, 1900, p.1. His practical manuals were already well known; *The Claims of Decorative Art*, 1892 and *The Bases of Design*, 1898.

27. Crane, p.10.

28. Crane, pp.16–17.

29. Dierkens-Aubry, p.38.

30. Howard, p.202.

31. Ashby, Charlotte, 'The Pohjola Building: Reconciling contradictions in Finnish architecture around 1900', in Raymond Quek and Darren Deane with Sarah Butler (eds.) *Nationalism and Architecture*, Farnham: Ashgate, 2012, pp.135–46.

32. Norri, Marja-Riitta, Standertskjöld, Elina, and Wang, Wilfried, 'Finland', *20th-Century Architecture*, Munich/London/New York: Prestel, 2000, pp.30–31, 153.

33. Glancey, Jonathan, *Twentieth-Century Architecture*. London: Carlton Books, p.79.

34. René II, Duke of Lorraine inherited the two-barred cross as a symbol from the House of Anjou. He placed the symbol on his flag before the Battle of Nancy.

35. Uglow, p.214.

36. Kellow.

Chapter Four

Materials and Techniques

The Age of Glass, Ceramics and Iron

The Eiffel Tower (1889) encapsulates the new era of iron and glass, materials that were transformed from utilitarian into beautiful architectural forms. These materials, already commonplace for railway stations and warehouses, were applied to civic and domestic architecture. Iron provided not only the structure but also the embellishment in the form of balconies and awnings. Ceramics, used both externally and internally, and stained glass brought colour and light. Ceramics were also hygienic and easy to clean given the high levels of pollution at the close of the century. Plus, then as now, graffiti was a problem. No longer restricted to ecclesiastical commissions, the scope of stained glass expanded. Designers were given a free hand to work in the New Art idiom: cafés, restaurants, banks, pharmacies, department stores were all enriched with stained glass. The attention given to metalwork, the use of ceramics and glass raised the status of the applied arts, bringing them closer to the fine arts. They give New Art buildings their distinctive character.

Stained Glass

Stained-glass production underwent a technical and stylistic revolution largely due to the endeavours of Morris in England and Louis Comfort Tiffany (1848–1933) in America. Morris looked back to medieval precursors in his quest to reinvent stained glass. During the eighteenth century, the practice was to use clear glass painted with enamels rather than coloured glass. The lead cames, a divider bar used to join pieces of glass together to make a larger glazing panel, were no longer required to hold individually cut pieces of coloured glass. Instead windows were made up of regular square or rectangular panes. The Gothic Revival (c.1815–70), which saw the construction of many new churches, demanded a return to traditional stained glass windows. Many Victorian families commissioned memorial windows for their local parish church. Commercial manufacturing

Kempe (1837–1907), *Annunciation*, Mary Seymour memorial window (1899) All Saints, Carshalton, Sutton, London.

responded to the high demand and by the close of the century the British stained glass industry was enormous, with centres in London, Birmingham, Liverpool, Newcastle-upon-Tyne, Edinburgh and Glasgow. Many windows were exported, notably to the British colonies. However, decorative quarry glass was mass-produced, moulded and printed, rather than hand-cut and painted. Patterns became standardized and often lacked imagination; many windows relied on an architectural framework, Gothic-style canopies and tracery surrounding individual figures or story panels. Windows became very repetitive, as prospective purchasers simply ordered them from catalogues.

By the 1880s the Arts and Crafts movement was arguing for a return to individuality and experimentation with new types of glass, as well as using different thicknesses and plating or layering. Plating, the leading up of two or more pieces of glass of the same shape, one over the other, was used to achieve depth of colour or three-dimensional effects. Morris and Tiffany used plating to enhance the colour or texture of their windows. The technique of layering was developed in France by Charles-Laurent Maréchal of Metz (1801–87). Flashed glass, laying a colour or colours over clear glass, was skilfully employed to enhance deep folds in robes. Cameo glass, a technique perfected by the Romans, was also revived. The Portland vase in

Tiffany, William Edgar Webb memorial window, All Saints Episcopal Church, Pasadena (1923, Roland Coate, Reginald Johnson and Gordon Kaufmann).

the British Museum, dating to the first century CE, is the most famous exemplar. This was painstakingly cut with a lapidary wheel, the top layer of white glass cut away to reveal the blue glass below. Hand-cut cameo

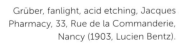

Grüber, fanlight, acid etching, Jacques Pharmacy, 33, Rue de la Commanderie, Nancy (1903, Lucien Bentz).

Grüber, dichroic glass. Interior (warm colours). Villa Majorelle or Villa Jika, 1 Rue Louis Majorelle, Nancy (1901–02, Henri Sauvage).

Grüber, dichroic glass. Exterior (cold colours) Villa Majorelle or Villa Jika, 1 Rue Louis Majorelle, Nancy (1901–02, Henri Sauvage).

glass, as perfected by Gallé, was both time-consuming and expensive. However, acid etching, using hexafluorosilicic acid, enabled Gallé and Daum to commercially manufacture cameo glass.

During the 1880s John La Farge (1835–1910) and Tiffany perfected new types of glass commonly known throughout Europe as American glass. La Farge is credited with developing opalescence; he patented his technique in 1879. Milky opalescent glass, its variegated colour resembling opal, can be almost opaque. La Farge's stained glass elicited great excitement at Paris 1889. Iridescence, a technique particularly associated with Tiffany, was achieved by adding or exposing the surface to metallic oxides thereby creating a lustrous film. A chenille or undulated pattern was produced by pressing an embossed roller onto the glass while it was still hot. Manufactured in multicoloured sheets, with colours spread throughout in whorls and darting lines rather like marble, the new glass had movement when illuminated. These new materials revolutionized design, as the colouristic effects and textures meant you could paint with glass. Stained glass came to resemble mosaics of glittering, translucent colours.

Dichroic glass, two different colours caused by changing lighting conditions, was used by several

Wagner, mosaic window designed by Adolf Böhm (1873–1941), Villa Wagner I, Hüttelbergstraße 28, Vienna (1912–13).

Grüber, *Le Paysage Vosgien* (Vosges Countryside), chenille or undulated surface, Chamber of Commerce and Industry, 40, Rue Henri-Poincaré, Nancy (1908, Émile Toussaint and Louis Marchal).

master glass-makers including Grüber and Tiffany. It is beautiful to look at from either side. From the inside a window will glow with rosy light, while externally the colours will be cool blues. The technology dates back to the Roman period, as seen in the fourth-century Lycurgus cup in the British Museum; this is green when lit from the front in reflected light, and purplish-red when lit from inside or behind so that the light passes through the glass. The effect is achieved using colloidal gold and silver particles dispersed through the glass matrix; certain wavelengths of light either pass through or are reflected.

New types of glass induced Horta and Guimard to create simple linear compositions based on strong lines, moving away from imitating paintings. Figural designs were influenced by the Japanese print, clear outlines created with the leading lines. Posters also played their part in shaping a new aesthetic, with many designers like Eugène Grasset (1845–1917) designing for both mediums. The cloisonné style can also be linked to post-Impressionist artists, notably Paul Gauguin (1848–1903) and Les Nabis (Prophets), a group of artists working in the later 1880s and 1890s who pursued the unity of the arts.

Guimard, window, Musée d'Orsay (c.1898).

Morris's medieval-inspired aesthetic and respect for hand-craftsmanship transformed stained glass window manufacturing. His ethos was pragmatic; he realized that 'a good craftsman was not necessarily a great artist'[1]. Production of stained glass windows requires many specialist skills. An alliance between the imaginative artist and the skilled craftsman was needed. Morris never attempted to make his own glass; he relied on Powell of Whitefriars. By 1854, Powell of Whitefriars, established by James Powell in 1834, were experimenting with chemical mixes in order to replicate the quality of medieval coloured glass for the antiquarian Charles Winston (1814–64), the authority for cathedral and church window restoration. His *An inquiry into the difference of style observable in ancient glass paintings especially in England, with hints on glass painting* (1847) provided a benchmark for architects working in the Gothic Revival style. Powell's glass, its mix of air bubbles and brilliant natural colours matching medieval glass, was supplied to several firms. The company also fabricated windows, commissioning cartoons from Burne-Jones, Henry Holiday, Robert Anning Bell, Edward Poynter, Ford Madox Brown and George Cattermole.

After 1875, Burne-Jones provided the designs for all the windows produced by Morris & Co.[2]. The east window created for St Martin's, Brampton, Cumbria (1879, Philip Webb), includes a remarkable *Pelican in her Piety*, the nest set on a sinuous, twisted tree. Like Mackmurdo's design, Pevsner singled this out as a precursor of Art Nouveau[3]. Morris took sole responsibility for the colours, combining brilliant hues especially the vibrant reds of his later windows. These are seen at their best in Burne-Jones' *Last Judgement* (1889–97) window for St Philip's Cathedral, Birmingham. Both Morris and Burne-Jones deemed the four windows for St Philips, *Nativity* (1887–88), *Ascension* (1884–85), *Crucifixion* (1887–88) and *Last Judgment* (1896–97) to be their greatest achievement, although it could be argued the bold colours and dramatic compositions are at odds with the calm neo-Classical

Burne-Jones, *Pelican in her Piety* (1879), St Martin's, Brampton, Cumbria (Philip Webb).

interior. Nevertheless, they are a technical tour de force, each window a single picture, their density resembling a mosaic. This pictorial approach, unimpeded by any internal divisions, was very influential.

Christopher Whall (1849–1924) is recognized as the leading Arts and Crafts stained glassmaker,

Burne-Jones, *Ascension* (1884–85), St Philip's Cathedral, Birmingham.

Whall, four-light window, *The Holy Spirit and Pentecost*, Mrs Frederick Cook in memory of her husband, Wyndham Francis Cook (c.1905), Holy Trinity Church, Sloane Street, London (1888–90, John Dando Sedding).

in effect 'England's Tiffany'. He used a wide range of colours and textures, experimenting with new materials such as Prior's 'Early English' glass, a slab glass which replicated the luminosity and varied colouring of early medieval glass. This had been developed by the architect Edward Schroeder Prior (1852–1932) in 1889; it was made by blowing glass into a rectilinear box and then cutting off the sides. This yielded flat panes of uneven thickness, often streaked with colour, which could be used to create more abstract patterns[4].

Arts and Crafts, and Glasgow School

From the outset Morris made both ecclesiastical and domestic windows; natural light could be limited, filtered and directed through stained glass. Diffused light was ideal in the dining room, creating a mellow, muted, ambience. During the 1870s and 1880s, the House Beautiful was enhanced with door panels, fanlights and above all impressive staircase windows. The trend continues in the Arts and Crafts house, Baillie Scott favouring strong outlines. His stunning three-light window (1901) featuring stylized birds and pendulous blooms for the music room of the Villa Kahn-Starre, Manheim, Germany, is now in the Museum Künstlerkolonie, Darmstadt[5].

Arts and Crafts furniture often features inserted glass panels. Mackintosh's furniture was similarly enriched with glass, gesso or pewter panels; the wardrobe doors in the master bedroom at Hill House (1902) have inserted pink glass panels that complete a stylized rose tree. The back of the washstand is also protected with an abstract design in leaded glass.

For the Rose Boudoir (1902–03), created for Turin 1902, the glass continues the theme of stylized roses. While Mackintosh did not design pictorial windows, Oscar Paterson (1863–?) made this his speciality. According to *The Studio*, Paterson had 'realized the secret mystery of an opal, he has caught the amber of a sunset sky, and has dreamed (if not seen) the magic phosphorescence of midnight seas in the tropics'. Rather than shedding a 'dim religious light'[6], Paterson's windows were pitched in a high key, lemon and white with neutral greys contributing to his distinctly novel colour schemes. His motifs recall Voysey and Baillie Scott, sun bursts with flying birds, peacocks and galleons, a popular pun on 'craft-man-ship'. Paterson collaborated with Harry Thomson, producing both ecclesiastical and domestic windows: the Argyll window for St Giles Cathedral, Edinburgh (1896) and

the nativity for Mayfield Church, Edinburgh (1912). Paterson's domestic windows epitomize the Glasgow style.

American Glass: Tiffany

Tiffany began his career firstly as a painter and then a decorator. Around 1875 he became interested in glassmaking; an opalescent floor-to-ceiling glass screen in the entrance hall of the Whitehouse, commissioned by President Chester Alan Arthur, was a groundbreaking commission. He established his company L. C. Tiffany & Co. in 1883; this became the Tiffany Glass and Decorating Company in 1892, its workshops located in Corona, Queens, New York[7]. At the World's Columbian Exposition held in Chicago

Tiffany, drapery glass, All Saints Episcopal Church, Pasadena (1923, Roland Coate, Reginald, Johnson and Gordon Kaufmann).

Tiffany, *Garden Landscape*, fountain, (1905–15), The American Wing, Metropolitan Museum, NY.

(1893), he headhunted Arthur Nash (1849–1934), the manager of Thomas Webb and Sons of Stourbridge. 'Crystal King of England', Webb was at the forefront of technical innovation. The company was particularly noted for the high quality of its cameo glass; the first pieces were produced by John Northwood in the 1870s. Tiffany was clearly influenced by ancient glass, particularly Roman and Syrian specimens he had seen on a trip to the South Kensington Museum in 1865. He was fascinated by the iridescence of ancient glass; buried for many centuries, the surface degrades causing a shelly layer. Tiffany also admired the luminous colours of medieval glass.

With the aid of Nash, Tiffany developed his famous iridescent Favrile glass. This was patented in 1894; metallic oxides are blended into the molten glass creating stunning colours and unique effects. Respecting the innate nature of the material, Tiffany integrated forming and decorating into one process. The original trade name was Fabrile after the old English word meaning hand-wrought or handcrafted. Tiffany changed this to Favrile, as allegedly this sounded better. He gave his colours exotic names, 'Gold Lustre', 'Samian Red', 'Mazarin Blue', 'Tel-el-Amarna' (or Turquoise Blue), and 'Aquamarine'. Tiffany's windows also benefitted from other technical innovations; folded 'drapery' glass was first made in 1877, while his opalescent and iridescent glass was manufactured by Louis Heildt & Co. from 1881. Favrile glass was also used in mosaics; the largest and most significant mosaic is the *Dream Garden* (1916), designed by Maxfield Parrish (1870–1966) and commissioned for the Curtis Publishing Company's headquarters in Philadelphia (Pennsylvania Academy of the Fine Arts). It took a year to make the twenty-four panels, taking a further six months to install. Tiffany may have made the shimmering *Garden Landscape* (1905–15, Metropolitan Museum, New York) as a preliminary study for the Curtis commission. It graced the Tiffany showrooms until their contents were auctioned in 1938.

Tiffany's Dream Home

Laurelton Hall (1902–05), on Long Island, New York, was developed as a showcase for Tiffany's artworks, windows, glassware, pottery, enamels, oil paintings, and watercolours. The Tiffany Chapel, originally made for the 1893 World Columbian Exposition, was reconstructed in the grounds. The three million dollars he inherited from his father barely covered the cost. Every aspect of the project was designed by Tiffany, from the eighty-four-roomed mansion surrounded by fountains, pools, and terraced gardens to the stables, greenhouses, chapel, studio, and art gallery. The interiors reflect his taste for the Orient, an Arabian Night's dream come to life; its over-the-top, theatrical décor became the most publicized in America. Falling into neglect after the Second World

Tiffany, four-column loggia, Laurelton Hall (1902–05), Charles Engelhard Court, The American Wing, Metropolitan Museum, NY.

Tiffany, *View of Oyster Bay* leaded window, originally designed in 1908 for the Manhattan home of silk industry scion William C. Skinner, Charles Engelhard Court, The American Wing Metropolitan Museum, NY.

War, Laurelton Hall was badly damaged by fire in 1957. However, Hugh and Jeannette McKean of the Charles Hosmer Morse Museum of American Art salvaged many windows and architectural features, shipping them to Winter Park, Florida. The monumental four-column loggia with its colourful glass and pottery floral capitals (magnolia, poppies) has graced the Metropolitan Museum of Art's American Wing since 1980, a gift from the McKeans. The Daffodil Terrace, an extraordinary outdoor room adjoining the Laurelton Hall dining room, has been reconstructed at Winter Park, a tribute to Tiffany's passion for flowers. Its marble columns are topped with capitals smothered with glass daffodils. In the dining room Tiffany composed a blue-green harmony, integrating the medallion rug, magnificent leaded glass ceiling ornament and marble and glass mosaic chimney breast. The *toutes ensemble* was completed with a series of six spectacular Wisteria transom windows. The living room was also called the 'forest room' as the walls and ceiling were painted with horse chestnut leaves that shaded, top to bottom, from light to dark green. It came to resemble a museum,

his exhibition windows providing a retrospective of his career: *Eggplants* (1879); *Flowers, Fish and Fruit* (1885); *Feeding the Flamingos* for Chicago 1893 and the magnificent *Four Seasons* panels created for the Paris 1900. *The Bathers*, intended for exhibition in San Francisco, filled an alcove. The most magical space was the double-height entrance hall or Fountain Court, in effect a winter garden, where his flower-filled portrait (1911, the Hispanic Society of America, New York) by Joaquín Sorolla y Bastida (1863–1923), was hung.

Brussels

Raphaël Évaldre (1862–1938) was the principal glass master active in Brussels during the Art Nouveau era. Évaldre was a student and disciple of Tiffany, bringing American glass to Brussels; he collaborated with Horta, Hankar, Paul Saintenoy (1862–1952) and Léon Delune (1862–1947)[8]. Évaldre's most famous pictorial window is *La Vague* (The Wave) (1896), after a design by Henri Privat-Livemont (1861–1936). It can be found in the dining room of l'Hotel Saintenoy, the home of the architect. The motif combines Hokusai's famous *Under the Wave off Kanagawa* with a Mucha-style maiden[9].

The most famous feature of Horta's house and studio (1898) is the staircase fanlight, filled with textured American glass, which bathes the whole stairwell with light. By day it glows yellow, but at night, under artificial light, the hues are a mysterious blue. Such theatricality is typical of Horta. In the dining room, a wooden partition is filled with Horta's whiplash motifs in textured rose-coloured glass. The frame is integral to the glass composition, with wooden uprights playing the role of a fictive trunk or branch. The network of curves, in wood and leaded glass, are inseparable from the architectural décor.

Horta's most audacious winter garden, crowned with a magnificent stained glass cupola, was created for the Van Eetvelde House (1895, fabricated by Évaldre). Centrally placed, connecting the drawing

Privat-Livemont (designer) and Évaldre (maker), *La Vague* (The Wave) l'Hotel Saintenoy, Rue de l'Arbre Bénit 123, Ixelles, Brussels (1896–97).

Horta, house and studio, staircase fan light, rue Américaine Saint-Gilles, Belgium (1898–1901).

room with the salon, when filled with plants it must have resembled an exotic jungle. The analogy would have been fitting; the client Baron Edmond van Eetvelde (1852–1925) was administrator of the Belgian Congo. The open plan, enabling the diffusion of light, and the integration of structure and decoration, mark Horta as the supreme Art Nouveau architect. The fate of this winter garden is instructive; the light well above the glass dome was blocked to provide extra office space when the Fédération de l'Industrie du Gaz (FIGAZ) made the property its headquarters. Fortunately, the structure was dismantled and stored, so that when FIGAZ were persuaded to restore the building, they were able to remove the offending office floors and reinstate the light well (c.1988). For the Solvay House (1894), Horta designed his most beautiful staircase, its magisterial American glass skylight bathing the interior with pink and yellow light (fabricated by Évaldre). The fan-shapes of its construction recall Gothic fan-vaulting. Its sinuous patterning is picked up in the stair carpet and the balustrade, a *toutes ensemble*.

The Hotel Hannon (1903–04), designed by the

Évaldre, impost, Hotel Hannon, Avenue Brugmann, Saint-Gilles, Brussels (1903–4, Jules Brunfaut).

Évaldre, winter garden, Hotel Hannon, Avenue Brugmann, Saint-Gilles, Brussels (1903–04, Jules Brunfaut).

eclectic architect Jules Brunfaut also boasts a remarkable staircase, painted by Paul-Albert Baudouin. The windows are attributed to Évaldre. The imposts over the doorways, filled with golden American glass, cast an autumnal glow. The hall opens out into a winter garden, the exterior window filled with a tangle of iron, lead and glass. This is another good example of the integration of structure and decoration. Édouard Hannon (1853–1931), who became a director and manager (1907–25) of the Solvay company, came to know Gallé and Majorelle through his visits to Dombasle, their plant near Nancy. Hannon commissioned both to decorate his new home.

Paris: Pictorial and Abstract approaches

Encouraged by Morris, French artists attempted to break down the barrier between the fine arts and decoration. The Nabis, who numbered Maurice

Denis (1870–1943) and Pierre Bonnard (1867–1947), designed stained glass, murals, wallpaper, tapestries and Japanese-style screens, alongside posters, theatre sets and costume design. By turning their attention to décor, they hoped to unify art and life. Thinking along the same lines, Bing enhanced his gallery L'Art Nouveau with windows designed by the Nabis artists and fabricated by Tiffany.

The Swiss-born Eugène Grasset, best known for his poster designs, created several notable windows in the pictorial tradition. Described as an industrial designer, he collaborated with commercial firms as well as skilled craftsmen. His female figures show affinity with the Pre-Raphaelites and Crane's graphic style, with Botticelli-style long, flowing hair and enigmatic expressions. The Grasset Maiden is as distinctive as Mucha's *femme fleur*, being a woman of her

Grasset, *Spring* (1894), Musée des Arts Décoratifs, Paris.

et le Commerce, enrichit l'Humanité (Work, Industry and Commerce enrich Humanity) for the Paris Chamber of Commerce (c.1900)[10].

Like Horta, Guimard integrated his windows into an over-arching architectural scheme, the simple abstract curvilinear forms echoing the whiplash of surrounding iron and wood. Some of his most striking designs were created for the Castel Béranger (1895–98). His other notable use of stained glass is the skylight in the Hotel Mezzara, 16th arrondissement, Paris. The dramatic double-height entrance hall, its second-floor gallery reached by a sweeping staircase, is lit with an intricate tangle of leaded lines and glass.

Nancy

Nancy's architects favoured pictorial windows. They had plenty of bow windows, verandas and winter gardens to fill. They could draw on the services of France's 'Tiffany', Jacques Grüber, as well as Joseph Janin (1851–1910), another local glassmaker and painter. Given Lorraine's grand tradition of glass-making, inherited from the Middle Ages and the Renaissance, the region was bound to be at the fore-front of technological innovations. The Daum Brothers, whose family originated from the glassmaking region centred on Bitche in the Vosges, turned the fortunes of their *crystallerie* around by producing art glass. By 1891 Antonin was leading the design department, while Auguste supervised overall management. Antonin understood the importance of collaborating with leading artists; Grüber was hired in 1893.

Grüber: The 'French Tiffany'

A man of many talents, Grüber is best known for his stained-glass windows; like his American counterparts, his experimental windows featured acid etching, plating, iridescent and dichroic glass. He used the lead came to his advantage, inscribing his motifs with solid outlines. After training at l'École

time; *Spring* (Musée des Arts Décoratifs, Paris), and its pendant *Autumn*, exhibited in the architecture section of the Salon du Champ-de-Mars in 1894, are exemplary. A collaboration with the Parisian painter, glassmaker and mosaic artist Félix Gaudin (1851–1930), the pair also created *Le Travail, par l'Industrie*

Grüber, *Roses and Seagulls* (1904), Maison Bergeret, 24 Rue Lionnois, Nancy (1903–04, Lucien Weissenburger).

Grüber, Crédit Lyonnais, rue Saint-Georges, Nancy (1901, Félicien César).

des Beaux Arts in Nancy, he studied at l'École des Arts Décoratifs and l'École des Beaux-Arts in Paris, as well as frequenting the studios of the Symbolist painter Gustave Moreau. This accounts for his interest in poetic and Symbolist subjects. Upon returning to Nancy in 1893 he collaborated with the Daum glassworks, Majorelle and René Wiener (1855–1939), who commissioned book bindings. He opened his own workshops in 1897. As a founder of the École de Nancy, Grüber pursued not only the alliance of art and industry but also the gesamtkunstwerk ideal. His finest windows in Nancy number the staircase window, *Roses and Seagulls* (1904), for the Maison Bergeret (1903–04, Weissenburger); the five windows for the Chamber of Commerce (1909, Émile Toussaint and Louis Marchal) and the stupendous *Clematis* ceiling of the Crédit Lyonnais (1901, Félicien César).

The Chamber of Commerce windows, which took over three years to fabricate, are technically the most complex; they are entitled *La Verre* (Glass), *La Chimie* (Chemistry), *La Siderurgie* (Iron and Steel Industry), *Le Village Lorraine* (Lorraine Village) and *Le Paysage Vosgien* (Vosges Countryside). They were also very expensive, being mostly paid for by syndicates of local manufacturers. However, Ernest Solvey (1838–1922), whose plant was at nearby Dombasle-sur-Meurthe, contributed *La Chimie*; it shows the chemist in his laboratory, perhaps engaged in the Solvay process, the ammonia-soda process for the manufacturing of soda ash. Using plating, Grüber was able to create the illusion of depth; the blast furnaces can be seen in the background of *La Siderurgie*. *La Verre* is dedicated to the production of glass, a heroic worker gathering molten 'metal' from a furnace. The acid-etched panel that commemorates the various benefactors captures the flames of the furnace. *Le Paysage Vosges* appears to represent the natural beauty of the Lorraine forests, but a closer inspection reveals the paper mills of Henri Boucher, the sponsor. At the time he

Grüber, *La Siderurgie*, Chamber of Commerce and Industry, 40, Rue Henri-Poincaré, Nancy (1909, Émile Toussaint and Louis Marchal).

was President of the Chamber of Commerce of Épinal and President of the Société Industrielle de l'Est.

However, the most idiosyncratic setting for Gruber's stained glass can be found in the garden of Eugène Corbin's villa, the Aquarium designed by Weissenburger (c.1911–12). This remarkable confection, topped with a viewing platform protected by a glass awning, was designed with fish tanks that doubled as its windows. The spectacle of ornamental fish apparently freely swimming through the interior must have impressed his visitors. The remarkable door, *Algues et Poissons*, was shown in the Pavilion de l'École de Nancy at the Exposition Internationale de L'Est de la France (1909). A series of rectangular acid-etched panels replicate the underwater world. Above the door and encircling the interior as imposts are six lunettes filled with aquatic plants, frogs and seagulls, recreating Monet's water lilies

Grüber, *Le Paysage Vosgien*, Chamber of Commerce and Industry, 40, Rue Henri-Poincaré, Nancy (1909, Émile Toussaint and Louis Marchal).

Grüber, *Dove and Peacock* (c.1904), Musée l'École de Nancy.

in stained glass[11].

Like many stained glass windows now in museums, Grüber's masterpiece, a window known as *Doves and Peacock* (c.1904) was removed from the veranda of the Maison La Salle on the Rue du Général-Drouot in Nancy. Sometimes windows are rescued when a building is demolished. Also, as their value has increased, being left to the elements or vandalism has become too risky. *Doves and Peacock* is a technological masterpiece, combining painted glass, American glass, plating, acid etching and iridescent and dichroic glass. The motifs illustrate Grüber's botanic knowledge: tulip, maple and sycamore trees, ipomoea, honeysuckle, arum lilies, arrowhead, irises and marsh flowers.

Winter Gardens

Janin's masterpiece, the winter garden in the Maison Bergeret (1904, Weissenburger) combines beauty with ingenuity. The hollow glass bricks, alternating green and white, provide insulation. They resemble *Falconnier briques en verre soufflé*, named after their inventor Gustave Falconnier (1845–1913). Patented in 1886 and made under license, Falconnier glass bricks were used by Guimard and Le Corbusier (Charles-Edouard Jeanneret-Gris, 1887–1965) for their modern translucent glass walls. The panels of stained glass, using American and dichroic glass, depict the beautiful but deadly Datura (Devil's Trumpets or Moonflowers); these white trumpets open at night, emitting a pleasant fragrance. They are suitably decadent, as ingesting Datura will lead to drowsiness and hallucinations. The pink and purple

Grüber, door, Aquarium Villa Corbin, 38 Rue Sergent Blandan, Nancy (1904–09, Lucien Weissenburger).

Janin, winter garden, Maison Bergeret, 24 Rue Lionnois, Nancy (1903–04, Lucien Weissenburger).

Janin, impost, winter garden, Maison Bergeret, 24 Rue Lionnois, Nancy (1903–04, Lucien Weissenburger).

Belles-de-nuit (*Mirabilis jalapa*) are also known as the 'four o'clock flower' as the blooms open at dusk. They emit a strong, sweet-smelling fragrance throughout the night, closing for good, like Morning Glory, in the morning. Both flowers are perfect for a winter garden that would have been used during the evening. The magnificent *Peacock* (1902) impost, also by Janin, was moved here from Albert Bergeret's factory; it originally separated the accounting department from the director's office.

Miksa Róth: 'Hungary's Tiffany'

Considered the finest stained-glass artist of the Magyar Szecesszio, Miksa Róth's (1865–1944) work was repeatedly awarded prizes at international exhibitions. In 1899 he was officially appointed Imperial and Royal Court Glass Painter. Working with many of the best architects and designers of the day, Róth created windows in many styles: Historic, Art Nouveau, Jugendstil, Viennese Secession and Hungarian Secession! The windows for Budapest's famous

Hungarian Parliament building (1885–1904, Imre Steindl) were prepared in 1890. Respecting the neo-Gothic character of the overall decoration, Róth opted to use a Grotesque style.

However, Róth wanted to prove his worth as an independent designer; he did not want to be just a 'simple copier of the cartoons delivered by painters'[12]. Visiting the 1893 Chicago World Exhibition, Róth was inspired by Tiffany's opalescent and Favrile glass. In 1897 he made his first purchase of opalescent glass from the Hamburg glass painter Karl Engelbrecht. Marking a turning point in his career, opalescent glass enabled his artistic self-awareness. The glass painter was now encouraged to assert his own artistic taste, 'use the accidentalities of opalescent glass creatively… he has to study his glass material, its characteristics and its nuances carefully'[13]. Returning to first principles, respecting the material's nature, motifs were chosen that brought out the beauty of various glass surfaces. Like Tiffany, Róth learnt to paint with glass; 'The glass painter, who has been lowered to work as an industrialist, through using opalescent glass has been elevated again to be an autonomous, inventive artist'[14].

While Róth designed simple windows that relied on the effects of colour and line, he also composed complex figurative windows. One of his most beautiful Tiffany-style windows, red tulips framed by two peacocks, was made for the Alpár Villa, Rózsadomb

Róth, *Nocturnal Landscape with Lilies* (1898) Miksa Róth Memorial House, Budapest.

Róth, Grotesque style, Hungarian Parliament building (1885–1904, Imre Steindl).

Róth, Kossuth staircase, Gresham Palace, Széchenyi István tér 5–6, Pest (1905–07, Zsigmond Quittner and József Vágó).

Róth, *Glasgow Rose* (pre-1907), Miksa Róth Memorial House.

(1903); the architect Ignác Alpár was one of Róth's many clients, commissioning windows for the Magyar Nemzeti Bank (1902–05) and the Museum of Agriculture in the rebuilt Vajdahunyad Castle, originally created for the 1896 Hungarian Millennial celebrations (1904). Such massive commissions also called for new products, windows that brought in the maximum amount of light and were cost effective as well as beautiful. The answer was etched glass, which also allowed him to devise delicate floral and arabesque patterns. Many etched windows were ordered for Lechner's Hungarian Secession Geological Society building (1898–99). For his skylights he favoured *kunstgeld* or artistic yellow tempered glass.

Róth was clearly aware of New Art trends. The window he created for the Gresham Palace's Kossuth staircase (1905–07), honouring Hungary's great revolutionary leader, is in a linear Secession idiom. A window in the Miksa Róth Memorial House replicates the Glasgow Rose. The Museum of Applied Arts held regular exhibitions featuring international artwork thanks to its forward-looking director, Jenő Radisics. The exhibition 'Modern Art' (1898) was intended to showcase the new trends coming from Western and Northern Europe. Bing provided a selection of works from L'Art Nouveau, including Tiffany Favrile glass. Gallé sent a selection from Nancy. The English contingent included wallpapers by Crane. In 1900 Crane was honoured with a one-man show, which he attended in person; as Crane was 'by now arguably the best-known decorative artist in Britain since the death of William Morris... Academics, museum directors, journalists and the Minister of Culture, Gyula Wlassics, danced attendance on him'[15]. However, simply copying these foreign forms would lead nowhere. The renewal of Hungarian art depended on cooperation between artists and industry. Artists and craftsmen were to strive for the same level of excellence in both the fine and applied arts.

Mosaics

Following a trip to Venice, where he mastered the art of mosaic making, Róth established his own workshop. Italian artisans Giovanni Barbus and Pietro Labuss brought their technical expertise to Budapest. Rather fortuitously, Róth's father-in-law Josef Walla was the largest producer of high-quality terrazzo in Hungary. Róth won the silver medal at Paris 1900 with the *Pax* and *Rising Sun* mosaics, made with Murano and opalescent glass. He experimented with different combinations: 'I even tried to make mosaic from Zsolnay's beautiful eosin material and to amplify the effect of the iridescence of the eosin's lustre I even applied mildly three-dimensional embossed elements among the mosaic'[16].

Róth, *Rising Sun*, Murano mosaic (1900) Miksa Róth Memorial House.

Róth, *Kossuth* mosaic, Zsolnay eosin-glazed components and Zsolnay lustre ceramic insets (1899–1900), Miksa Róth Memorial House.

He went further than simply responding to Art Nouveau floral forms, developing a style based on distinctly Hungarian motifs, a Hun-Hungarian Secession. Inevitably he turned to Lechner in search of what could be construed Hungarian; the result was the *Kossuth* mosaic (1899), named in honour of Lajos Kossuth, the motif resembling a convex palmette or tulip echoing Lechner's style. These elements are made from Zsolnay's eosin. The geranium, the national flower, the tulip, a folk-art motif and the peacock were declared 'Hungarian'. Embroidery provided many patterns that could be identified as Hungarian. The quest for a style that expressed the nation's spirit acquired legitimacy when Crane visited Transylvania in search of pure Hungarian folk art and culture[17].

Collaborations

Róth's international reputation spread to Mexico City, where he worked with the Hungarian architect and sculptor Géza Maróti (1875–1941) executing his design for the dome of the National Theatre, Palacio de Bellas Artes (Palace of Fine Arts), Mexico City (1904–08, Adamo Boari); the theme chosen was Olympus with Apollo surrounded by nine muses.

Maróti and Róth worked on several projects together; the Liszt Ferenc Academy of Music (1907, Flóris Korb and Kálmán Giergl) is adorned with Maróti's sculptures and Róth's glass and mosaics.

Róth also collaborated with Sándor Nagy and Ede Toroczkai Wigand, members of the Gödöllô artists' colony. Together they created the Hun-Hungarian Secession style windows for the Palace of Culture, Marosvásárhely, today Târgu Mureş, Romania (1911–13); a cultural complex, this building is comparable to the Municipal House, Prague[18]. In Budapest, his most accessible work is the giant mosaic on the façade of the former Török Bankház (1906, Armin Hegedűs and Henrik Böhm).

After his death in 1943, Róth's reputation fell into obscurity. Born into a Jewish family, Róth was baptised into the Catholic faith in 1897 in order to marry Jozefa Walla. In an era of pro-assimilation this was not uncommon. However, following the First World War and the collapse of Hungary, the Jews were marginalized; even those, like Róth, who had converted could not escape victimization. He was forced to close his workshops in 1939.

Róth, Liszt Ferenc Academy of Music, Liszt Ferenc tér 8, Pest (c.1907, Flóris Korb and Kálmán Giergl).

Ceramics

Today wall tiles tend to be restricted to the utilitarian parts of a house, the kitchen and the bathroom. This was not the case in the Victorian home where tiles were used in areas that took a lot of 'wear and tear', such as the entrance, hallway and stairs. The fashion for smoking rooms led to entirely tiled rooms, the most dramatic example of a fully tiled interior being Lord Leighton's Arab Hall, Kensington (1879–81, George Aitcheson and William de Morgan).

Often pictorial adverts, tiles were used extensively in commercial contexts for shop fronts and interiors. They were bright and colourful, easy to clean and relatively inexpensive. Moreover, in restaurants they resisted fire, steam and food odours. For Café Mollard (1895, Édouard-Jean Niermans), opposite the Gare Saint-Lazare, 8th arrondissement, Sarreguemines, one of the largest tile manufacturers, created panels that illustrate local destinations: Deauville, Saint-Germain-en-Laye and Avray. There is a festive atmosphere, as befitting a restaurant, with one panel featuring a boating party. Hidden from sight for many years after Art Nouveau fell out of fashion, the tile panels were recovered and restored in the late 1960s.

As tiles are hygenic, they had an obvious application in hospitals and schools. They are used for utilitarian and decorative purposes throughout the Hospital de la Santa Creu i Sant Pau (1901–30, Lluís

Guimard, Maison Coilliot, Rue de Fleurus, Lille (1898–1900).

Domènech i Montaner) Barcelona's largest Modernista project. Many of the exterior tiles bear the initials of the Catalan banker Pau Gil i Serra, the hospital's patron. Believing that people would recover better if they were surrounded by beauty, every surface is covered with exquisite ornament. The building is also joyous, with plenty of humorous or endearing animals; a cat chasing a mouse and a monkey toying with a snail.

Used in public contexts, pictorial tile panels and ceramic façades fulfilled the New Art's democratic mission, achieving Art for the People. Townscapes were transformed, as novelty made people stop and stare. This is especially true of the Maison Coilliot, Lille (1898–1900), designed by Guimard for the ceramic manufacturer Louis Coilliot. The façade, showcasing his enamelled 'lava', is show-stopping. The calligraphy of the signage is especially striking, recalling Guimard's lettering for the Paris Métro.

Domènech i Montaner, Hospital de la Santa Creu i Sant Pau, Barcelona (1901–30).

Curtain Walls

Elaborately patterned façades, resembling textiles, fulfilled the tenets of the architectural theorist Gottfried Semper (1803–79). In *The Four Elements of Architecture* (1851), Semper argued the 'enclosure' (the walls) had their origins in weaving. The most basic spatial divider was a fabric screen. It was only when structural weight bearing came into play that walls needed to be solid. With new building techniques using structural steel or reinforced concrete frames, the façade, no longer weight bearing, could be hung like a curtain. The curtain wall simply divides the outside from the inside.

Today the curtain wall is often glass, allowing the maximum amount of light into the building. The concept of the curtain wall developed from iron and glass constructions such as the Crystal Palace (1851). Following the Great Chicago Fire (1871), architects looked for new solutions for larger and taller buildings. This was achieved using a framework of steel girders, which carried the building's weight. Walls, floors, ceilings and windows were suspended from a relatively lightweight steel skeleton. The so-called 'column-frame' construction pushed buildings up rather than out. The steel weight-bearing frame also accommodated larger windows. Interior walls were thinner, creating more usable floor space. With weight-bearing masonry rendered obsolete, architects were freed from former constraints; there was no need to follow historical precedent in terms of style. This new freedom resulted in a technical and stylistic revolution.

Tile and Terracotta

The idea of building colour into the fabric of a building, 'structural polychrome', was advocated by Ruskin in his *Seven Lamps of Architecture* (1849) and *Stones of Venice* (1851–53). Ruskin cited Tuscan and Venetian Romanesque and Gothic buildings, such as the Doge's Palace in Venice, as exemplars. Drawing on such continental precedents, Gothic

Strauven, Maison de Beck, 9 Avenue Paul Dejaer, Brussels (1902).

Revival architects embraced 'structural polychrome'; William Butterfield's Keble College, Oxford (1868–76), is a prime example. With Britain's damp climate, using bricks of different colours (typically brown, cream and red), in patterned combinations (bands, stripes and crosses), was more practical than plastered or painted surfaces. Colourful brickwork was also abundantly used in Brussels, Gustave Strauven and Ernest Blerot successfully combining the neo-Gothic with Art Nouveau.

Red and buff terracotta, meaning 'baked earth', came into its own as a means of decoration. This ceramic material could be easily moulded or carved by hand or cast in moulds. Reusable moulds enabled the production of identical pieces; each piece of sculpture or tile could be repeated many times using the same mould, saving time and money. Godfrey Sykes

(1824–66) collaborated with engineer and architect Francis Fowke (1823–65) with the ornamentation of the new buildings for the South Kensington Museum; visitors are treated to a wealth of terracotta, tiles and mosaics.

Doulton's of Lambeth

Although, Henry Doulton (1820–97) had established his firm's reputation manufacturing stoneware drainage pipes and sanitary wares, he wanted to exhibit more glamorous products at the international exhibitions. George Tinworth (1843–1913), 'the most famous terracotta sculptor of the Victorian era', who trained at both the Lambeth School of Art and the Royal Academy Schools, won Doulton many accolades with his sculptural panels; some thirty were shown at the 1867 Paris Exposition Universelle[19]. Southbank House, Lambeth (1876–78, possibly Robert Stark Wilkinson or F. W. Tarring), the only surviving part of the Doulton Pottery complex in Lambeth, acted as a 'living advertisement' for the factory's products. The entrance retains the high-relief terracotta tympanum by Tinworth, *Mr Doulton in his Studio* (1878), which shows Doulton and his artists including Hannah Barlow (and her cat Tommy) and Tinworth.

Tinworth, *Mr Doulton in his Studio* (1878), Southbank House, Lambeth (1876–78, possibly Robert Stark Wilkinson or F. W. Tarring).

Carrara Ware and Marmo

In the 1890s, Doulton's Carrara ware, a stoneware with a white matt glaze that imitates a dull marble effect, was used extensively as its glazed surfaces could be easily cleaned. It was ideally suited to Edwardian Baroque: London's Savoy Hotel, on the Strand (1899, Thomas Edward Collcutt); the Debenhams building on Wigmore Street (1906–07, William Wallace and James Gibbs), Edwardian Baroque with a touch of Art Nouveau; and Asia House, Lime Street (1912–13, George Valentine S. Myer). Doulton extended the palette of colours, introducing a soft grey and blue as seen on the flamboyant New Art façade of the Turkey Café, Leicester (1900–01, Arthur Wakerley).

Burmantofts Pottery of Leeds, Doulton's rival in the

Doulton Carrara Ware, Turkey Café, Granby Street, Leicester (1900–01, Arthur Wakerley).

North, also developed a wide range of architectural materials; Faience, a glazed stoneware, and Marmo, an artificial marble. Lefco, which had a granite appearance, was also used for garden ornaments. James Holroyd, the works manager, brought in sculptor Edward Caldwell Spruce (1865–1922) and architect Maurice Bingham Adams (1849–1933) to work on architectural projects. Many, like Atlas House, Leeds (1910, William Perkin and George Bulmer) are in the Edwardian Baroque style. The County Arcade and Cross Arcade, Leeds (1897–1900), designed by architect Frank Matcham (1854–1920), best known for his theatres, are ornamental extravaganzas. Gilded mosaics made of Burmantoft vitreous tiles fill the pendentives of the three glazed domes. The cast-iron balustraded gallery is lined with a Burmantoft's Faience frieze of fruit. While the architectural style is a mix of neo-Renaissance and neo-Baroque elements,

using pink brick and Burmantoft terracotta, the mosaics are distinctly Art Nouveau. The central dome carries full-length figures representing Leeds; the cloth industry, mining, architecture/engineering and manufacturing. In the smaller domes Mucha-style female heads symbolize 'Art', 'Liberty', 'Peace', 'Justice', 'Commerce', 'Agriculture', 'Labour', 'Industry'. While they recall the style of Neatby, Burmantoft's best-known designer had been lured away to Doulton's by 1890. Doulton probably hoped Neatby would bring some of Burmantofts' clients with him; they were not disappointed, winning the contract for the Refuge Assurance Company building in Manchester (1891–96, Alfred Waterhouse).

Terracotta and Carrara: William James Neatby

Head designer of Doulton's architectural department, Neatby was responsible for major projects in both terracotta and Carrara ware, the most famous being Harrods Meat Hall (1902). Collaborating with many architects, Neatby's style evolved from Historicism to exemplifying English New Art. His terracotta work on the South Building, Royal Observatory at Greenwich (1891–99, William Crisp), offers us *fin de siècle* themes intended to express the function of the building as an astronomical observatory. The decoration of the bay window incorporates a sleeping woman, her head surmounted by a bat (vision at night) and a six-pointed star, representing *Night*; her sinuous, curvilinear hair references Art Nouveau mascarons. Neatby's panel *Astronomia* (1895) also uses a symbolic woman, one arm outstretched holding the sun, the other a crescent moon. Behind her are the astrological symbols for Aquarius, Scorpio, Leo and Taurus.

Neatby would have been aware of the New Sculpture movement, led by Alfred Gilbert, George Frampton, Alfred Drury, Albert Toft and Frederick Pomeroy.

Projects using brightly coloured Carrara ware include the Fox and Anchor, Charterhouse Street,

Burmantofts vitreous mosaic, The County Arcade and Cross Arcade, Leeds (1897–1900, Frank Matcham).

Neatby, *Night*, Royal Observatory, Greenwich (1891–99, William Crisp).

Neatby, *Astronomia*, Royal Observatory, Greenwich, (1891–99, William Crisp).

City of London (1897–98, Latham A. Withall); the Royal Arcade, Norwich (1899, George Skipper); the Turkey Café, Leicester (1900–01, Arthur Wakerly) and the Everard Building, Bristol (1901, Henry Williams).

Royal Arcade, Norwich

The Castle Street entrance of the Royal Arcade, Norwich, perhaps the most imposing New Art façade in England, brings many elements together; Neatby's distinctive calligraphy, his sculptural work and his relief tiles. As in the case of the Turkey Café there is a distinct Moorish/Islamic influence. The apex is crowned with a winged female head, perhaps the goddess of 'retail therapy'! The window below is filled with blossom-laden trees and doves. The interior is decorated with Carrara ware and Parian ware, another ceramic product designed to simulate marble; panels of confronting peacocks or scrolling foliage are positioned over the shop fronts.

The focal point of the complex is the junction of the main arcade with its south arm where mystical female figures, wearing ornate Renaissance-Mucha-style head-dresses, surround the skylight. Each holds an orb, originally intended to carry signs of the zodiac but for some reason these were never executed. Neatby may have been aware of Crane's *Sphaera imaginationis* (Sphere Imagination) a design for a stained-glass window (1899, Budapest Museum of Applied Arts). Most strikingly the outlines of the decorative forms are in white rather than the conventional black, the effect resembling stencilling. The

Neatby, Royal Arcade, Norwich (1899, George John Skipper).

background trees are reduced to square heads containing a pyramid of six dots; such extreme stylising suggests Neatby was familiar with Lethaby's *Architecture, Mysticism and Myth* or was already aware of the emerging linear Glasgow style.

There is nothing obtuse about the Turkey Café, its pediment crowned with a large turkey. Neatby's authorship is assumed as it was planned while he oversaw Doulton's architectural ceramics department. Like the Royal Arcade, the façade draws on Moorish/Islamic sources.

Everard Building, Bristol

The Everard Building is regarded as Neatby's finest work, although the scheme was probably chosen by Edward Everard, the building's owner, who saw himself as the inheritor of the tradition of fine-quality printing. The decorative scheme, a 'monument to the history of printing', commemorates Johannes Gutenberg and William Morris' Kelmscott Press. Behind each figure can be seen their distinctive typefaces. Between them stands the Spirit of Literature holding an open book. The figure in the gable, holding a lamp and a mirror, represents Light and Truth.

The ornamental pavilions that top the skyline are decorated with heart-shaped leaves, while the frieze of highly stylized trees, above the entrance, alludes to the Tree of Knowledge. When the building was unveiled, so many people stopped to stare at this remarkable edifice that the police were called to regulate the traffic. With this project, more than any other, Neatby achieved a work of public art.

Although Neatby left Doulton to set up in partnership with E. Hollyer Evans, his erstwhile employers still called on his services. He was responsible for the scheme, executed in Parian ware tiling, for the Harrod's Meat Hall (1902), the most famous English New Art interior. The lower frieze consists of twenty hand-painted medallions, illustrating medieval hunting themes (archery and falconry) set within a background of stylized fish and birds. Each medallion is topped by a heart-shaped tree, the splayed branches bearing heart-shaped leaves. The tiled ceiling also appropriately features game birds. The whole scheme was miraculously completed in nine weeks.

Glazed Stoneware: Alexandre Bigot

With the wide application of architectural ceramics at Paris 1889, the demand for such products grew rapidly. As the leading player in the field, Alexandre Bigot (1862–1927) collaborated with many of the greatest sculptors and architects of the time:

Neatby, Everard Building, 37–38 Broad Street, Bristol (1901).

Lavirotte, Guimard, Majorelle, Sauvage, and Anatole de Baudot (1834–1915). A physics and chemistry instructor, Bigot became interested in ceramics after viewing Chinese porcelains at Paris 1889. In 1894 he established a factory at Mer (Loir-et-Cher) to produce *grès flammés*, a stoneware fired at high temperatures. With his knowledge of chemistry, Bigot was able to create glazes in many colours and finishes including crystalline and matte glazes using acids to corrode the surface. His early work, small vases and plates with applied newts, frogs and snakes, recalls the manner of the famous French master potter Bernard Palissy (c.1510–89). Unveiling his wares in 1894, Charles Holme remarked 'the whole of [Bigot's] exhibit was modelled by his own hands', setting his work apart from factory-made products[20]. His art pottery, figures, vases, tiles and other decorative ceramics were sold through Bing's L'Art Nouveau. In its heyday, the factory employed around one hundred and fifty workers and operated ten industrial kilns.

Bigot's stoneware was particularly suitable for the panelling and decoration of the façades of 'ferrocement' buildings[21]. An extensive range of products was offered in the trade catalogue issued in 1902; frost-resisting glazed and unglazed tiles, roof tiles, including ridge-tiles of various shapes, as well as a wide variety of architectural components, such as columns, pillars, lunettes, lintels, banisters, arches, friezes and parapets. For the interior, floor and wall tiles could be purchased, as well as fireplace surrounds.

Bigot and Lavirotte

In addition to fabricating Joseph René Binet's (1866–1911) designs for the main entrance to Paris 1900, Bigot's ceramics pavilion, designed by Lavirotte, caused a sensation. Awarded the Grand Prix, contemporary photographs show a remarkable ensemble of architectural ceramics: columns, pillars, balconies, friezes, entire doorways and ridge-tiles and finials. Some of these items were used on Lavirotte's Avenue Rapp projects; 3, Square Rapp (1899–1900) and 29,

Avenue Rapp (1901) were 'living advertisements' of the ceramist's art. The Bigot Pavilion was purchased by Jenő Radisics, the director of the Museum of Applied Arts in Budapest. Understandably Bigot's technical innovations drew Radisics' interest, as Lechner's Museum of Applied Arts (1896) is a prime example of the use of ceramics in architecture.

The Lavirotte building, described as 'ornamental delirium', is undoubtedly the most eccentric and whimsical Art Nouveau building in Paris. The façade, a relief-sculpture composed of various ceramic materials, is a veritable catalogue of erotic symbolic motifs. It must have raised several eyebrows at the turn of the century. The centrepiece is the extravagant doorway, framed with full-length statues of Adam and a very sexy Eve (sculptor Jean-Baptiste Larrivé); Adam appears to be calling out a warning! Positioned over the lintel, a female head (said to be Lavirotte's wife, the painter Jane de Montchenu) is a

Bigot, 29 Avenue Rapp, 7th arrondissement, Paris (1901, Jules Aime Lavirotte).

Bigot, a double-headed tortoise, 29 Avenue Rapp, Paris (1901, Jules Aime Lavirotte).

modern femme fatale, her shoulders draped with a fashionable fox fur. The wit extends to a 'bestiary of sin': preening peacocks (beauty), their fanned tails filling the window embrasures; a double-headed tortoise (sexual dimorphism); bull's head corbels (masculinity) supporting the central window, while the bronze lizard that serves as the door handle refers to Parisian slang for male genitalia.

Lavirotte deserved to carry off the city's prize for the most original façade. He won the prize again for

34, Avenue De Wagram, 8th arrondissement, known as the Ceramic Hotel (1904). Constructed of reinforced concrete, the sculptural decoration of climbing plants (wisteria growing out of pots at ground level) is signed by the sculptor Camille Alaphilippe (1874–1934), who assumed directorship of Bigot's factory in 1914. Originally a *maison meublée*, a furnished house or an establishment that rented furnished rooms, the original interiors were lost when it became a hotel.

Other collaborations

Other Bigot projects in the capital include the apartment block 14, Rue d'Abbeville 10th arrondissement (1901, Alexandre and Edouard Autant), famed for its luxuriant vegetal decoration topped with bats; the more restrained 25 Rue Franklin, 16th arrondissement (1903, Auguste Perret) with vertical panels of stylized leaves and the church of Saint Jean de Montmartre, 18th arrondissement (1894–1904, Anatole de Baudot). Here, brick and stoneware mosaic patterns conceal the reinforced concrete structure.

Alexandre Charpentier's (1865–1909) dining room for Adrien Bénard's villa in Champrosay (Essonne)

Bigot, wall fountain for Adrien Bénard's villa in Champrosay, Essonne (1901, Alexandre Charpentier) Musée d'Orsay.

illustrates the novel use of ceramics in the Art Nouveau interior, Bigot's magnificent wall fountain forming the centrepiece of the ensemble. Its grey-green colour contrasts with the dark red mahogany panelling. Charpentier chose appropriate themes, roses, raspberry bushes, pea and bean plants, the panelling gracefully and fluently inserted into the powerful lines of the structure. In the foliage you can make out two laughing children's heads, one of Charpentier's favourite themes. *L'Illustration* praised the ensemble, which was 'characterized by its originality and individuality; everything was done specifically for the destination. That's why it looks strangely stunning.' Bénard was a keen supporter of the New Art; under his directorship the Compagnie du Métropolitain Parisien chose Guimard to design the entrances to the underground railway.

Beyond Paris

In Nancy, Bigot was involved in three important projects: the balcony balustrade of the Villa Majorelle (1901–02, Henri Sauvage), bedecked with aquatic plants, and the remarkable fireplace in the dining room; the flower-head tiles on the Graineterie Génin (seed merchant's shop), Rue Bénit (1901, Henri Gutton (1851–1933) and Henry Gutton (1874–1963) and the funerary monument of Georgette Vierling, wife of the writer Jules Rais (1901, architect Xavier Girard and Parisian sculptor Pierre Roche), surmounted by Bigot's enamelled stoneware lily. Originally in the Cimetière de Préville, it has been relocated to the grounds of the Musée l'École de Nancy.

Bigot had rivals; Émile Müller and Co. claimed to be 'the largest factory of ceramic products for buildings,

Bigot, balcony balustrade, Villa Majorelle or Villa Jika, 1 Rue Louis Majorelle, Nancy (1901–02).

Bigot, dining room fireplace, Villa Majorelle or Villa Jika, 1 Rue Louis Majorelle, Nancy (1901–02).

Bigot, ceramic lily, funerary monument of Georgette Vierling (1901, Xavier Girard and Pierre Roche) Musée l'École de Nancy.

industries and works of art in the world'. The trade catalogue is full of coloured bricks, lintels, balusters, friezes, fireplaces and flamboyant female mascarons. The founder Émile Müller (1823–89) established the Grande Tuilerie d'Ivry (Ivry Port, Seine) in 1854. He perfected his *grès* by 1884; the company fabricated the stoneware balustrades for the Eiffel Tower (1889). After his death in 1889, Müller's son Louis took over the company. By 1900 Grande Tuilerie was made up of five factories in Ivry with between 300 and 400 workers. Notable commissions include the friezes for the domes of the Grand Palais and Petit Palais for Paris 1900. The company collaborated with many famous artists, sculptors and architects: Grasset, Toulouse-Lautrec, Charpentier and Guimard. They competed against Bigot, their ceramics for the House of Thistles, 16th arrondissement (1903, Charles Klein) securing the city's Façade of the Year award.

Gentil and Bourdet, founded by Alphonse Gentil (1872–1933) and François Eugène Bourdet (1874–1952) were active in Nancy. Their factory at Billancourt, on the outskirts of Paris, was founded in 1901. Like Bigot, they specialized in *grès flammés* high-fired stoneware with lustrous glazes. The staircase for the Villa Victor Luc (1901–02, René Hermant)

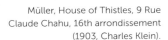

Müller, House of Thistles, 9 Rue Claude Chahu, 16th arrondissement (1903, Charles Klein).

Gentil and Bourdet, staircase, Villa Victor Luc,Rue de Malzeville, Nancy (1901–02, Rene Hermant).

is outstanding. They also provided tiles for Maison Geschwindenhammer, Quai de la Bataille (1905, Henri Gutton and Joseph Hornecker) and the water lily tiles on the gateposts of the Villa Les Roches, Parc Saurupt (1902–04, Émile André).

Tiles or Sgraffito: Brussels

Alongside tile, sgraffito, which involves incising a pattern into the upper layer of the mortar revealing the darker layer below, was particularly popular in Brussels[22]. The clearly defined patterns could be filled with colours. The technique has a long history going back to the Italian Renaissance. Although much of the sgraffito work in Brussels is anonymous, four masters of the art stand out; Paul Cauchie (1875–1952); Adolphe Crespin (1859–1944); Henri Antoine Théodore Livemont, known as Privat-Livemont (1861–1936) and Gabriel van Dievoet (1875–1934) who sometimes collaborated with his brother, the architect Henri van Dievoet (1869–1931).

Paul Cauchie

Beginning his career as a student of architecture at the Academy of Fine Arts, Antwerp, Cauchie changed direction, studying painting under Constant Montald (1862–1944). However, his new expertise was applied to sgraffito. The façade of the Cauchie House (1905) advertises the skills of Cauchie and his wife Caroline Voets, known as Lina. They provided many services, from painting and sgraffito to embroidery and wall hangings. On the façade, Mucha-style maidens, each holding an attribute, personify the fine and applied arts; stone carving (hammer and chisel); drawing (dividers); sculpture (figurine); painting (brushes and palette); music (Greek harp); architecture (building) and applied arts (jewellery). These figures may also represent the nine muses, with the caryatid, possibly Clio, holding up the message *'Par Nous, Pour Nous'* (By Us, For Us). This declaration of faith extends into the interior, the dining room also decorated with sgraffito. Here we find references to music, eating and drinking as well as love. The abundance of stylized roses, both on the exterior and interior, reveals the influence of Mackintosh and the Glasgow school.

Adolphe Crespin

The remarkable sgraffito on the façade of the Hotel Ciamberlani, No. 48 Rue Defacqz, (1897, Paul Hankar) was carried out by Adolphe Crespin. The

Cauchie, Maison Cauchie, Rue des Francs, Etterbeek, Brussels (1905).

Adolphe Crespin, sgraffito, Hotel Ciamberlani, 48 Rue Defacqz, Saint-Gilles, Brussels (1897, Paul Hankar).

scheme was devised by the owner, Albert Ciamberlani (1864–1956), a well-known Italian Symbolist painter. The seven medallions running under the cornice resemble Roman mosaic hunting scenes, men hunting animals and animals hunting one another[23]. Reading from left to right, three appear to reference the Labours of Hercules; the Cretan Bull (2), the Stymphalian birds (3) and Diomedes' man-eating horses (5). The fourth roundel depicts a dog attacking a horse, the sixth a bull goring a horse. The main section of the frieze represents the ages of man from childhood (right spandrel) to old age (left spandrel). The central section is dominated by a great tree, also symbolic of the passage of time; to one side its leaves are falling (left) while on the other flowers are in bloom and fruits hang from the branches. The two kissing peacocks perhaps symbolize love or light, a

beehive and ears of wheat suggest fruitfulness and hard work. Below, a heroic man holds a flaming torch over a young child playing with flowers. This may allude to enlightenment, or perhaps Prometheus who brought humans the gift of fire. This gift enabled man to develop both science and the arts.

Crespin often collaborated with Hankar. He was responsible for the sgraffitio on Hankar's studio-house (1893): *Morning* (bird and chestnut leaves); *Day* (bird and bright sun), *Evening* (swallow) and *Night* (bats and stars). The two panels on the oriel window, strikingly overlaid by the wrought-iron balustrade, feature cats playing amongst nasturtiums. The panels owe a clear debt to Japonisme. Crespin studied at the Académie des Beaux-Arts in Saint-Josse-ten-Noode, a proving

Adolphe Crespin, sgraffito, Maison Hankar, 71 Rue Defacqz, Saint-Gilles, Brussels (1893, Paul Hankar).

ground for Art Nouveau, alongside Privat-Livemont, Saintenoy and Léon Govaerts.

Privat-Livemont: The 'Belgian Mucha'

The multi-talented Privat-Livemont is best known for his posters *Absinthe Robette* (1896) and the *Brussels International Exposition 1897*. Winning a scholarship to study in Paris in 1883, Privat-Livemont remained there for six years working on the interiors of the Théâtre-Français and the Hôtel de Ville. Marrying Madeline Brown in 1889, his wife often served as his model. His Mucha-style ladies were transferred to pictorial tiles for the striking façade of La Grande Maison de Blanc, Brussels (1897, Oscar François). A department store selling lingerie and hosiery, the tile panels celebrate 'Commerce' and 'Industry'. Several panels illustrate the wares on offer, ribbons and wool. The tiles were manufactured by Boch Frères, also known

Privat-Livemont, Maison Beukman, Rue Faider, Ixelles (1900, Albert Roosenboom).

as Royal Boch, which marketed its wares under the trade name Keramis[24]. Factories were established at La Louvière (1844) and Tournai (1851). Crespin also designed for Boch Frères; on the façade of 20–20A Chaussée de Forest, Saint-Gilles (1911) female heads are surrounded by stylized peacock feathers.

Privat-Livemont's sgraffito work can be found on the Maison Beukman, Rue Faider, Ixelles (1900, Albert Roosenboom). One of the most beautiful and enigmatic pictorial designs, at its centre a femme fatale appears to impose silence by putting a finger to her lips and closing her eyes. To either side, two infants stand surrounded by poppies, emblems of Hypnos, the Greek god of sleep and Morpheus, god of dreams. This nocturnal peace frames the bedroom window. The sgraffito frieze on the house and studio of Alfred Ruytinx, Rue Vogler (1905–06) is equally beautiful. An allegory of painting, a typical Art Nouveau maiden holds a palette and brushes. The child behind her alludes to youth and beauty.

Collaborating with Henri Jacobs (1864–1935), Privat-Livemont worked on the Josaphat School, Rue de la Ruche (1907); the external sculptural frieze of bees and sgraffito flowers is fittingly emblematic of the street name – *ruche* means hive. The courtyard is decorated with a frieze of sgraffito, female heads surrounded by stylized foliage. The intention of the municipal administration was not only to instruct but also educate, 'to render better men, to raise the moral level of the people and to give them a taste for

Privat-Livemont, la Grande Maison de Blanc, 32 Rue Marche aux Poulets, Brussels (1897).

Good and Beauty'. The building was to be a 'permanent lesson'[25].

Terracotta and Glazed Tiles: The Grand Duke's Ceramics Factory, Darmstadt

Grand Duke Ernst Ludwig channelled all his energy and personal fortune into a Darmstädter Renaissance. The local economy was rejuvenated by initiating art-industries modelled on English and French precedents; Darmstadt would eventually be recast as a *ville et métiers d'art*. The Grand Duke's ceramics factory, supervised by Jakob Julius Scharvogel (1854–1938) operated from 1904–13, the precious glass factory under Josef Schneckendorf (1865–1949) commenced in 1906, while the Ernst-Ludwig-Presse, directed by Frederick Wilhelm Kleukens (1878–1956) from 1907, could be likened to Morris's Kelmscott Press. But this alliance of the arts and crafts was no utopian dream; if a venture proved unprofitable it was closed.

Scharvogel secured his reputation with the opening of a workshop in Munich (1898); over the next few years he won prizes at the international exhibitions. His high-fired stoneware, based on Japanese models, was decorated with newly developed glazes. Hand-crafted, bold colouristic effects made each piece unique. He looked for inspiration to the French artist-studio potters: Bigot, Auguste Delaherche (1857–1940), Pierre-Adrien Dalpayrat (1844–1910), Jean-Joseph Carriès (1855–94) and Ernest Chaplet (1835–1909), considered the father of French studio pottery. From the outset, Scharvogel was interested in the use of ceramics in architecture, interior décor and furniture. His patron, Ernest Ludwig, was probably encouraged by the Olbrich Haus and Behrens Haus, created for the 1901 Darmstadt exhibition, which were both clad with tiles.

The most ambitious project undertaken by the

Scharvogel and Jobst, Schmuckhof, Badehaus 7, Bad Nauheim (c.1908).

Scharvogel and Jobst, Schmuckhof, Badehaus 7, Bad Nauheim.

Scharvogel and Huber, ceramic capital, waiting room, Badehaus 7, Bad Nauheim (c.1908).

Scharvogel and Jobst, Badehaus 2, Bad Nauheim (c.1908).

Grand Duke's ceramics factory was the spa and sanitorium complex at Bad Nauheim. A natural mineral spring, Bad Nauheim literally means 'effervescent bath'. Architect Wilhelm Jost (1874–1944) orchestrated a grandiose scheme, which included the Trinkkuranlage (pump room), Sprudelhof (courtyard of the major spring) and seven bathhouses. This magnum opus is the most complete Jugendstil complex in Germany. Scharvogel created many elements that could be used in combinations; moulded palmettes, capitals and gargoyles. He was assisted by the sculptor Heinrich Jobst (1874–1943), who had succeeded Ludwig Habich as the colony's sculptor in residence in 1906. He was responsible for the sculptural work of Badehaus 2 and 7 as well as the central fountain of the Sprudelhof. Sculptural terracotta dominates Badehaus 2, offset with blue glazed tiles, and the Schmuckhof (ornamental courtyard) of Badehaus 7 (1906–08). Badehaus 2 is classical in tone, with mermaids, nymphs, centaurs and fauns/satyrs. Badehaus 7, which resembles a medieval cloister, features figurative columns, male and female nudes, and reliefs all related to water; otters catching fish, ducks, pelicans, and even jellyfish. The most eye-catching element is the fountain, with water spurting from the mermaid's breasts. While the Schmuckhof's terracotta was bespoke, the glazed ceramics in the waiting hall, based on designs by the sculptor Karl Huber, were for general sale. Their colour range – brown, greenish

grey and white, with either smooth or speckled surfaces – contrasts with the warm Mediterranean orange-buff terracotta of the courtyard. Both the ornamental courtyard and waiting hall were exhibited at the 1908 Darmstädter Künstlerkolonie Exhibition to demonstrate the successful union of art and industry. Although critically well received, the pottery was not a financial success. Scharvogel's contract was rescinded in 1913.

Pyrogranite and Eosin: Zsolnay Pécs

Lechner's iconic buildings, the Museum of Applied Arts (1896), the Geological Museum (1896–99) and the Postal Savings Bank (1900–01) are all distinguished by their use of Zsolnay ceramics. Much that is odd about Lechner is explained by his background and training. His father ran a brickworks, which encouraged his interest in all types of ceramic materials[26]. Finishing his architectural training in Berlin at the Bauakademie, he absorbed Gottfried Semper's theory, which argued cladding was a 'garment' on the building's structure. Mimicking textiles, hanging patterned ceramics on an iron or steel frame seemed a logical way forward. On his trips to England in 1879 and 1889, Lechner would have seen ceramic-clad buildings, such as the Natural History Museum (1873–81, Alfred Waterhouse), the first building in England to be completely clad in terracotta[27]. The Thonet house (1888–89), on the main shopping street in Pest, is seen as a turning point, as although it is still stylistically Historicist its steel structure is entirely clad in Zsolnay pyrogranite.

Vilmos Zsolnay

Famous for its stoneware and earthenware with brightly coloured glazes, Zsolnay Pécs, southern Hungary, was founded by Miklós Zsolnay (1800–80) in 1853. It was his son Vilmos Zsolnay (1828–1900), a technical innovator, who led the factory to worldwide recognition after he assumed control in 1863. Zsolnay architectural ceramics were used throughout the Austro-Hungarian Empire and even beyond; in Vienna, Max Fabiani's (1865–1962) Portois & Fix (1898) building was clad in Zsolnay's pyrogranite. This new durable material was in production by 1886. Fired at high temperature, pyrogranite was frost-resistant and fireproof making it ideal for all forms of architectural work, particularly roof tiles. The roof of Matthias Church, Buda (1874–96, Frigyes Schulek) is especially colourful, with repeating geometric patterns in yellow, green and ochre. Lechner used this material throughout his buildings. Motifs derived from Hungarian embroidery were enlarged for the

Pyrogranite, Atlas figures, Hungarian National Geological Institute, Stefánia út 14, Pest (1896–99, Ödön Lechner).

patterned tiles of the Museum of Applied Arts. The same floral motifs were transformed into sculptural components for staircase banisters and railings. The roof tiles of the Geological Institute form a

Pyrogranite, Aladár Árkay, Reformed Church of Fasori, Városligeti fasor 5–7, Pest (1912–13).

Pyrogranite, Párisi Nagy Áruház (Great Parisian Department Store), Andrassy Avenue, Pest (1909–12, Zsigmond Sziklai).

contrasting pattern of light and dark blue, the pyramidal central tower surmounted by a globe supported by four Atlas figures. When questioned about the intricate detailing of the Postal Savings Bank roof (bullheads, winged serpents), which could not be seen at street level, Lechner is said to have retorted 'only God and the birds will see them'.

The Gellért Thermal Baths and Swimming Pool (1912–18, Izidor Sterk, Ármin Hegedűs, and Artúr Sebestyén) use Zsolnay ceramics throughout, for cladding columns, fountains, benches and statues[28]. In the steamy atmosphere, the aquamarine tiles create a fairy-tale aquatic world. The relief tiles reinterpret Hungarian folk-art motifs. A similar adaptation, including traditional tulips, also distinguishes the façade of Aladár Árkay's Reformed Church of Fasori (1912–13).

The Párisi Nagy Áruház (Great Parisian Department Store), one of the landmarks on Andrassy Avenue (1909–12, Zsigmond Sziklai), also makes use of Zsolnay's pyrogranite. The site was redeveloped by Samuel Goldberger, who created a modern store along Parisian lines. The façade is distinguished by its great parabolic arch, regarded at the time as a distinctly Hungarian feature, clad with Zsolnay tiles. The atrium cut through five floors, revealing all the levels of the store.

Eosin

Influenced by the multi-coloured iridescent glazes of the French art potter Clément Massier, Zsolnay perfected its own lustre glaze, named eosin, by 1893. Eosin takes its name from the Greek *eos*, the first flush of dawn. According to the angle of reflection, the metallic surface flashes different colours; shades of green, red, blue, and purple. Over time different eosin colours and processes were developed. Eosin tiles were used throughout the Liszt Ferenc Academy of Music (1904–07), cladding the lower portion of the walls and as decorative roundels featuring musical motifs. At the other end of the spectrum, the tiles and improbable elephant, rhino and hippo heads on the famous Elephant House, Budapest Zoo, are also in eosin.

The former Árkád-Bázar toy store of Késmárky and Illés (1909–10, Jozef and Laszlo Vágó) is almost entirely clad in terrazzo slabs and ceramic panels, the distinctive Secession style calligraphy of the shop sign in eosin. The figural motifs, children playing with their toys, are charming.

Zsolnay eosin, Liszt Ferenc Academy of Music, Liszt Ferenc ter 8, Pest (1904–07, Flóris Korb and Kálmán Giergl).

Zsolnay eosin, Arkad-Bázar toy store, Dohány utca 22–24, Pest (1909–10, Jozef and Laszlo Vágó)

Trencadís: Barcelona

Drawing on Iberia's Moorish heritage, Catalan Modernista architects used ceramics extensively both externally and internally. They particularly favoured trencadís (meaning 'chopped'), also known as pique assiette or broken tile mosaics. This form of mosaic is made from irregular broken tile and glazed ceramics cemented together. Patterns can be random, geometric, pictorial or a hybridization. Trencadís is thus a form of bricolage, 'found object' or recycled art. Gaudí first used trencadís for the Güell Pavilions, Pedralbes (1884–87). He favoured brightly coloured glazed ceramic shards. He often used flawed and discarded pieces of tile collected from the Pujol i Bausis factory, in Esplugues de Llobregat, Barcelona (c.1858–c.1960) popularly known as 'The Rajoleta' (The Little Tile)[29]. The company also supplied Domènech and Puig i Cadafalch. Jaume Pujol took control of the factory in 1876. With the help of his son Pau, he remained manager until his death in 1892. From 1901 to 1904 Joan Baptista Alós served as artistic director. Pujol i Bausis joined the team Domènech assembled for the construction of the Castell de Tres Dragons (1888). The demands of the Modernista architects undoubtedly led to a revival of local crafts and sparked the development of art industries.

Gaudí tended to create patterns in his trencadís work, as seen on the fourteen chimney stacks of the

Gaudí, trencadís chimney, Güell Palace, Carrer Nou de la Rambla, Barcelona (1886–88).

Güell Palace (1886–88). One features a bold black-and-white geometric pattern, another black squares within a blue grid on a bold yellow background and one predominately white with regularly spaced black circles. The latter is made of white pottery from domestic cups and plates. The brand name can be seen on some of the shards. Another chimney stack is composed of spirals of trencadís in a rainbow of colours: red, pink, blue, green, orange, red.

Gaudí: Parc Güell

Parc Güell's serpentine bench (1909) is Gaudí's most famous use of trencadís. At first sight the collage appears random, but a closer inspection reveals abstract and pictorial sections including the signs of the zodiac (Sagittarius, Pisces, Cancer and Aries) on the exterior surface. Five-branched palmettes abound. Figurative designs include six-pointed starfish, fish, crabs and twisted seaweed. A commercially made

Gaudí and Jujol, serpentine bench, Parc Güell, Gracia, Barcelona (c.1909).

Gaudí and Jujol, *Sun*, Parc Güell, Gracia, Barcelona (1909–14).

tile decorated with a butterfly has been deliberately broken and reset. The work was undertaken in collaboration with Josep Maria Jujol (1879–1949). According to legend Gaudí and Jujol gave the labourers a free hand on the condition they respected certain guidelines. Although the colours mix randomly, with blue, green and yellow predominating, they had significance for Gaudí, symbolizing Faith, Hope and Charity. Jujol also included roses and allegorical phrases that paid homage to the Virgin Mary.

Jujol was responsible for the rosettes on the ceiling vaults of the marketplace. These incorporate all kinds of broken material; tiles, plates, saucers, bottles and even a china doll. The four largest (3m in diameter) are suns representing the four seasons. They are all based on a twenty-pointed star. The lunar cycle is represented by fourteen smaller rosettes, variations of swirls and spirals.

The entrance to the marketplace is spectacular;

the monumental staircase (1903–06) bears symbolic sculpture expressing the ideals and concepts of the garden-city project. Made up of three flights, the staircase is split in half by fountains; the division represents the 'Catalan countries' – northern Catalonia, the French side and south Catalonia, the Spanish side. On the second fountain a shield with yellow and red bars replicates the Catalan flag, while the serpent alludes to the beneficial properties of the water. A natural spring was found on the site; perhaps to recoup his investment, Güell decided to market this 'medicinal' spring water under the brand name SARVA. The bottles were labelled with an image of the staircase, which read 'Source: Parc Güell' ('Neighbourhood of Health'). Located on the third flight is the famous dragon or salamander, *El Drac*, covered in bright trencadís, which acts as an overflow for the water cistern below the marketplace. It used to boast sharp teeth and claws. Its meaning is hotly debated: it could be the mythological dragon Python, protector of the subterranean waters of the temple of Delphi; an alchemic salamander representing fire or even the symbol of Nîmes, the French city where Güell spent his youth. The meaning of the ceramic sculptural tripod, on the upper part of the fountain, is equally problematic; this could be the Delphic Oracle of the Sanctuary of Apollo or the tail of the serpent from the fountain below.

Gaudí's love of tiles can be traced back to his first

Gaudí, *El Drac* [dragon] or salamander, Parc Güell, Gracia, Barcelona (1909–14).

Gaudí, Casa Vicens, Carrer de les Carolines, Barcelona (1883–85).

major commission, Casa Vicens (1883–85), which reflects neo-Mudéjar architecture, a revival of Moorish forms such as horseshoe arches, arabesque tiling, and geometric brick ornamentation. Having invested in the Pujol i Bausis ceramics factory, perhaps Manuel Vicens i Montaner was keen to utilize his asset.

Domènech: Hospital de la Santa Creu i Sant Pau

Domènech was equally committed to the use of tile although trencadís plays a minor role at the Hospital de la Santa Creu i Sant Pau (1901–30) and the Palau de la Música Catalana (1905–08). Domènech's principles were based on 'structure, function and ornament'. Trained as an engineer, he drew on his comprehensive knowledge of Romanesque and Gothic forms as well as Byzantine sources; his knowledge of patterns suggests he was familiar with Owen Jones' indispensable *The Grammar of Ornament* (1856). He had a thorough knowledge of the nature of materials; it was a subject he taught at the Barcelona School of Architecture. Following Arts and Crafts precepts, he believed in respecting and bringing out the best of the materials. He used ornament, integrating many different materials, to create his own symbolic code that frequently references Catalan traditions. Like Ruskin, he believed the goal of architecture was beauty; colour was paramount, as seen in the tile-clad roofs and domes of the Hospital de la Santa Creu i Sant Pau. Resembling fish scales, the scalloped tiles are laid in bold patterns; against a vibrant yellow the geometric patterns mix terracotta red with blue, buff, white and black. Vivid yellow fleurons and pinnacles bristle on the skyline. The vaults of the central hall of the Administrative Pavilion are covered in glazed pink tiles. The staircase vault shimmers with buff glazed ribs supporting an impressive coloured glass skylight.

The conception of the glazed ceramic mosaics depicting the history of the Hospital, decorating the two lateral wings of the Administrative Pavilion, was entrusted to the painter Francesc Labarta (1883–1963). They were fabricated by the Italian-born artist

Labarta, *Founding of the Hospital,* ceramic mosaic, façade, Hospital de la Santa Creu i Sant Pau, Barcelona (1902–30, Domènech).

Domènech, Administrative Pavilion, Hospital de la Santa Creu i Sant Pau, Barcelona (1902–30).

Mario Maragliano (1864–1944). In sixteen sections, the mosaics tell the entire history of the Hospital from its medieval foundation to the unification as Santa Creu i Sant Pau. The rear façade features mosaics of St George, patron saint of Catalonia and Saint Martin, soldier and benefactor of the poor, flanked by heraldic devices of the city of Barcelona, the Hospital and its patron Pau Gil. The iconographic scheme includes St Eulalia of Barcelona and St Elizabeth of Hungary, representing charity and the care of the sick, alongside the doctor saints Cosmas and Damian, who gave their services free of charge. A range of different techniques was used in the interior, including ceramic mosaics, moulded tiles and trencadís. In the Sala Domènech i Montaner conference hall, the red brick walls are clad to dado level with yellow honeycomb-shaped tiles surmounted by a mosaic frieze featuring flowers and flowing tendrils in blue, red and yellow. This is capped with a band of moulded white flori-form discs, which resemble flower heads. This sophisticated combination of colours and textures creates unparalleled visual diversity.

Domènech relied on Lluís Bru i Salelles (1868–1952) and Mario Maragliano for his ceramic and mosaic projects. Both worked on the Hospital de la Santa Creu i Sant Pau. Travelling to Venice to learn how to make mosaics in 1904, Bru worked on the Casa Lleó Morera (1902–05, Domènech) and the Casa Comalat (1911, Salvador Valeri i Pupurull) and outside Barcelona, on the Pere Mata Institute in Reus (1897–1912, Domènech) and the mosaics of the North Station, Valencia (1913). He also designed ceramics for the Pujol i Bausis manufactory.

Azulejos: Arte Nova in Porto and Aveiro

In Portugal, Arte Nova buildings are often distinguished by their azulejos or painted tile panels. Azulejo comes from the Arabic *zellige* meaning 'polished stone' as the original idea was to imitate Roman mosaics. The earliest azulejos dating to the thirteenth century were alicatados, panels of tile-mosaic. Single colour tin-glazed earthenware tiles were cut into geometric shapes and assembled to form repeating angular patterns. Many examples can be admired in the Alhambra of Granada. These techniques were introduced into Portugal by Manuel I after a visit to Seville in 1503. Adopting the Moorish tradition of *horror vacui* ('fear of empty spaces'), the Portuguese covered walls completely with azulejos. They were not merely ornamental; they were also for temperature control, keeping interiors cool. Tiles can cover the entire façade or be arranged in panels. Many of the late nineteenth-century apartments around the Mercado do Bolhão, Porto's central market dating back to the 1850s, are covered with azulejos creating a rainbow of colours: green, pink and yellow. However, traditional blue and white pictorial panels remained popular.

It was through tiles that the New Art forms gained visibility throughout Portugal. They can be found on houses with no other Arte Nova characteristics. Manufacturers embraced floral forms and natural motifs (flowers, birds, insects, female figures). Hand painting resulted in a more naturalistic approach, while stamping and moulding produced graphic and linear designs with clear contours. Tiles were made to order; in this context they were often signed and dated. They were also mass-produced, being selected for friezes and panels through catalogues.

Jorge Colaço

Azulejos are found on the interior and exterior of every type of building from churches to railway stations, the most notable example being the 20,000 azulejos used to decorate the vestibule of Porto's São Bento railway station (1900–16, Marques da Silva). The first tiles were placed on 13 August 1905. The blue and white tile pictures represent important moments in Portugal's history. To the left of the entrance is the *Battle of Arcos de Valdevez* (1140) and *Egas Moniz before Alfonso VII, King of León and Castile* (twelfth century) while to the right, is *John I and Phillipa of Lancaster entering Oporto* to celebrate their wedding in 1387 and the *Conquest of Ceuta* (14 August 1415), marking the beginning of the Portuguese Empire in Africa. On the wall leading to the platforms are panels representing the famous Douro valley; the vineyards, harvesting and shipping the wine down the Douro. The polychrome upper frieze that runs around the entire interior depicts the history of transport, culminating in the arrival of the train.

This imposing scheme was undertaken by the painter Jorge Colaço (1868–1942). They were made at the Sacavém Factory, also known as Fábrica de Loiça, founded by Manuel Joaquim Afonso (c.1856). The factory was acquired by John Stott Howorth (1829–93), who later naturalized to become Baron of Howorth de Sacavém.[30] New machinery was brought in from England, as well as fine quality white kaolin clay. Keeping abreast of the latest technologies, an

Colaço, azulejos, São Bento railway station (1900–16, Marques da Silva).

Colaço, *History of Transport*, polychrome upper frieze, São Bento railway station (1900–16, Marques da Silva).

85m-long tunnel kiln was installed in 1912. Stylistically, Sacavém was influenced by Minton & Co., Stoke-on-Trent, importing moulds and enamels. Tile manufacturing started in 1890; mass production using press-moulding ensured Sacavém tiles were affordable. They can be found throughout Portugal.

Colaço worked at Sacavém from 1904 until 1924. In addition to the São Bento project, he also painted the tile panels for the Palace-Hotel do Buçaco, Luso (1888–1907, begun by Luigi Pietro Manini). A romantic neo-Manueline palace, evoking the sixteenth-century architectural style that marks the high point of the Age of Discovery, the tiles commemorate Portugal's great poets and playwrights as well as historical events like the Battle of Bussaco (1810).

Rafael Bordalo Pinheiro

Known as the 'Portugese Pallissy' due to his love of insects and reptiles, Rafael Bordalo Pinheiro (1846–1905) began his career as a cartoonist. Founding the Fábrica de Faianças Caldas da Rainha in 1884, Pinheiro created whimsical pottery vegetables, flowers, insects, fish and animals for the table as well as tiles. The factory employed several techniques including hand-painting and moulding. Pinheiro's products can be likened to Minton's Majolica, a glazed earthenware that reinvented sixteenth-century Italian Maiolica. Minton presented their new material at the 1851 Great Exhibtion. Majolica was created by Joseph Leon Francois Arnoux, who was appointed Art Director at Minton in 1848. Brightly coloured and hard wearing, it was ideal for tiles and garden ornaments, as well as highly ornate tablewares. Pinheiro's embossed tiles

Bordalo Pinheiro, *Grasshopper and Wheat* (1902) Rafael Bordalo Pinheiro Museum, Campo Grande, Lisbon.

Grasshopper and Wheat, and *Butterfly and Wheat* (1902) were first made for the Panificica Mecânica, Lda (Mechanical Bakery), Campo de Ourique, Lisbon, to decorate the interior of the pastry and bakery shop.

Aveiro: Fábrica da Fonte Nova

The hand-painted blue and white azulejos on Averio's station capture the locale, with scenes of the town's canals that gave rise to its ephitet 'Portugal's Venice'. It was the arrival of the railway line between Porto and Lisbon that secured Averio's prosperity.

Tiles were used extensively in Aveiro, where most of the Arte Nova buildings are built in adobe (sun-dried clay bricks). A thriving ceramics industry grew up around the Ria de Aveiro, a region rich in fuels, clay, fine white sands and crystallized pebbles. Founded in 1882 by the Melo Guimarães brothers, Fábrica da Fonte Nova was the main tile producer in the Aveiro district[31]. Hand painting predominates,

Seagull tiles, interior, Casa Mário Pessoa, Rua Doutor Barbosa Magalhães, Aveiro (1906–09, Silva Rocha and Korrodi).

much of the work being undertaken by Francisco Pereira, Carlos Branco and Licínio Pinto. The factory developed an individual style, with green, purple, yellow and pink dominating their designs. On the Casa de Anselmo Ferreira, also known as Casa da

Pinto, for Fábrica da Fonte Nova, Casa da Cooperativa Agrícola, Rua João Mendonça, Aveiro (1913).

Belvedere, rear courtyard Casa Mário Pessoa, Rua Doutor Barbosa Magalhães, Aveiro (1906–09, Silva Rocha and Korrodi).

Cooperativa Agrícola (Agricultural Co-operative building) (1913, Silva Rocha), the tiles were hand-painted by Licínio Pinto, being signed and dated 1913.

Casa Mário Pessoa (1906–09, Silva Rocha and Korrodi), built for the entrepreneur Mário Belmonte Pessoa, is ornamented with commercially printed tiles and unique hand-painted panels. On the ground floor, the walls are covered with a dado, a continuous frieze of seagulls on a turquoise ground. The tiles lining the enclosed porch are decorated with swimming ducks, surrounded by curvilinear plant motifs. A hand-painted panel, cows in an idyllic landscape, can be found in the belvedere of the rear courtyard. Surrounded by purple arum lilies on a yellow ground, it bears the stylistic traits of the Fonte Nova pottery. The belvedere was created as a quiet spot, also affording good views of the patio and the square behind the property, for the young ladies of the house.

Vila Africana

Silva Rocha was a teacher at and then director of Aveiro's Industrial Design School for almost forty years. He taught the next generation; Jaime Inácio dos Santos (1874–1942) and José de Pinho, the architect of the Vila Africana, in nearby Ílhavo (1907–08). This was built for Dr José Vaz, who had served in the African Maritime Partnership, Cape Verde. After the Casa Mário Pessoa, this is the most exuberant Arte Nova residence, adorned with polychrome and blue-and-white painted panels against a background of bright yellow tiles. Purple irises and flowing stems surround the name Vila Africana. A frieze of pink flowers on a purple ground runs under the entablature. The blue-and-white tile panel on the entrance staircase, attributed to Fonte Nova, is painted with an idyllic landscape, swans floating serenely on the water. Two birds, holding up swags in their beaks, highlight the owner's initials.

Landscape tile panel, Vila Africana, Rua Vasco de Gama, 135, Ílhavo (1907–08, José de Pinho).

American Terra Cotta: Louis Sullivan

Embracing the potential of the steel frame, Sullivan initiated a new grammar of structural form: base, shaft and cornice. His mantra, 'that form ever follows function', became the basis of modern architecture leading eventually to a total rejection of ornament, which was condemned as superfluous. This was not Sullivan's intention, as he developed his ethos from the Roman architect Marcus Vitruvius Pollio; a structure must be 'solid, useful, beautiful'. Sullivan's buildings are beautiful, his surfaces covered with lush decorative forms ranging from vines and ivy to Celtic interlace inspired by his Irish heritage. His trademark complex organic forms called for malleable materials; terra cotta, which was lighter and easier to work with than stone masonry and ironwork, seen at its best in the writhing canopies of the Carson Pirie Scott and Co. store, Chicago[32].

While Sullivan's ornament is undoubtedly original it was not without precedent. He drew on both European and American precursors, notably Frank Heyling

Furness (1839–1912) of Philadelphia who reworked Ruskinian polychrome Gothic juxtaposing styles and elements in a forceful manner. Although many of Furness' buildings have been demolished, the Fisher Fine Arts Library (1888–91), on the campus of the University of Pennsylvania, is a testament to his originality. Combining red sandstone, brick and terra cotta this Venetian Gothic giant – part fortress and part cathedral – was built to be the primary library of the university. Like his English counterparts, Furness boldly combined stone, iron, glass, terra cotta, and brick.

The Guaranty/Prudential Building, Buffalo, NY (1894–95), designed by Sullivan in partnership with Dankmar Adler (1844–1900), exemplifies Sullivan's use of terra cotta. The building was divided into four zones: the basement (utilities); ground floor for public areas (shops and lobbies); office floors and finally the upper zone for elevator equipment and utilities. The supporting steel structure was cloaked with burnt orange slip-glaze terra cotta blocks, with different styles of block defining the three visible zones of the building; the critic Montgomery Schuyler knew of 'no steel-framed building in which the metallic construction is more palpably felt through the envelope of baked clay'. Sullivanesque patterns had reached their maturity; 'The entire façade of this building is clothed in ornament, like hieroglyphs on the columns and walls of temples in ancient Egypt'[33].

Terra Cotta

The terra cotta was manufactured by the Chicago-based Northwestern Terra Cotta Co. (1877–1956). The hollow units were hand cast in moulds or carved in clay; modular casts, that could be used repetitively, reduced costs. The final effect does indeed resemble a fabric, yet this seeming homogeneity is composed of complex individual components. The Guaranty/Prudential Building façade culminates in a riot of organic curvilinear forms merging into the branches of a tree at its corners; with its trunk extending down the edge of the building to ground level, the metaphor of growth is obvious.

The Norwegian-born Kristian Schneider modelled the ornament under the guidance of Sullivan and George Grant Elmslie (1869–1952), his chief draftsman and ornamental designer. Schneider's talents as a modeller of decorative plasterwork were recognized during the construction of the Auditorium Building, Chicago (1889, Sullivan and Adler). This resulted in a lasting collaboration between Schneider and Sullivan, who employed him separately to make the clay models for the cast-iron ornament surrounding the shop windows of the Carson Pirie Scott and Co. store.

The Northwestern Terra Cotta Co. became a major producer of terra cotta, opening plants in St Louis and Denver. They supplied decorative mouldings for many of Chicago's landmark buildings including the Civic

Sullivan and Adler, Guaranty/Prudential Building, Church and Pearl Streets, Buffalo, NY (1894–95).

Opera House (1885, Cobb and Frost; demolished), the Chicago Theatre (1921, Cornelius W. Rapp and George L. Rapp) and the Wrigley Building (1921–24, Graham, Anderson, Probst & White), a skyscraper completely clad 'from sidewalk to searchlight' in terra cotta. In 1906 Schneider left Northwestern Terra Cotta Co. to work for the American Terra Cotta and Ceramic Company.

From its founding (c.1876), in time to rebuild the fire-ravished city of Chicago, until its closing in 1966, the American Terra Cotta and Ceramic Company was the major producer of architectural terra cotta in North America[34]. The company operated for eighty-five years in the little town of Terra Cotta, Crystal Lake, Illinois fabricating architectural terra cotta for more than 8,000 buildings throughout the United States and Canada. Founder William Day Gates developed the products from utilitarian bricks and drain tiles to decorative, glazed terra cotta. The company commercially marketed stock designs of Sullivanesque ornament.

Metalwork

Of all the elements used to enrich New Art buildings, three-dimensional metalwork stands out as the most effective. Both wrought and cast iron offered a perfect medium for expressing the fluidity of organic motifs. Buildings were adorned with grilles, window-guards, balconies, railings and canopies. Alessandro Mazzucotelli's balconies bring the flat façades of Milan's Liberty apartment blocks to life. Louis Majorelle used ormolu mounts to emphasize the sinuous lines of his furniture, as well as fabricating staircases and balconies. However, many makers remain anonymous, their work the only record of their skill and imagination.

Style Métro

Guimard's whiplash style is superbly expressed in the fluid cast-iron forms of the Paris Métro (1899–1904/13). The glass lamps and signage perfected by 1902 created a distinct identity quickly dubbed Style Métro. The initial network was planned and built to open in time for Paris 1900. Fearing the entrances might mar the cityscape, a competition was held, stipulating they were to be 'as elegant as possible but above all very light, prioritizing iron, glass and ceramic'[35]. Financier Adrien Bénard (1846–1912), whose bank was underwriting the construction, favoured Art Nouveau. He commissioned Alexandre

Sullivan and Schneider, iron work, former Carson Pirie Scott & Co. store, South State Street and East Madison Street, Chicago, Illinois (1896).

Guimard, *entourage*, Paris Métro Gare du Nord (1899–1904).

Guimard, Métro cartouche or baluster shield, Paris Métro Abbesses, 18th arrondissement (1899–1904).

Charpentier (1856–1909) to design a dining room for his villa at Champrosay, Essonne, in the new style. Bénard persuaded the Compagnie du chemin de fer métropolitain de Paris (CMP) to appoint Guimard to design the entrances to the underground stations.

Guimard opted for cast-iron set in concrete to reduce costs as well as to express his sinuous Art Nouveau forms[36]. Painted green to emulate weathered brass, they have been restored using two different shades; for green-field sites they are painted *vert*

Guimard, holder for a map and advertising, Paris Métro Gare du Nord (1899–1904).

Guimard, Paris Métro Bastille station (1899–1904). Destroyed.

wagon ('train-car green') and in dense urban locations a slightly bluer shade, *vert allemand* ('German green'). All the components were standardized, including the railing cartouches, also known as baluster shields, which incorporate the letter 'M' for Métro. The signage was extended incorporating a holder for a map of the system and for advertising materials (*porte-plan*) with the station name above[37].

The standard unroofed entrance was known as an *entourage*. It was normally surmounted by a 'Métropolitain' or 'Métro' sign arch held between two risers in the form of sinuous stalks that have been compared to lily-of-the-valley. Each stalk bears a light, a red-orange globe reminiscent of an eye or a flower, possibly a lily or an orchid. These were

not ready until 1901, the year after the first system opened. Three entrances, one at Bastille and two on Avenue de Wagram at Étoile, took the form of free-standing pavilions, small stations including waiting rooms. They were loosely based on Japanese pagodas. Eight elaborate structures, designated 'Édicule B' by Guimard, were installed at the termini of Line 1 and at two other major stations. Enclosing the stairway on three sides and glass roofed with a projecting canopy, they are known as *libellules* as they resemble dragonflies. Inaugurated on 13 December 1900, Porte Dauphine, the western terminus of Line 2, has survived, even retaining its decorative wall panels. Another, with open sides, can now be found at Abbesses, 18th arrondissement, having been moved

Guimard, Paris Métro Porte Dauphine (1899–1904).

Guimard, Paris Métro Abbesses, 18th arrondissement (1899–1904).

Guimard, cast iron balcony, Tremois Apartments, 11 Rue François-Millet, 16th arrondissement, Paris.

from Hôtel de Ville in 1974.

Guimard's entrances received a mixed reception; many were hostile to the *libellules* and the lettering, which was deemed 'unreadable'. The sinuous stalks were dubbed *nouille* or 'noodle style'. His design for the Opéra station (1904), ridiculed in the daily newspaper *Le Figaro*, who disliked its 'enormous frog-eye lamps', was rejected. Severing their relationship with Guimard, the CMP bought his moulds and rights; a total of 141 entrances were ultimately constructed, the last in 1913. Eighty-six are still extant and protected as historical monuments.

Le Style Métro popularized Art Nouveau, hitherto a style known only to connoisseurs. It certainly aroused the imagination of both writers and artists, the Surrealist Salvador Dalí (1904–89) declaring 'those divine entrances to the Métro, by grace of which one can descend into the region of the subconscious of the living and monarchical aesthetic of tomorrow'[38]. Art historian Robert Schmutzler saw them as 'arousing…

expectations of the abode of Venus deep down in the mountain rather than a democratic subway'[39].

Following his success with the Métro style, Guimard designed a range of cast iron balcony balustrades and grills made by the Fonderies de Saint-Dizier, Haute-Marne; they could be easily purchased through sales catalogues. They can be seen on many of his buildings in Paris including 17–19 Rue Jean de la Fontaine, Hôtel Mezzara and the Tremois Apartments, 11 Rue François-Millet. They also appear further afield, even in Nancy. The metalwork covering the door in the entrance to his apartment block, 17–19 Rue Jean de la Fontaine, is a perfect expression of his whiplash.

Guimard, entrance, apartment block, 17–19 Rue Jean de la Fontaine and Rue Agar, 16th arrondissement, Paris.

Majorelle: *Maître Ferronnier*

The artistic recuperation of ironwork is credited to the Parisian Émile Robert (1860–1924). During the 1880s the medium was elevated to the point where it rivalled bronze. With the advent of Art Nouveau's grammar of floral ornament, Robert sought assistance from Victor Prouvé, one of the leading lights in l'École de Nancy. In Nancy the artistic status of wrought and cast iron was already recognized due to the work of master ironsmith Jean Lamour (1698–1771). His Rococo 'Golden Gates' and grilles for the Place Stanislas (1755) are legendary, providing both a stylistic exemplar and benchmark. The Art Nouveau *ferronnier* had much to live up to.

Louis Majorelle rose to the challenge, installing a forge in his workshop on the Rue Girardet in 1890.

Majorelle's first recorded ironwork, banisters and lamps, was reported in *La Lorraine artiste* in 1899. Majorelle's ornamental wrought iron found its finest expression in light fittings, the glass shades provided by Daum. The fluid plasticity of his forms, attenuated flowers and plants, belied the rigidity of the material. In his hands, wrought iron acquired a 'personality' of its own[40].

His large projects in Nancy include the staircases of the Banque Renauld (1907–10, Émile André and Paul Charbonnier) and Maison Bergeret (1903–04, Lucien Weissenburger). Although different designs, both take the plant Honesty as their theme. They terminate in a fluid, swirling wave-formation of stems highlighted in copper. Honesty was also the basis for a set of gates displayed at the Salon des Artistes Décorateurs in 1906 (Toledo Museum of Art). Majorelle was clearly fond of Honesty, using the motif throughout his villa, notably for the magnificent

Majorelle, staircase, Maison Bergeret, 24 Rue Lionnois, Nancy (1903–04, Weissenburger).

Majorelle, entrance, Villa Majorelle or Villa Jika, 1 Rue Louis Majorelle, Nancy (1901–02, Sauvage).

Majorelle, entrance, Weissenburger house and studio, Cours Leopold, Nancy (1904, Lucien Weissenburger).

Majorelle, entrance and canopy Chamber of Commerce and Industry, 40, Rue Henri-Poincaré, Nancy (1909, Émile Toussaint and Louis Marchal).

front door. Batch production allowed for the repetition of elements; motifs could be used for staircases, gates and grilles. *Algue* or seaweed was taken as the theme for the Weissenburger house and studio (1903–04), the ginkgo leaf for the Ginkgo Pharmacy (1915, Paul Charbonnier) and ferns for the staircase in the Chamber of Commerce (1909, Emile Toussaint and Louis Marchal). This is a modest affair compared to the entrance, which is protected by a magnificent canopy. The metalwork of the door is based on

Majorelle, balconies, Galeries Lafayette, Boulevard Haussmann, 9th arrondissement, Paris (1907–12, Georges Chedanne).

sycamore maple (*Acer pseudoplatanus*) leaves and distinctive seeds, nicknamed 'copters'.

The staircase and balconies created for the Galeries Lafayette (1907–12, Georges Chedanne) were his magnum opus. Polished copper flowerheads and foliage, which sprout from entwined and undulating stems, provided accents; the key motif was the passionflower, very apt in a Temple of Commerce that aroused many desires. Majorelle's forms were more abstract and robust than those of Gallé.

Exposition Internationale de L'Est de la France

By 1900, large smelting works had replaced wood-fired forges. A secondary industry was born, foundries springing up in the vicinity of the mines. The new Iron Age was celebrated at the Exposition Internationale de L'Est de la France (1909) held in Nancy; the façade of the Palace of Metallurgy, conceived by Louis Lanternier and Eugène Vallin, replicated a gigantic factory supported at its corners by fictive blast-furnaces. Equipped with lamps, these glowed red like the fiery exhaust from factory smokestacks[41]. Decorative plasterwork continued the theme of flames.

Charbonnier's monumental entrance made by La Société Anonyme de Forges et Aciéries de Pompey celebrated their success in the industry: the company had supplied the iron for the Eiffel Tower. Two tall pylons, 23.5m high, linked by an ogival arch, 12.50m across, were decorated with common products: axles, cartwheels, gears and locks were crowned by Nancy's coat of arms. The pylons supported arc lamps; emulating the grandiose entrance to Paris 1900, Nancy had its very own Porte Binet symbolizing the power and boldness of Nancy's steel and iron industries.

Alessandro Mazzucotelli: The 'Magician of Iron'

Born in Lodi, as a young lad Mazzucotelli dreamed of becoming a painter or sculptor, but his family did not have the means to satisfy his ambitions. Aged eighteen, he was apprenticed to the Milanese blacksmith Defendente Oriani. Committed to the medium, he would style himself an 'ornamental blacksmith'. In 1891 he succeeded his master, the workshop changing its name to Mazzucotelli-Engelmann; later he worked alone, first in Via Ponchielli and then opening a new workshop in Bicocca (1909). By this time, he was developing an international market, notably in South America. Commissions came from Buenos Aires, Mexico City and even Bangkok.

Abandoning Historicism, Mazzucotelli distinguished himself at Turin 1902. Collaborating with Sommaruga, Pirovano, Campanini and Stracchini,

Lanternier and Vallin, Palace of Metallurgy, Exposition Internationale de L'Est de la France (1909). Destroyed.

Mazzucotelli, Villa Faccanoni-Romeo, Via Michelangelo Buonarroti, 48, Milan (1911–13, Giuseppe Sommaruga).

Mazzucotelli, Casa Campanini, Via Bellini 11, Milan (1904–06, Alfredo Campanini).

his ironwork can be seen all over Milan. His work stands out both stylistically and through his choice of motifs, oversized dragonflies and butterflies. They seem to alight on the top of lamps or on balconies as seen on the Casa Ferrario (1902, Ernesto Pirovano). Their fantastic size is surreal. Intricate, often excessive, there is a Baroque splendour to his work; his lamps for the Municipal Casino San Pellegrino Terme

Mazzucotelli, *The Gate of the Butterflies*, Casa Moneta, Via Ausonio 3, Milan (1904, Giuseppe Borioli).

Mazzucotelli, Casa Maffei, San Donato, Turin (1904–06, Antonio Vandone).

(1906, Romolo Squadrelli) are stupendous.

Under Sommaruga's direction, he created the awesome staircase and light fittings of the Palazzo Castiglioni (1901–04). While the entrance gate is composed of oversized foliage and flowers, naturalistically rendered, the exterior grilles are completely abstract, simply pieces of sinuous twisted metal. The ironwork for the Villa Faccanoni-Romeo (1911–13) is equally impressive, with typically oversized insects alighting on the gatepost and on a lamp. His ironwork is often the defining Liberty element, as seen in *The Gate of the Butterflies*, Casa Moneta (1904, Giuseppe Borioli).

Following an extensive European tour (1903–04), Mazzucotelli moved away from the naturalism seen at the Palazzo Castiglioni. His ironwork for Casa Campanini (1904–06) shows awareness of Mackintosh and the Viennese Secession in its use of controlled linearity. The *Cancello dei Gladioli* (Carlo Rizzarda Modern Art Gallery, Feltre), shown at the 1906 International Sempione Exposition, Milan, illustrates this transition, its geometrical plant forms combined with

abstract lines. Sometimes referred to as his 'ribbon' style, it can be seen at its best in the gates of the Casa Maffei in Turin (1906). Prepared to move with the times, Mazzucotelli made the transition to postwar Art Deco exhibiting the gate *Groviglio di serpi* (Tangle of Snakes) (restored, Largo Domodossola, Milan) at the Milan International Biennial Exhibition of Applied Arts (1923).

Porto

The cast-iron shop fronts (*devantures*), unique to Porto, defy classification being a convoluted combination of eighteenth-century Rococo and Arte Nova forms. They were fabricated by the Porto Companhia Aliança iron foundry (Massarelos foundry) established circa 1852.[42] A product of increased wealth and urban development, they can be found in Santo Ildefonso, a cosmopolitan area of the city. Tourists still flock to the famous Majestic Café (1916–21, João Queiroz), on the Rua de Santa Catarina, its magnificent interior on

Teixeira Lopes, cast-iron shop front (*devanture*), Ourivesaria Reis & Filhos, Rua de Santa Catarina Santa, Porto (1905).

a par with Parisian Belle Époque brasseries.

Close by, the former Ourivesaria Reis & Filhos (1905, José Teixeira Lopes, 1872–1919), in a prominent position on the corner of Rua de Santa Catarina and Rua 31 de Janeiro, stands out from the crowd. Originally a jeweller's, founded by António Alves dos Reis in 1880, its lavish cast-iron façade reflects the opulent commodities being sold. Scrolls, shells and curves are twisted into exaggerated New Art forms topped with a gilded femme fatale, perhaps Porto's version of *La Parisienne*, the woman who loves to shop! An urban myth maintains this is a bust of Dinamene, a beautiful Chinese woman, beloved by Portugal's national poet Luís Vaz de Camões (1524–80). Dying in a shipwreck on the Cambodian coast she was personified by Camões as a sea nymph. Fortuitously, a bust of Camões can be seen directly opposite, on the Latin bookstore. The romantic theme continues inside, with painted vignettes on the celling in *fête galante* style, lovers choosing tokens of their affections, attributed to the architect's brother António Teixeira Lopes. A plaster frieze aptly features putti playing with jewels.

Casa Vicent (1914), Rua de 31 de Janeiro, another important commercial artery, is equally eccentric, exaggerated undulating Rococo scrolls attempting to replicate moulded and chiselled silver. It was originally created for Ourivesaria Miranda & Filhos.

Ourivesaria Cunha (1914) continues the Rococo theme with *Grupo de Amores* by the sculptor José de Oliveira Ferreira, a putto offering a necklace to

Camões, Latin bookstore, Rua de Santa Catarina, Porto (c.1905).

Cast-iron shop front (*devanture*), Casa Vicent, Rua de 31 de Janeiro, Porto (1914).

his sweetheart, at its apex. A combination of marble and cast iron, the shop front was created for Alfredo Pinto da Cunha.

Conclusion

Metal, ceramics and glass came together to create the monumental gateway of Paris 1900, a fitting entrance to the greatest show on Earth. Flanked by two pylons, the Porte Binet on the Place de la Concorde recalled a Byzantine palace; the name honoured its creator Joseph René Binet (1866–1911). Vilified by Remy de Gourmont as 'a hideous carnival mask but quite original in its hideousness', it was a daring and innovative structure[43]. With fifty-six ticket booths, 1,000 people could be admitted every minute. Using polychrome ceramic decoration by Bigot, glass and electricity, Binet sought to create an architecture of colour and light: 'This door has been noticed not by the polychrome itself, but as the first attempt at domestication of electricity at the service of colour

and architecture'[44]. 'Under the sun's fires', glass cabochons sparkled by day, while at nightfall inner lighting achieved a transformation; the glass cabochons on the pylons were graded, the darkest ones at the bottom, the clearest at the top. Some of the globes created a halo that doubled the effect; by day and night, the gateway recalled a 'vast luminous mosque with glittering minarets'[45]. It was nicknamed the Salamander, as it resembled the elaborately decorated Salamander stoves popular at the time.

Overlooking the Porte, watching the thousands pouring through the entrance, was *La Parisienne*, a monumental sculpture some 15ft tall by M. Moreau-Vauthier. This was not a traditional allegorical figure; rather this was a woman of the times, robed by the great couturier Paquin in a very modern dress: 'This woman is Paris, Paris of 1900', declared *Le Petit Journal*, 'emerging from the past and turning to the future, Paris, with a welcoming wave of her arms, seems to invite the world.'

A dream city was created on the banks of the Seine; 'a shimmering city of décor in which all the sections

Grubhofer, *Illumination of the main entrance to the Paris Exhibition* (Porte Binet) *The Studio*, Vol.20, No.89, August 15 1900, opposite p.141.

of every nation… tried to outdo each other in the imaginative richness of their luxurious displays'[46]. It was a new magical force, electricity, that transformed this 'common effort' into a wonderland. With over 50 million visitors, the Universal Exhibition was the greatest the world had seen; it was a millennial moment, an opportunity to review the progress of the century. It was the apogee of Art Nouveau.

Notes

1. Sewter, A. C., *Stained Glass of William Morris and his Circle*, Vol.1, New Haven: Yale University Press, 1974. p.22.

2. Morris bought out his partners in Morris, Marshall, Faulkner & Co., the company simply becoming Morris & Co. in 1875.

3. Penn, Arthur, *St Martin's: The Making of a Masterpiece*, Brampton: David Penn/ Millyard Studios, 2008, pp.46, 47.

4. Cook, Martin Godfrey, *Edward Prior: Arts and Crafts Architect*, Marlborough: Crowood Press, 2015, pp.46, 152–3.

5. Baillie Scott, Mackay Hugh, *Houses and Gardens* (1906), reprinted Woodbridge: Antique Collectors' Club, 1995, p.308.

6. White, Gleeson, 'Some Glasgow Designers and their work', Part IV, *The Studio*, Vol.13, No.59, Feb 15 1898, p.18

7. In 1902 this was reorganized as Tiffany Studios, with Tiffany Furnaces set up at Corona.

8. He is said to have fabricated the windows for: l'Hotel Tassel (1893, Horta); Maison Frison (1894, Horta); l'Hotel Solvay (1895, Horta); l'Hotel van Eetvelde (1895, Horta); l'Hotel Saintenoy (1896–7, Saintenoy); Maison Devalck (1900, Gaspard Devalck); l'Hotel Hannon (1903, Jules Brunfaut); Rue du Lac 6 (1904, Leon Delune).

9. Saintenoy is best known for the Brussels department store Old England (1898–99).

10. Arwas, Victor, *Berthon and Grasset*, London: Academy Editions, 1978, p.18. From 1879 Gaudin's workshops were in Clermont-Ferrand, manufacturing religious and civil stained-glass windows and mosaics.

11. Moving to Paris in 1916, the master glassmaker transitioned into the Art Deco idiom.

12. Fenyi, Tibor, *The Glass paintings of Miksa Róth from Historicism to Art Nouveau*, Budapest: Miksa Róth Historical House, 2016, p.70.

13. Karoly Lyka quoted Fenyi, p.70.

14. Karoly Lyka quoted Fenyi, p.70.

15. *Hungarian Quarterly*, Vol. XLII, No. 163, Autumn 1900; Konody, Paul G., *The Art of Walter Crane*, London: George Bell & Sons, 1902, pp.125–29.

16. Fenyi, p.74.

17. Konody, p.126.

18. Gerle, p.26.

19. Atterbury, P. and L. Irvine, *The Doulton Story*, Stoke-on-Trent: Royal Doulton Tableware, 1979, p.71.

20. Holme, Charles; Arthur, Paul, *French Art Nouveau Ceramics: An Illustrated Dictionary*, Paris: Norma Editions, 2015, pp.57–58.

21. Ferrocement or ferro-cement was invented by the Frenchmen Joseph Monier and Joseph-Louis Lambot. French engineer and self-educated builder François Hennebique patented his pioneering reinforced-concrete construction system in 1892.

22. Good examples of sgraffito can also be found in Ghent, Namur and Charleroi.

23. Warren, Richard, *Art Nouveau and the Classical Tradition*, London: Bloomsbury, 2017 pp.63–4.

24. The company is now styled Villeroy & Boch.

25. Demey, Thierry, *History of Brussels Schools*, Coll. Brussels, City of Art and History No.39, Ministry of the Brussels-Capital Region, Directorate of Monuments and Sites, 2005, p.48.

26. Gerle, p.12.

27. Gibbs & Canning supplied the terracotta.

28. The site was redeveloped following the construction of the Liberty Bridge, one of the city's Millennium projects.

29. Elias Peris in Onda (Castello) and Cristofòl Guillamont in Alcora (Valencia) were also suppliers.

30. Later managers, James and Raul Gilman, Herbert and Clive Gilbert, all English nationality, maintained strong commercial links with England, importing materials and machinery.

31. A fire destroyed the factory in 1937.

32. In this section I have adhered to the American spelling, terra cotta.

33. Sprague, Paul Edward, *The Drawings of Louis Henry Sullivan: A Catalogue of the Frank Lloyd Wright Collection at the Avery Architectural Library*, Princeton: Princeton University Press, 1979, p.38.

34. William Gates purchased the Spring Valley Tile Works factory that year. In 1887, fire destroyed the drain tile factory. Gates rebuilt his operation, expanding the clay works and starting the production of decorative, glazed terra cotta. It was at this time that the company name was changed to American Terra Cotta and Ceramic Co..

35. Canac, Sybil, *Paris Métro: Histoire et design*, Issy-les-Moulineaux: Massin, 2014, p.39.

36. The production of all the cast iron was entrusted to the Val d'Osne Foundry, except for gutters and drainpipes. These were supplied by Bigot-Renaux.

37. Ovenden, Mark, *Paris Underground: The Maps, Stations, and Design of the Métro*, London and New York: Penguin Random House, 2009, p.25.

38. Rheims, Maurice, *Hector Guimard*, trans. Robert Erich Wolf, New York: Abrams, 1988, p.88.

39. Schmutzler, Robert, *Art Nouveau*, trans. Édouard Roditi, New York: Abrams, 1978, p.214.

40. Little is known about the individual craftsmen who worked in the Majorelle metalshop. Jean Keppel, Desgrey and Mahier are listed as *ferronniers*.

41. Clericuzio, Peter, 'Modernity, Regionalism, and Art Nouveau at the Exposition Internationale de l'Est de la France, 1909', *Nineteenth-Century Art Worldwide*, 10, no.1 (Spring 2011). Accessed 29/09/2019.

42. The Companhia Aliança was founded by Baron Massarelos and Gaspar da Cunha Lima.

43. Jullian, Philippe, *The Triumph of Art Nouveau: Paris Exhibition 1900*, London Phaidon Press, 1974, p.42.

44. Lydwine Saulnier-Pernuit and Sylvie Ballester-Radet (eds.), *René Binet, 1866–1911: An Architect of the Belle Époque*, Sens: Museum of Sens, 2005.

45. Anonymous writer, *Le Petit Journal*, March 20, 1900; https://fr.wikipedia.org › wiki › René_Binet_(architecte) accessed July 2019.

46. Jullian, p.16.

Chapter Five

Iconic Buildings

WHAT MAKES A BUILDING ICONIC? A building that is the first of its kind, breaking new ground in terms of its style, layout or use of 'cutting-edge' materials, would be an obvious choice. However, it could also be an architect's masterpiece, demonstrating the maturity of their style. So many New Art buildings have been lost due to accidents, two World Wars and demolition in the post-war era that a perfectly preserved building is justifiably iconic. With these caveats in mind, the buildings considered here have also been chosen to illustrate the importance of stained glass, ceramics and metalwork, showing how these applied arts contributed to the unique character of Art Nouveau/Jugendstil buildings. These case studies include a private residence, a shop, an apartment block, a tea room, a church, a concert hall and a commemorative tower to judge whether the New Art was really 'For the People'.

Horta's l'Hotel Tassel (1892–93)

In terms of his legacy, Horta has been especially unlucky; L'Innovation department store, on the Rue Neuve in Brussels, was tragically destroyed by fire in 1967 killing 251 people. L'Hotel Aubecq (1899–1902), designed for the industrialist Octave Aubecq, could not be saved, although the main façade was dismantled. Its furniture is now scattered in private and public collections, most notably Musée d'Orsay, Paris and Musée de Fin-de-Siècle, Brussels. However, this prompted a crusade led by architect Jean Delhaye (1908–93) to save Horta's houses; he purchased l'Hotel Tassel and l'Hotel Deprez-Van de Velde, 3

Avenue Palmerston (1895–96), as well as preserving the extension to l'Hotel van Eetvelde, 2 Avenue Palmerston (1899) which had been acquired by his parents.

Ranked the first full expression of the new architectural style, l'Hotel Tassel, a private residence for the scientist Professor Emile Tassel (1862–1922), is defined by his signature whiplash; flowing lines integrate all elements of the architecture. The contemporary Maison Autrique (1893), by comparison 'without luxury or extravagance', only hints at what is to come. The arabesque sgraffito panels decorating the loggia and the floor mosaics are the only overt Art Nouveau elements. Horta designed everything for the Tassel, door handles, stained glass and light fittings, at that time an unheard-of freedom of expression. Horta commented, 'The crazy idea of creating a completely new architecture did not exist at the time... developing a personal language and not a conventional stylistic vocabulary'[1].

L'Hotel Tassel broke with past styles and architectural conventions, forging a new alliance of iron and glass. The entrance, located centrally rather than to one side, was given the place of honour; the Egyptian-style door surround suggests one is entering a temple. Immediately above a bow-shaped central window rises to a recessed loggia; the use of iron beams, with clearly exposed rivets, made large window openings feasible. On the bow window, the base and capital of the stone columns grab the sill and iron lintel above like foliate claws. Although expensive, composed of fine ashlar rather than brick, the decoration is restrained; ostentatious displays of wealth were no longer the order of the day. Following the 1885 elections and ensuing workers' riots, the Belgian bourgeoise became more

Horta, exterior l'Hotel Tassel, 6, Rue Paul-Emile Janson, Brussels (1892–93).

cautious. As one entertained at home, it was wiser to lavish one's wealth out of sight.

The interior spatial arrangement was novel, experimenting with open plan and split levels. The standard pattern was a semi-underground basement for services (kitchen, cellar) with an elevated ground floor composed of three adjoining rooms, *enfilade* or back to back, and two floors of bedrooms above. These arrangements were driven by commercial demands, as the house had to be saleable. Horta dispensed with such conventions, rising to the challenge of adapting the construction to the specific demands of his client, requirements that might not suit subsequent buyers: 'I proclaimed that the house should not only be built in the image of the occupant, but it should also be his portrait'. This was not a family home, but a 'bachelor pad'. Tassel, who lived with his grandmother, liked to entertain; he belonged to an elite circle of

intellectuals, scholars and artists, the Loge des Amis Philanthropes (Philanthropic Friends Lodge), which had accepted Horta as a member in 1887[2]. Dominated by its reception areas, l'Hotel Tassel is a mansion, whereas the Maison Autrique is still a family house.

Horta borrowed ideas from the theatre; the open plan, mobile partitions, use of reflecting mirrors to multiply the sense of space and top-lit glass roofs over the staircase and the winter garden. The narrow entrance is flanked by a cloakroom and parlour; Tassel received his university students here, not wishing to admit them into his private sanctum. Mackintosh would copy this arrangement for Hill House, Helensburgh (1902), with Walter Blackie's study and office positioned to the right of the entrance before a flight of steps leads you up into the hall. Public and private are carefully demarcated. In l'Hotel Tassel the entrance opens out into an octagonal vestibule; the mosaic floor takes the form of an octopus spiralling around the heating vent. A short flight of steps rises to the winter garden (left) and staircase (right) that extends to the mezzanine and upper floors. This central circulation area, lit by a skylight, is the most dramatic part of the house.

The floor, ceiling and walls of the winter garden and staircase are integrated through decorative arabesques. The whiplash whorls across the mosaic floor,

Horta, staircase, l'Hotel Tassel (1892–93).

Horta, double mirrors and skylight, Horta house-studio, Rue Americaine, Brussels (1898–1901).

loops up the wall, into the metalwork of the staircase and above our heads in the stencils on the ceiling. The cast-iron columns branch out like trees. Crane's 'That reddening on the Triton's spear', from *Flora's Feast* (1889) has been cited as a potential source for Horta's arabesques. He commissioned Henri Baes to execute a mural intended to suggest liana, a long-stemmed woody vine that springs from the ground and climbs up trees to gain access to light. They can also form canopies. Liana can be found in moist tropical forests, especially the Congo rainforest. During the 1890s, much of Belgium's wealth came from exploiting the Congo, which had been personally colonized by Leopold, King of the Belgians. While Horta may have been referencing Belgium's imperial domains, the decoration was also linked to the function of the space, suggesting the dense vegetation of a tropical hothouse[3]. Potted plants were integrated through the murals and metalwork into a harmonious whole. With its reflecting mirror, the winter garden is a magical space, far from the world outside. Horta used the same trick in his own house at the top stairs, although here the illusion of infinity is multiplied as two mirrors face each other.

The smoking room installed on the mezzanine was an intimate space. A divan was placed in the recess of the bow, its leaded glass window in an abstract-linear Japanese style. The curling motifs unfurl like wisps of cigar smoke[4]. This was Tassel's private spot, where he entertained his closest friends. He installed a projector; the lantern cast images from the mezzanine onto a large screen placed in the salon. The gaze plunges into the salon and beyond as the space flows into the dining room, a curtain dividing the two functional areas. A staircase provided access to the kitchen below. Some of the furniture was designed by Horta. He also accompanied Tassel to Paris, purchasing pieces from Bing's L'Art Nouveau, which had just opened. Contemporary critics were downright rude; 'I told you that it was a house… isn't it ridiculous, if he thinks he's accomplished something, he's much mistaken… who's the crackpot who's going to live in it?'[5]

Bing's L'Art Nouveau (1895; destroyed)

La Maison l'Art Nouveau on Rue de Provence opened in December 1895. Bing, who began his career as a purveyor of oriental goods, may have been inspired by Liberty's and Morris & Co., whose showrooms opened on Oxford Street in 1877. However, it was Belgium who deserved the 'honour of having first devised truly modern formulas for the interior decoration of European dwellings'[6]. Bing acknowledged the role of Octave Maus and La Libre Esthétique in promoting modern art; 'this was the first occasion when the aristocratic arts of painting and sculpture admitted without blushing to their companionship the commonality of industrial productions'. He admired Serrurier-Bovy, who succeeded in conjoining 'beauty, hygiene and comfort'. But the designer who really stood out was van de Velde, who created the 'first important examples (ensembles) of modern decorative art' based on the 'line in its full and single power'[7]. Naturally Bing turned to van de Velde for the interiors of his new gallery L'Art Nouveau, an exemplary 'total artwork':

at heart a collector, with a passion for beautiful things, Bing sought 'unity with complexity'[8].

L'Art Nouveau was not a new build; renovations to an existing building were carried out by Louis Bonnier (1856–1946), who added a glass cupola, while the impression of newness was achieved by resurfacing the principal façade. Bing favoured a pictorial treatment; having commissioned Frank Brangwyn (1867–1956), an artistic 'jack-of-all-trades', he approached Horta, whom he invited to Paris to see the project at first hand. A preliminary scheme was suggested but never carried through. Reverting to Brangwyn's proposal, a painted frieze divided the floors, the upper section accented with horizontal bands. A second frieze sat under the eaves. The lower section was decorated with random square-shaped stencils of highly stylized flowers and abstract forms. The most striking feature was the entrance, flanked by giant plaster sunflowers, clearly a homage to English Aestheticism.

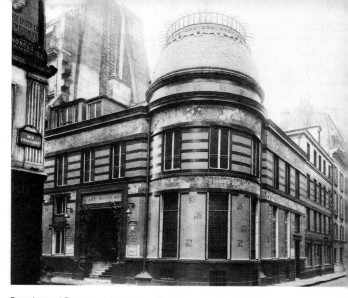

Bonnier and Brangwyn, La Maison l'Art Nouveau, Rue de Provence, Paris, opened 1895.

Lautrec and Tiffany, *Au Nouveau Cirque, Papa Chrysanthème* (At the New Circus, Papa Chrysanthemum) (Musée d'Orsay).

In 1894 Bing was sent on a mission by the Director of the Beaux Arts, tasked with investigating the American arts scene. His report, *The Artistic Culture in America*, followed (1895–96). He succeeded in obtaining exclusive rights to Tiffany's glass in Europe and Britain. Bing commissioned a series of windows clearly intended for promotional purposes; they were shown at the Salon du Champ de Mars, Paris in 1894. They were then installed in L'Art Nouveau. For this project, he opted for the most progressive artists of the day, commissioning Henri de Toulouse-Lautrec, Paul-Albert Besnard and the Nabis artists: Ker-Xavier Roussel's *Le Jardin*, Pierre Bonnard's *Maternity*, Jean-Édouard Vuillard's *Les Marroniers* (Chestnut Trees) and Félix Edouard Vallotton's *Les Parisiennes* were executed in a bold, linear style reminiscent of posters. Toulouse-Lautrec's (1864–1901) *Au Nouveau Cirque, Papa Chrysanthème* (At the New Circus, Papa Chrysanthemum) (Musée d'Orsay) has survived. The subject was taken from a Japanese-inspired ballet performed at the Nouveau Cirque, Rue Saint-Honoré, in 1892. Lautrec's stained-glass panel was prominently displayed in l'Art Nouveau, above the entrance leading to the section where Japanese goods were displayed. The panel received high praise from Jacques-Émile Blanche in *La Revue blanche*: 'The most astonishing of these pieces is probably

de Feure, boudoir, L'Art Nouveau, Paris. *Deutsch Kunst und Dekoration*, Vol. XII, April–Oct 1903, p.333.

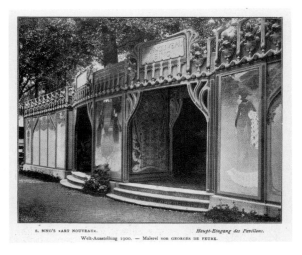

Bing's Pavilion L'Art Nouveau, Paris 1900, *Deutsche Kunst und Dekoration*, Vol. VI, April–Sept 1900, p.550.

that by M. de Lautrec who has managed to make the most beautiful and most modern decorative motif from a circus scene and a courtesan's hat'[9]. Unfortunately, the project was not a commercial success, as it seems Bing received no commissions. Nevertheless, they had a profound influence on the development of Art Nouveau stained glass. Tiffany was awarded the *Legion d'Honneur*, the highest accolade, at Paris 1900, for his Favrile glass; across Europe, Tiffany's glass would be known as American glass.

The room settings were overseen by van de Velde; the dining room was decorated with panels by the painter Paul Ranson, while Georges Lemmen collaborated on the smoking room. The Glasgow Four contributed posters, probably Mackintosh's *The Glasgow Institute of Fine Art* (1894–95) and the Macdonald sisters and McNair's poster of the same name, both exemplars of the 'Spook School'. They form a manifesto for The Four's radical graphic style: 'the elongated treatment of the human figure, the framing

devices of stylized plant forms, symbolic motifs and, most importantly, the proportional division of the picture plane for the arrangement of the design'[10].

Establishing his own workshops, Bing sought an alliance of art and industry. The lesson he learnt in America, a reflection of republican democracy, was 'that the machine can propagate beautiful designs intelligently thought out and logically conditioned to facilitate multiplication. It will become an important factor in raising the level of public taste'[11]. Bing advanced the careers of several designers; Eugène Gaillard (1862–1933), Georges de Feure (1868–1943) and Edward Colonna (1862–1948). All three collaborated on Bing's Pavilion L'Art Nouveau for Paris 1900.

Bing faced competition from La Maison Moderne (1899–1903) established by art critic and art historian Julius Meier-Graefe (1867–1935). Born in Hungary, Meier-Graefe studied in Munich before heading for Berlin where he was one of the founders of the avant-garde arts and literary magazine *Pan* (1895). Leaving after barely a year he launched *Dekorative Kunst* (1897–1929), which was published by Alexander Koch. Relocating to Paris, he opened La Maison Moderne on the Rue des Petits-Champs. Like Bing, Meier-Graefe favoured 'scenography', devising integrated room settings; consumers were offered 'populuxe' objects that harmonized with one another, creating an ideal

van de Velde, 'Vitrine in the Maison Moderne, Paris', *Deutsche Kunst und Dekoration*, Vol. VII, Oct 1900–March 1901, p.103.

and La Maison Moderne were the leading taste-makers promoting the applied arts on an international stage. Their carefully designed and crafted environments demonstrated that theory and practice could work cohesively. They also granted architecture and interior décor the same status. When Bing retired in 1904, his premises were acquired by Majorelle, giving l'Ecole de Nancy a Parisian showcase.

Guimard's Castel Béranger (1895–98)

Guimard's Castel Béranger lives up to its name; it really does resemble a magical castle[12]. Considered the first Art Nouveau building in Paris, it secured Guimard's reputation, wining the city's prize for the best façade in 1899. Although composed of thirty-six individual apartments, Guimard conceived these interiors as gesamtkunstwerk, the prospectus providing a catalogue of fixtures and fittings that extends to the fireplaces and furniture as well as the treatment of the walls. Due to the high cost of unique pieces, the concept of the 'total artwork' was normally restricted to single-owner houses, like Guimard's l'Hotel Mezzara (1910–11), also on the Rue Jean de la Fontaine. However, by forging an alliance with established manufacturers, Guimard was able to build up a repertoire encompassing all aspects of interior décor: door handles, key escutcheons, window catches, balustrades and balconies that could be used on projects large or small. His cast iron was produced by three foundries: Durenne, Le Val d'Osne and Bigot-Renaux.

Collaborating with the Leclerc foundry at Saint-Dizier, Guimard made his designs available to the general public through catalogues. A whole series of architectural, garden and even burial cast-iron products could be purchased. Hence, his balconies even pop up in Nancy. Serial production brought down costs, as did using cheaper materials. His leaded glass, composed of simple arabesques rather than complex pictorial designs, was executed using inexpensive industrial glass in a limited range of colours. All his designs are linked through

vision of unity. They were shown in beautiful cabinets and vitrines, which enhanced their aesthetic qualities. Delicate Danish porcelains produced by Bing and Grondahl glowed in soft lighting, while Max Laeuger's robust pots were used for floral arrangements. Van de Velde was called on to provide the architectural framework; line provided both structure and ornament, the latter achieved through freely moving abstract linear patterns. A similar environment was cultivated in a Budapest branch.

Yet despite a broad promotional campaign, including eye-catching posters by Manuel Orazi and Maurice Biais and adverts in *L'Art Décoratif*, Meier-Graefe failed to win enough clients; many purchases were made by directors of applied arts museums in Germany, Austria and Scandinavia. He was forced to close in 1903, although the gallery in Budapest continued to operate until c.1910. Most importantly L'Art Nouveau

line, from the plasterwork friezes and Lincrusta Walton panels to the mosaic floors and stair carpets[13]. While Guimard's gesamtkunstwerk was more affordable, it took a leap of the imagination, as his prospectus for the Castel Béranger shows, to surround oneself with his whiplash motifs on every conceivable surface. En masse they do have a hallucinatory effect[14].

Born in Lyon, Guimard appears to have run away from home in order to pursue his dream of becoming an artist. Attending the École des Arts Décoratifs in Paris, he was taught by Charles Genuys, the chief architect for the Commission of Historic Monuments, and Eugène Train, the municipal architect for the city of Paris. Genuys, a disciple of Viollet-le-Duc, introduced Guimard to the theory that Gothic forms could be adapted for modern use. Iron rather than stone could be used for arches and vaults. But following Viollet-le-Duc, all materials had to be employed according to their qualities and properties. As 'honesty' was paramount, metal beams had to be exposed. The revealed iron beam of Guimard's first experimental building, the École du Sacré Coeur, 16th arrondissement (1895), is supported by cast-iron, 'V' shaped supports.

Graduating to the École des Beaux-Arts, he befriended Henri Sauvage, another Art Nouveau pioneer best known for the Villa Majorelle, Nancy. In 1894 he was granted a travel scholarship enabling him to visit London; he might have seen Queen Anne buildings by Norman Shaw or popped into Liberty's or Morris & Co.'s showrooms. His conversion to Art Nouveau was inevitable following his meeting with Horta in 1895. Horta stressed the importance of

Guimard, central courtyard, Castel Béranger, 14 Rue Jean de la Fontaine, 16th arrondissement, Paris (1895–98).

Guimard, 'Hippocampi' (seahorses), Castel Béranger (1895–98).

Guimard, entrance portal and gate, Castel Béranger (1895–98).

Guimard, staircase, Castel Béranger (1895–98).

unity; the structure and decoration (furniture, wallpaper, carpets) should all be in harmony. Seeing the newly completed l'Hotel Tassel at first hand would have sealed his conversion.

Guimard had been contracted to build an apartment block in traditional style for Madame Anne-Elisabeth Fournier, a wealthy widow, before his trip to Brussels. Upon his return he convinced his client to embrace the new style. He benefitted from changes to the long-established building codes. The rules instituted in 1884 permitted larger projecting features on the façade, such as bow windows and corner domes. Architects were able to break from the monotonous Haussmann style. Castel Béranger is built around a courtyard; every façade is varied, with different sized and shaped windows. Alongside dressed stone, Guimard used a myriad of contrasting materials: *pierre*

de taille (cut stone); red, grey and glazed bricks; millstone-grit; cast iron; copper; wood and polychrome stained glass. The prospectus provides all the names of the craftsmen and manufacturers involved in the project. All the cast-iron creations were produced by Durenne à Sommevoire, Haut-Marne, except for the roof gutters and drainpipes. The windows were supplied by Georges Néret, the terracotta and glazed bricks by La Tuilerie de Choisy-le-Roi, run by Gilardoni Fils et Cie, and the stoneware by Bigot.

Picturesque variety, seen in both architectural forms and range of materials used, recalls the Gothic; the overhanging turrets on the corners, oriel windows and the plethora of gargoyles. The fantastic cast-iron balconies feature bizarre masks that resemble a cat with massive whiskers. The ironwork braces are formed into hippocampi (seahorses), although they look more like dragons. Guimard's use of cast iron aroused astonishment, as it was still associated with railway stations and factories. Fish appear to leer at you from ceramic panels under windows or over doorways. While much of the patterning is purely abstract, masses of swirling asymmetric lines, the eye tries to pick out forms. Inevitably, Castel Béranger was nicknamed 'Castel dérangé' (Crazy Castle) or House of the Devils by Guimard's detractors. Legend has it that the old ladies of the neighbourhood crossed themselves when they had to walk by.

The entrance gate exemplifies Guimard's whiplash. His organic forms are more abstract than Horta.

Guimard, water-tap-cum-fountain, courtyard, Castel Béranger (1895–98).

He took the latter's advice grasping the stem, but he goes further reducing his arabesques into pure line. It is said he created his door handles by squeezing clay through his fingers. The gate, flanked by two squat columns, leads to a cavernous entrance, the ceiling lined with glowing beaten copper. The walls are covered with glazed stoneware tiles, attributed to Bigot, which resemble molten lava. The whole surface is covered with a lacey tangle of whiplash metalwork, which extends over the walls and ceiling. Opening out into a lighter foyer, the staircase sweeps upwards, its curvilinear banister echoed in the mosaic floor and stair carpet. The inclusion of a lift was another innovation. A stained-glass door leads to the courtyard, where one finds the most extraordinary water tap-cum-fountain. The flow of water appears to be fossilized in molten metal; Art Nouveau is often

categorized as deliquescent, with solids melting or dissolving into liquids.

Guimard did not forget his debt; when the building was completed, he sent Horta the lavishly illustrated prospectus, which included all aspects of the construction, with the inscription, 'to an eminent master and friend, Victor Horta, affectionate homage from an admirer'. Clearly proud of his achievement, Guimard moved into one of the apartments. The interiors were used to publicize his practice; a postcard shows him working in his studio. The post-Impressionist painter Paul Signac (1863–1935) and the architect and decorator Eugène Pierre Selmersheim (1869–1941) became his neighbours, perhaps indicating that you had to be 'arty' to appreciate the quirkiness of the Castel Béranger.

Guimard did not develop a school of pupils or followers. Although he initially supported himself by teaching at the École des Arts Décoratifs, he gave up this post in 1900 when his career took off. He remained a loner by choice, relying on a relatively small circle of artistically adventurous clients who gave him the opportunity to cultivate his art. For the Nozal family, Guimard not only built a town house, 52 Rue de Ranelagh, 16th arrondissement (1902–06) but also a country house, La Surprise (1903–07) Cabourg, Normandy and a warehouse for the Nozal Company (1902).

In 1909, Guimard married the American-Jewish painter Adeline Oppenheim; his wedding present was a new house on the Avenue Mozart, 16th arrondissement. In 1938 the Guimards wisely moved to New York, where Guimard is buried[15].

Mackintosh's Willow Tea Rooms (1902–03)

Of the tea rooms Mackintosh had a hand in designing for Miss Cranston, the Willow Tea Rooms is the only one to survive almost intact. Catherine Cranston (1849–1934) began to build her empire in 1878, opening her first tea room, the Crown Luncheon

Room, on Argyle Street, Glasgow. From the outset she set high standards not only in terms of the quality of the food and service but also as regards the décor of her establishments. She realized she could attract a better class of clientele by offering surroundings in the latest fashion. There was plenty of competition in Glasgow; tea and luncheon rooms abounded, partly due to the temperance movement. Moreover, women who were out and about shopping or even part of the work force could enter a tea room unaccompanied. By the time of the 1901 Glasgow Exhibition, Britain's Second City of Empire had become 'a very Tokio for tea rooms'[16]. In fact, these tea rooms did a great deal more than just serve tea or coffee, cocoa and chocolate. They expanded into luncheon rooms and offered facilities for both ladies and gentlemen to relax in. Men were catered for with smoking rooms, which also provided recreational activities such as billiards. The simple refreshment rooms, first seen at the international exhibitions, were transformed into palaces for leisure and entertainment. Increasingly sophisticated customers demanded more than *café au lait* and French pastries; they were prepared to pay a premium for artistic refinement. Nevertheless, Miss Cranston made some daring choices when she engaged the services of George Walton and Charles Rennie Mackintosh.

With her marriage to John Cochrane in 1892, Miss Cranston's ambitions expanded: as a married woman, being in business broke social norms so she kept her maiden name. In 1897 she opened her second establishment on Buchanan Street; Edinburgh architect George Washington Browne remodelled the exterior, while Walton was tasked with decorating and furnishing the interior. Mackintosh received his first tea room commission. The Four, Mackintosh, McNair and the Macdonald girls, had already achieved notoriety. In 1894 their contribution to the Glasgow School of Art 'Art Club' exhibition provoked public outrage; posters shown the following year stoked the fires of disapproval[17]. Their figures likened to ghouls and gas pipes earnt them the derisory epithet 'Spook School'. More 'howls of rejection' followed when The Four exhibited posters, metalwork and furniture at the Arts and Crafts Exhibition in London (1896). Amidst all this negativity, Miss Cranston, perhaps wishing to capitalize on a cause célèbre, handed Mackintosh a commission that would turn 'the tide of public opinion'[18].

Asked to design stencilled murals for three spaces, the most striking scheme was created for the ladies' luncheon room. Based on an earlier watercolour *Part Seen, Part Imagined* (1896), the frieze is dominated by stately women, a likeness of Margaret Macdonald dressed in a white kimono and entwined in a rose tree, interspersed with abstract trees. The plethora of roses appears to have been intended as a pun on the tea rose, named for its fragrance which is reminiscent of Chinese black tea. Writing in *The Studio*, the editor Gleeson White was impressed by this 'honest attempt at novelty', which he likened to poster designs; 'a very important enterprise', the simplicity of the technique belied the sophistication of the result[19]. White added, 'As a rule, money is lavished on the walls of popular restaurants, but thought is scantily expended'. Mackintosh would soon be admitted into the ranks of 'the advanced but tolerated': 'when a man has something to say and knows how to say it, the conversion of others is usually but a question of time'[20].

Walton and Mackintosh's efforts won immediate approval. *The Bailie* considered the decorations to be 'in excellent taste and showing to much effect'; Miss Cranston's new tea rooms were 'unique… handsome, artistic, replete with every novelty'[21]. They were one of the sights of the city nobody could afford to miss. Upon seeing the Buchanan Street Tea Rooms, the young Edwin Lutyens concluded the Glasgow school was ahead of its competitors south of the border:

[Miss Cranston] has started a large Restaurant, all very elaborately simple on very new school High Art Lines. The result is gorgeous! And a wee bit vulgar! She has nothing but green handled knives and all is curiously painted and coloured… It is all quite good, all a little outre[22].

Returning the following year to those 'queer funny

rooms' for a hearty breakfast, he again waxed lyrically: 'Greens, golds, blues, white rooms with black furniture, black rooms with white furniture, where Whistler is worshipped and Degas tolerated, Rodin… admired for the love of oddity, sometimes called originality'. Miss Cranston had made 'a fortune by supplying cheap clean foods in surroundings prompted by the New Art Glasgow School'[23].

At the same time, the premises at 106–114 Argyll Street were expanded; the Glasgow architectural practice H. & D. Barclay redesigned the exterior, while the interiors were given to Walton and Mackintosh, with Walton in charge of the general décor, including stencilled wall panelling, wooden screens, billiard tables and grates. Walton's decorative motifs, notably the pretty stencilling, contributed to the femininity of the spaces; his charming *Eros* panel, made from green marble, slate, coloured glass and mother-of-pearl, graced the end of the lunchroom[24]. Mackintosh contributed his famous 'Argyll' high-backed chair with bird-like cut-out in the oval back (1896), small tables, umbrella stands and electric lighting for the billiard tables.

Miss Cranston's third establishment, the Ingram Street Tea Rooms, was continuously redesigned from 1900 to 1912, with Mackintosh the sole designer working alongside his wife. The layout, colour scheme and furniture varied according to each room's unique theme. The White Room, the ladies' luncheon room, was decorated with two gesso panels, *The Wassail*, by Mackintosh, and *The May Queen*, by Margaret Macdonald, intended to represent winter and summer. The panels achieved an international reputation, being shown at the 8th Secession Exhibition in Vienna (1900). Mackintosh and Macdonald attended the exhibition in person, staying in the city for some five weeks. It was a life-changing experience, as the two Scottish designers were able to meet the leading players of the Viennese Secession, notably Hoffmann and Moser. The resulting interchange of ideas was a defining moment in the evolution of Mackintosh's design ethos. Likewise, the Glasgow style appears to have sent Hoffmann in a new direction. Turning away from the curvilinear forms he

created for Paris 1900, he developed a restrained linear approach reliant on squares and grids. Mackintosh similarly opted for the square and the lattice as his signature motifs; squares feature in the tall-backed chair he developed for Ingram Street. The square often forms a retaining frame for his abstract organic shapes. Black-and-white squares still dominate his last major project, 78, Derngate, Northampton (1916–19), the only house he designed in England.

Mackintosh's 'white rooms with black furniture, black rooms with white furniture' reach their maturity in the Willow Tea Rooms on Sauchiehall Street, considered the summation of Mackintosh's partnership with Miss Cranston. Here, at last, he controlled every aspect, the structure as well as the interior décor. Nevertheless, Macdonald was closely involved; their ideas had fused, as seen in various collaborative projects such as the competition entry A House for an Art Lover (1901) and the Rose Boudoir for Turin 1902. Until recently Margaret's contribution has either been negated or castigated. Some critics have gone as far as accusing her 'over-prettiness' of despoiling Mackintosh's modernist simplicity. Her 'lower' position embodies the 'invidious old oppositions between "masculine" architecture (pure, reasoned, essential) and "feminine" decorative art (distracting, trivial, superficial)'[25]. However, these feminine qualities ensured the success of Mackintosh's Willow Tea Rooms, designed as they were for a largely female clientele: *The Bailie* was enthusiastic:

Her new establishment fairly outshines all others in the matters of arrangement and colour. The furnishings, besides, are of the richest and most luxurious character. Indeed, Miss Cranston has carried the question of comfort fairly into that of luxury, when providing for the enjoyment of her friends and patrons. Her 'Salon de Luxe' on the first floor is simply a marvel of the art of the upholsterer and decorator. And not less admirable, each in its own way, are the tea-gallery, the lunch-rooms, the billiard-room and the smoking room.[26]

Mackintosh, front tea room, Willow Tea Rooms, Sauchiehall Street, Glasgow (1902–03), *Dekorative Kunst*, Vol.8, 1905, p.261.

Mackintosh, gallery, Willow Tea Rooms (1902–03).

The demur exterior belies the richness of the interiors. The wide window of the Room de Luxe stretches across the façade above the lattice-paned shop front. The chequered edging and elegant looping ironwork reprise the combination of austere square with abstract organic forms. The motif of the willow lay at hand, as Sauchiehall Street means 'ally of willows'. Upon entering, the customer passed a white-painted screen inset with leaded glass panels leading to the central cash desk. This offered a point of departure: on the ground floor, into the tea room at the front or lunchroom at the back, up the stairs to the tea gallery, built around a well overlooking the lunchroom, or to the Room de Luxe facing the street. Further up on the second floor was the male domain, the billiard and

smoking rooms. Essentially open-plan, the division on the ground floor, between the tea and luncheon areas, was demarcated by an eye-catching flower bowl suspended over two tables and the order desk with its iconic chair (1905), the semi-circular back pierced with a lattice resembling a tree.

The front tea room was white with dark-stained chairs. The principal decorative feature, on the side walls, was a rather strange relief plaster frieze which has been interpreted as willow trees. They are completely abstracted, as were the pink and green patterns on Macdonald's gauzy curtains. The ladderback chair was reinvented, with curved rungs from top to bottom; unfortunately, this novel approach resulted in a loss of strength. In the dining area and gallery,

Mackintosh, glass and mirror frieze, Room de Luxe, Willow Tea Rooms (1902–03).

vertical cut-out. A gesso panel encrusted with glass jewels and beads by Macdonald, inspired by Dante Gabriel Rossetti's sonnet 'O ye, all ye that walk in Willow-wood', added a mystical, fairy-tale quality to the room. The final touch was a chandelier of dangling pink glass baubles. This 'luxe' cost the customer an extra penny on a cup of tea. While many came to scoff, few failed to admire the audacity. While Mackintosh was called again, to transform the basement at Argyle Street into the Dutch Kitchen (1906) and to install the Oak Room at Ingram Street (1907), the Willow Tea Rooms was unequivocally his masterpiece.

Wagner's Kirche am Steinhof (1903–07)

St Leopold am Steinhof ranks as Wagner's masterpiece. Being an exemplary gesamtkunstwerk, it also demonstrates the collaborative nature of the

a boxy armchair with low inward sloping back was used. While the tea room was light, the back was darker, in keeping with a domestic dining room; grey canvas wall panels were relieved with stencilled ladies peeping from behind large roses. Light filtered down from the tea gallery, which was panelled in pink and grey, this time stencilled with large roses and a ladder trellis motif, which echoed the backs of the chairs.

By comparison, the Room de Luxe was sumptuous. The frieze of leaded panels of mirror, purple and white glass runs around three sides. The abstract pattern is continued on the magnificent double doors. The walls were originally lined with pale purple silk stitched with beads. High-backed silver chairs, upholstered in purple velvet, are inset with squares of pink-purple glass forming a lattice. Even the splat-shaped legs of the tables were decorated, with an oval set into a

Wagner, St Leopold am Steinhof, with statue of Leopold Steiner in foreground (1903–07).

Secession. Yet upon its completion, this full expression of the mature Viennese Secession style was defamed as 'a crazy church for crazy people'. St Leopold's was the centrepiece of the Niederösterreichische Landes-Heil-und Pflegeanstalt für Nerven-und Geisteskranke 'Am Steinhof' (Lower Austrian State Healing and Care Institution for the Neurologically and Mentally Sick, 'Am Steinhof'). The project was spearheaded by Leopold Steiner (1857–1927), a self-made man and gifted Christian Democrat politician; Am Steinhof became his life's work.

This was not Wagner's first ecclesiastical commission, having conceived the Orthodox Synagogue in Budapest (1868) and St Johannes Nepomuk Chapel, Vienna (1895). The latter, based on a Greek cross ground plan, all four sides of equal length, provided the model for St Leopold's some ten years later. Wagner's competition project for the Greek Orthodox St Andrew's Cathedral, Patras (1902), a commission he failed to secure, also shows many features of St Leopold's in embryo[27]. The Greek cross plan, the white marble clad walls, the gilded dome, the two frontal towers, the large semi-circular windows and the projecting awning. Many of these features are neo-Classical; Wagner's early buildings are indebted to Historicism. However, he developed a clear rationale and a disciplined language of form maintaining, 'The architect may... reach for the full treasure chest of tradition, not in order to copy what is selected, but rather to make it conform to his aims through remodelling'[28]. Having set out his rationale in a treatise, *Die Moderne in Kirchenbau* (The Modern in Church Construction) (1899), St Leopold's allowed Wagner to remodel traditional architectural forms, achieving 'modernism in sacral architecture'[29].

Above all Wagner strove to combine beauty with practicality. As he said himself, 'Something impractical cannot be beautiful'; 'Necessity' became a driving force, Wagner 'achieving increasingly "modern" expressive forms'[30]. His 'functional ornament' has a structural purpose, with the bolts securing the 2cm thick marble panels transformed into a distinctive pattern; he asserted 'having fulfilled their task to impede... any

Wagner, interior, St Leopold am Steinhof (1903–07).

Wagner, pulpit, St Leopold am Steinhof (1903–07).

shifting of the slabs, the heads of the white shining pretty nails remain a modern looking and novel ornament, born out of necessity'[31]. The grids of 4x4 squares adorning Am Steinhof's towers also have a symbolic meaning; squares represent the earthly while circles indicate the divine. Perhaps Wagner had read Lethaby's *Architecture, Mysticism and Myth*.

Being a church for a hospital, necessity certainly drove the conception of St Leopold's; Wagner consulted with doctors and nurses concerning their specific requirements. As hygiene was paramount, easily cleaned mosaics ousted painted surfaces. Continuously flowing water replaced holy water stoups at the entrance. Rather than fixed stalls, the pews, their bases protected by copper sheeting, can be easily moved for cleaning. The raked floor, which declines 30cm towards the high altar, allows attendees a good view. Safety was also paramount, with few sharp edges. Clerics were protected, the pulpit raised up on columns and entered via steps in the vestry. A marble communion rail prevented patients from disturbing the priest during mass. Emergency exits, in the side walls, enabled the speedy removal of any disruptive patients. There was even a first-aid room.

Wagner presented his model for the church at the 23rd Viennese Secession Exhibition in 1903. Building began in June 1905 and remarkably only two years later the church opened its doors in October 1907. His team included fellow architect Otto Schönthal (1878–1961), the sculptor Othmar Schimkowitz and the designer Kolo Moser.

Located at the highest point within the hospital complex, looking south on the plateau of a hill, Wagner transformed the church into a sacred gloriette. This dominant position created a hierarchy, with the pavilions for the sick and insane placed below. The axis formed separated the sexes, with women accommodated in the western section and men in the eastern. In the language of the day, 'the separation of the sexes was necessary to prevent its increase'. Although Wagner's overall plan was accepted, he was only entrusted with the construction of the church.

The skyline is dominated by the cupola covered with copper gilded sheets; it was re-gilded in 2000. This inevitably led to several rather derisory nicknames, '*Limoniberg*', as it recalled half a lemon, and '*Gugelhupf*', referring to the 'fools tower', a preceding insane asylum. On top of the bell towers are sculptures by Richard Luksch (1872–1936) of St Severin (right), a fourth-century missionary and St Leopold (left), patron saint of Lower Austria, who holds a model of the church. Unusually they are both seated. The entrance canopy, supported by elegant iron columns, shields three equally wide doorways, women entering through one and men the other. The central door was intended for special occasions. Above the canopy standing on four massive columns are Schimkowitz's gilded copper angels. Monsignore Henry Swoboda, who was entrusted with overseeing the project, complained, 'I thoroughly disapprove of the completely incomprehensible and unnatural shape of the wings. Neither from far nor near will anybody take them for angels' wings'[32]. Below the cornice, a rhythmic band of alternating gilded crosses and *Loorbeerkränzen* (laurel wreaths) completes the decoration.

The semi-circular glass mosaic window, concealed on the inside by the organ, depicts the Fall of Man. This and the great semi-circular side windows were designed by Moser; Wagner had every confidence, declaring 'I hope you'll soon enchant me with masterpieces'[33]. Totally in sympathy with Wagner's concept, rather than mystic darkness, the faithful are greeted with light. Moser's glass mosaics are 'paintings in light', the figures simply formed with shaped glass. Light colours were selected, white and yellow interspersed with blue, green and violet hues. The unusual east-west axis of the windows admits light throughout the day. It is worthwhile seeing the western window at dusk. This is dedicated to the physical world and the seven works of earthly charity: 'Verily I say unto you. Inasmuch as ye have done it unto one of these my brethren ye have done it unto me'. Facing towards the altar, their roles identified by inscriptions are:

St Elizabeth of Hungary: feed the hungry
Rebecca: the thirsty drink

St Bernard: the strangers house

St Martin: the naked clothe

John, the founder of the Order of the Brothers of Charity: visit the sick

John of Matha, founder of the Order of the Trinity: released prisoners

Tobias, with a shovel: bury the dead.

Panels of angels to either side, which recall Burne-Jones's angels, look down to earth. Above two peacock-winged angels bow their heads towards the *sudarium* of St Veronica, which bears the image of Christ's face.

The east window represents the intellectual virtues and the seven works of spiritual charity: 'Blessed are the merciful for they shall obtain mercy'. Facing towards the altar are:

John the Baptist: rebuke the sinner

Francis de Sales: instruct the ignorant

Moser, mosaic window, dedicated to the spiritual world, St Leopold am Steinhof (1903–07).

Clement Mary Hofbauer: advise the doubters right

St. Therese: the afflicted comfort

Joseph of Egypt: suffering injustice with patience

Stephan: those who have offended us a pardon

Abraham: pray for the living, for the dead are with God.

Here, the angels in the two flanking panels look up to heaven. Above two peacock-winged angels, also looking up, frame the Dove of the Holy Spirit. In the dome, lined with Rabitz panes (stucco on metallic lath), the four narrow windows represent the evangelists (Lion, Eagle, Angel and Bull).

The two windows flanking the high altar share a novel iconography; a distinctly Mackintosh-style rose tree intertwined with a passionflower grows from the font of life. Blue birds hover within the roses, while two squirrels descend the vine. Two birds drink from the font. Rabbits nestle in the foliage surrounding the basin, while two lizards appear at the base. This inventive Garden of Eden also annoyed Swoboda, who dismissed Moser from the project, despite protestations from Wagner, when he converted to Protestantism. His conversion had been to facilitate his marriage to Editha Mautner-Markhof.

Moser had been commissioned to design the mosaics above the high altar and the side altars. The latter were entrusted to Rudolf Jettmar (1869–1939): the left, the Annunciation and on the right, the

Schimkowitz, high altar, St Leopold am Steinhof (1903–07).

Guardian Angel. *Paradise Regained* above the high altar was eventually designed by Remigius Geyling (1878–1974) and executed by the Wiener Mosaikwerkstätte under the guidance of Leopold Forstner (1878–1936). It took eighteen months to complete, being consecrated in 1913. In the middle the blessing Saviour, framed by the Virgin Mary and St Joseph, is welcoming into heaven the intercessors and helpers of the sick. A kneeling St Leopold holds Am Steinhof in his hands. St Dympna, the patron saint of those afflicted with epilepsy or mentally ill, holds her sword aloft. The mosaic is a technical tour de force, composed of glass, vitrified enamel, the haloes being gilded tin sheets, the faces painted ceramic plaques, while the robes are cut from white, red and grey marble.

In the centre of it all is the awe-inspiring golden altar and baldachin created by Schimkowitz. Looking up through its central opening, the penitent sees the head of Christ. The opulent patterning and the angels with their rectangular gilded wings recall Klimt's famous 'Golden Period' paintings; *The Kiss* (Belvedere, Vienna) dates to 1907–08. The sacred vessels, the Monstrance and Chalice, the candle-holders, the cachepots as well as the four chandeliers were designed by Wagner and made by the Wiener Werkstätte. Even the liturgical vestments are in the Secession style. J. A. Lux, Wagner's biographer, paid tribute to the building's ingenuity as well as its beauty:

> *From every point about the city can be seen the golden cupola, flaming against its green setting. Of Palladian beauty, it is unmistakeably informed by the spirit of modernity, held together by a steel ring, which thus obviates the necessity of supports and buttresses. It is a child of modern constructional methods. At no other time than the present could it have been created in such a form*[34].

Inevitably, there was plenty of criticism, with one detractor observing, 'This building looks magnificent but gives the impression of the tomb of an Indian Maharajah'[35].

Domènech i Montaner, Palau de la Música Catalana, Barcelona (1905–08)

Opening to the public on 9 February 1908, the Palau de la Música Catalana is the most singular concert hall in the world, not only an outstanding example of Modernisme but also the embodiment of the Catalan spirit. At its heart lies the Orfeó Català, a choral society founded in 1891 by the composers Lluís Millet i Pagès (1867–1941) and Amadeu Vives i Roig (1872–1932). Interested in classical music and traditional folk songs, both initiated a renaissance of Catalan music[36].

As the Orfeó's importance increased, the need for its own premises became obvious. When Joaquim Cabot assumed the presidency, Domènech was formally commissioned in October 1904 to design a 'Palace of Music'. Construction was made possible through public subscriptions; this ensured that the citizens of Barcelona were truly invested in the Orfeó. It was to promote 'peace, patriotism and artistic culture'.

Aged fifty-four, Domènech was at the height of his career, currently constructing the Hospital de la Santa Creu i Sant Pau (1901–30). As an ardent *Catalanista* he was an obvious choice; the building had to express the 'full force of the *Renaixença*'. Domènech was faced with a difficult and irregular plot of land, hemmed in by existing buildings, in the Ciutat Vella (Old City). The narrow streets made an open perspective impossible. What he created has been described as a 'highly decorated glass box, an enormous shining jewel, lit from above and transparent'[37]. There is natural light everywhere, coming in at street level through the entrance porches, emanating from above on the staircase and the luminous aura of the auditorium created by the magnificent skylight. The Lluis Millet Hall, on the main floor, exemplifies the building's luminosity and transparency. Two storeys high, occupying the width of the main façade, the space is enclosed from floor to ceiling with leaded glass screens filled with stylized floral motifs. These are protected by a double colonnade of fourteen columns, all with different floral and arabesque patterns, on the balcony.

Using balconies and colonnades, plus the abundant use of tile and mosaics set against austere red brick, Domènech created a light, almost transparent façade. Rather than forming a barrier the façade plays with solids and voids creating a compositional rhythm. The windows are pulled back from the exterior wall allowing them to spread out horizontally and vertically as in the Lluis Millet Hall. The central section is crowned with a dome on the roofline; three arches define the next floor; seven columns on the first floor form a loggia and two large arches on the ground floor led to a vaulted portico, one originally for pedestrians and the other for cars. These are now closed off and incorporated into the vestibule. The side façade is clearly divided into four sections: the reception and foyer area, concert hall, backstage and administration. The concert hall is completely open, with five enormous windows, each divided vertically and horizontally into

Domènech i Montaner, Lluis Millet Hall, Palau de la Música Catalana, Carrer Palau de la Música, Barcelona (1905–08).

three sections corresponding to the three internal floors. A balcony runs the full width of this façade, pulling all these elements together, its balustrade of iron enclosed in green glass tubes. This novel use of glass can be found again on the grand double staircase, where the twisted iron supports of the balustrade are encased in yellow glass. The balustrade is composed of five different materials; iron, glass, ceramics and stone, topped with a smooth white marble handrail.

Looking from the rounded corner, the building resembles the prow of a ship with the two façades conceived as a whole, the same rhythms continuing across the full width and around the corner. Miquel Blay's monumental sculptural group *La cançó popular*

Domènech, Lluis Millet Hall, loggia, Palau de la Música Catalana (1905–08).

Domènech, corner showing continuation of the façade, Palau de la Música Catalana (1905–08).

Domènech, allegorical mosaic, Palau de la Música Catalana (1905–08).

catalana (The Catalan Folk Song) acts like a figure-head. Naturally as patron saint, St George takes pride of place; the first stone was laid on St George's day in 1905. He presides over the stonemasons and labourers building the Palau (a choir of workers) and a group of women and children singing. Below, a young woman, the spirit of song, looks out to the horizon. It was completed in September 1909 and paid for by the Marquis of Castellbell, Joaquim de Càrcer i d'Amat.

The decoration of the Palau is remarkable both technically and symbolically. Trencandís, free-form patterns, are combined with structured floral patterns in mosaic. The ingenuity of the tile designs is outstanding, with musical notes in relief found both inside and out. The play of colour is sophisticated; in the second-floor lobby (Circle) the tiles bear red and green flowers, in the corridor we find yellow and green leaves and in the side passages yellow and red flowers. There is a constant interaction of patterned, raised and plain tiles. The columns literally bloom into flowers. In the foyer they burst into hydrangeas and roses. In the loggia of the Lluis Millet Hall, each column, glistening with complex mosaic patterns, is capped with a stylized floral capital, although lilies and roses can be recognized.

The allegorical mosaic that stretches across the width of the façade, produced by Lluis Bru after a drawing by Domènech, depicts the Orfeó.

A monumental female figure, possibly the Virgin Mary holding a distaff and drop spindle, pulling out a thread, presides over rows of male choristers in smart black suits. She stands in front of the Senyera, the national flag with its distinctive four red strips on a yellow background. A chorister is holding the banner of the Orfeó Català designed by Antoni Maria Gallissà i Soqué (1861–1903). In the background the mountains of Montserrat rise. Below, the busts of Palestrina, Bach and Beethoven are framed within three arches. Wagner can be found on the side of the building. They were the work of Eusebi Arnau, a long-time associate of Domènech.

The vestibule and double staircase are luminous, bathed in a warm light that filters through the coloured glass windows and is reflected by the yellow and blue tiles of the walls and roof. Two lampposts, replicas of those found on the city's streets, make a direct connection to the outside. The stairs lead

Domènech, auditorium light fittings, Palau de la Música Catalana (1905-08).

Domènech, proscenium arch, homage to Josep Anselm Clavé i Camps and Catalan folk music, Palau de la Música Catalana (1905–08).

up to the stalls and the first floor of the auditorium.

Surrounded by two 'glass curtain walls', the beauty of the Concert Hall takes one's breath away. As architectural historian David Mackay declares, 'only a poem could translate into words this extremely humanized space'[38]. The rectangular auditorium, its height equal to the width, is flanked by lateral balconies, which seem to float. A Gothic element is introduced with the fan vaults of the ceiling; here, glistening ceramic peacock feathers splay out. The light fittings, composed of glass baubles and flower heads, which are suspended from these fan vaults, are ingeniously pulled back encircling the columns of the side naves, so they do not obscure the stage.

At the rear, winged horses fly out of stone buttresses supporting the ceiling. They are matched by the sculptures of the proscenium arch, the work of Didac Masana and Pau Gargallo. On the right the Valkyries ride out, with a bust of Beethoven beneath,

symbolizing classical music. On the left Catalan music is represented by a large tree spreading its branches over an idyllic scene of youths by a fountain, an allegory of the song *Les flors de maig*. They are watched over by Josep Anselm Clavé i Camps (1824–74), who encouraged Barcelona's choral societies.

The musical theme is continued in the rear wall of the semi-circular stage, a remarkable mixed media frieze composed of ceramics, wood and metal. Eighteen muses or goddesses of music emerge from a background of reddish-coloured trencadís mosaic. Each figure is outlined in white to make them stand out. They are linked by a mosaic garland of roses. The upper portion of each figure, moulded in terracotta, projects in the round from the flat background surface. Arranged in two groups of nine they tell the history of music; a bewigged eighteenth-century lady playing the violin, a Greek maiden blowing her double pipes, a medieval lady plucking her harp, and a Spanish dancer clicking her castanets. Remarkably, the musical instruments are made of wood. Following the iconographic program of the Palau, the figures represent both classical and popular music. The sculptural element was conceived by Eusebi Arnau, while the mosaic was the work of Lluís Bru.

Above all of this, the auditorium's crowning glory is the skylight. The inverted dome, like a giant water droplet just about to fall, radiates out into a sunburst. Alternatively, this might be a sun reflected in the waters of a lake ruffled by the waves. This central motif is surrounded by a choir of female faces. This

Arnau and Bru, rear wall of the stage, Palau de la Música Catalana (1905–08).

Tiffany style masterpiece was created by Antoni Rigalt i Blanch (1850–1914) at the Rigalt, Granell i Cia workshops.[39] The architectural importance of the Palau was immediately recognized; it was deemed the building of the year (1908). Despite recent changes and additions, allowing the Orfeó to continue its work, the Palau remains the most magical building in Barcelona.

Olbrich's Darmstadt Hochzeitsturm (Wedding Tower) (1907–08)

Unbeknownst to him, the third Darmstadt Künstlerkolonie Exhibition of 1908 was to be Olbrich's last; he died, shortly after the birth of his daughter Marianne, in August 1908 from leukaemia. Being the most experienced architect, Olbrich had been titular head of the colony since its founding in 1899. A strong bond developed between the architect and his patron, Grand Duke Ernst Ludwig:

The greatest of them all was Olbrich. I met him by chance. I saw his drawings for the Secession Exhibition in Vienna and a sketch for a portable candlestick, quite personal and different from the direction at that time. I felt immediately there's something fresh, something that suits me, something sunny that I didn't feel for all the others. [...] He was enthusiastic about my ideas and he appeared extremely sympathetic to me from the beginning. [...] I felt that more levity and taste was necessary for the German spirit and that he was exactly the right man as this finesse lay in his nature. [...] He helped realise many of my dreams – of which I was full[40].

Olbrich's legacy can still be seen on the Mathildenhöhe, on the edge of the city; the Ernst-Ludwig-Haus from the colony's first exhibition, entitled A Document of German Art (1901), and the Hochzeitsturm (Wedding Tower) from the third exhibition of 1908.

Olbrich, Hochzeitsturm (Wedding Tower) and Russian Orthodox Chapel, Mathildenhöhe, Darmstadt (1907–08).

Ernst Ludwig's ambitious plan, to revitalize the Hessian economy with an artistic 'naissance', was realized with the colony's first exhibition. Overnight Darmstadt was transformed into a centre of excellence, a shining beacon of modernity. Rather than creating only temporary structures, Olbrich laid out a small suburb, the seeds of an exhibition town. He declared:

We must build a city, a whole city! Anything less would be pointless! The government should give us [...] a field, and there we shall create a world. To build a single house means nothing. How can it be beautiful if an ugly one stands next door? What good are three, five, even ten beautiful houses [...] if the armchairs inside are not beautiful or the plates are not beautiful? No – a field [...] then we shall show what we can do. From the overall design down to the last detail, all governed by the same spirit, the streets and the gardens and the palaces and the cottages and the tables and the armchairs and the lamps and the spoons all expressions of the same sensibility...[41]

Olbrich did indeed 'create a world' with eight model houses clustered around the Ernst-Ludwig-Haus (1899–1901), 'The Temple of Work... a house of labour', both artists' studio and craftsmen's workshop. The temporary buildings, a fine art gallery, a theatre, a restaurant, a concert hall and an impressive entrance portal and ticket booth, fulfilled Ernst Ludwig's dream of building an Acropolis on the Mathildenhöhe.

Although critically acclaimed, the exhibition made a financial loss. The high cost of the beautifully crafted furniture and metalwork was beyond the reach of most consumers. The economic ramifications of producing Art for the People would lead to industrial serial production and an alliance with major manufacturers to produce cutlery and ceramics.

There was also tension within the 'First Seven', the artists called to Darmstadt to form the colony in 1899: Olbrich, Behrens, Patriz Huber, Hans Christiansen, Paul Bürck (1878–1947), Rudolf Bosselt (1871–1938) and Ludwig Habich. In the ensuing crisis, Behrens, Huber, Bürck, Christiansen and Bosselt left the Artist's Colony between 1902 and 1903. Although only Olbrich and Habich remained this was not the end of the story. A determined Ernst Ludwig rebuilt the team; 'It's named Artist's Colony, because everybody can go whenever he likes, and I can resolve his contract whenever I like'[42]. Ensuring the continuance of his politico-cultural-economic project, Ernst Ludwig invited the painter and illustrator Vincenz Cissarz (1873–1942), the architect and interior designer Paul Haustein (1880–1944) and the sculptor and graphic artist Daniel Greiner (1872–1943). This new team of five artists brought the second Artist's Colony exhibition to fruition in 1904. This was a more modest affair, focused on Olbrich's interlocking Dreihäusergruppe (Three House Group) on the Alexandraweg, conceived as an 'example of homes for the not over-wealthy citizen'[43]. More emphasis was placed on practicality and affordability; rather than silver, artists experimented with copper, brass and pewter. Olbrich designed a range of textiles, including a simple dish towel, reviving block-printing techniques, while Haustein attempted to reinvigorate the Upper Hessian pottery tradition. Overall the exhibition was praised as a 'reasonable compliance with the actual existing needs'[44].

After a four-year gap, the third exhibition, the Hessische Landesausstellung für freie und angewandte Kunst (Hessian Regional Exhibition for Free and Applied Arts) took place on the Mathildenhöhe. The aim was to demonstrate the revitalization of local industries thanks to the influence and input of the Artist's Colony. For the first time local artists, businesses and technical and vocational colleges participated. Now only Olbrich remained from the 'First Seven': architect Albin Müller (1871–1941), goldsmith Ernst Riegel (1871–1939), illustrator Friedrich Wilhelm Kleukens (1880–1954), sculptor Heinrich Jobst, ceramist Jakob Julius Scharvogel and glassmaker Josef Emil Schneckendorf (1869–1945) had joined the team. Scharvogel and Schneckendorf had been engaged to head the Grand Duke's ceramics factory and precious glass factory. The ornamental courtyard and waiting hall of Badehaus 7, part of the spa and sanitorium complex at Bad Nauheim, were exhibited to demonstrate the successful union of art and industry. Müller oversaw the conception as Olbrich had already left the colony to take up a post in Düsseldorf.

The 1908 exhibition was a splendid affair, the skyline dominated by the Hochzeitsturm (Wedding Tower), an observation tower Olbrich had originally conceived for the first exhibition. Ernst Ludwig's first marriage to his maternal first cousin, Princess Victoria Melita of Saxe-Coburg and Gotha ('Ducky'), had not been happy due to differences in character and attitude; while the serious Ernst Ludwig was driven by duty, the fun-loving Ducky avoided public commitments. The match being engineered by their mutual grandmother, Queen Victoria, divorce at last became possible with her death. Despite rumours that the Grand Duke was in fact homosexual, he married Eleonore of Solms-Hohensolms-Lich (1871–1937) on 2 February 1905. This marriage, which proved happy and harmonious, resulted in two sons: Georg Donatus (1906–37) and Louis (1908–68). So, there was much to celebrate, the Wedding Tower being a gift from the city. The tower provided views to the

Müller, clock face, Hochzeitsturm (1907–08).

Rhine and the hills of Vogelsberg and Odenwald. Olbrich explained his conception:

The vertical mass of the wedding tower, connected with the horizontal structures of the exhibition house, form a monumental entity that grows up like a landmark from the cityscape. Seen from a distance as close by, this fulfils a monument's requirement: To give dumb yet eternal news of the enthusiasm of a citizenry at a time of the happiest life celebration!

This remarkable tower looks to the past and the future; the five staggered gables resembling the fingers of a hand or a Hindu *Mudra* hand sign, presages Art Deco. However, by reiterating the bell tower of the Russian Orthodox St Mary Magdalene chapel that stands nearby (1897–99, Leon Benois), which also has a stepped profile, continuity is ensured. This equally

remarkable building, with its gold onion domes, was built by Ernst Ludwig as a private chapel for his sister Alexandra and her husband Nicholas II, the last Tsar of Russia. Another source could be the stepped gables commonly seen on medieval north German buildings, such as the Mecklenburg tower. However, a modernist feature is the way the continuous narrow horizontal windows are wrapped around the corners of the structure.

Unusually, local clinker brick was used for the structure, alongside red brick and tile. This rather coarse background contrasts with the decorative elements. The sundial in mosaic was contributed by Kleukens. In addition to bearing the signs of the zodiac, the inscription, from a poem by Rudolf Binding, reminds us of the transience of life. Müller added the clock whose gold-leaf face bears the symbols of Christian virtue: faith, hope and charity (cross, heart and anchor) (1914). Over the entrance the sculpture by Jobst features the coats of arms of the newly married couple. The figures are personifications of the four virtues of a ruler: Strength, wisdom, justice and gentleness.

The entrance lobby is dominated by two mosaics by Kleukens, which were installed for the last pre-war exhibition in 1914. *The Kiss* features two winged figures embracing; their wings join to form a sort of halo. *The Loyalty* represents a monumental winged female figure, perhaps the goddess of good fortune,

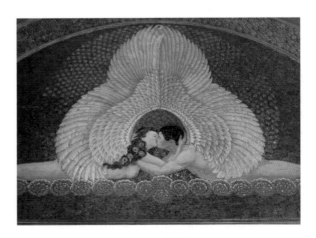

Kleukens, *The Kiss*, Hochzeitsturm (1914).

Hegenbart, the Grand Duke's Room, Hochzeitsturm (after 1908).

holding cornucopia under each arm filled with roses. Either side, two white doves fly away with the roses, spreading love in all directions. The goddess stands in front of a spreading Tree of Life. The two lions at her feet hold the arms of Ernst Ludwig and Eleonore (1914). The ceiling is designed as a star-spangled night sky.

The interior is divided into seven floors. The individual decorative schemes were only completed after the 1908 exhibition. The Grand Duchess' Room on the fifth level is known as the 'Wedding Room'. The murals by Philipp Otto Schäfer (1868–?) represent a princely wedding celebration in a neo-Italian Renaissance style. In the background 'the six (most beautiful) Hessian cities' can be seen: Gießen and Friedberg for Upper Hesse, Frankfurt and Offenbach for Starkenburg and finally Mainz and Worms for Rheinhessen.

The Grand Duke's Room on the fourth level, known as the 'Princely Room', was also lavishly painted by Fritz Hegenbart (1864–1943). The high barrel arched ceiling is covered with an intricate pattern of meandering lizards surrounded by blue leaves. Originally two allegorical wall paintings featured a mounted rider, a beautiful woman, and a youthful knight, leaping over a giant snail shell. They are said to represent 'the victory of modernity hurrying onwards'[45]. Only the female rider has survived. Today the Wedding Tower serves a very romantic

and apt purpose, used by the Darmstadt Registry Office for weddings.

Notes

1. Horta, Victor, *Mémoires*, Cécile Dulière (ed.), Brussels: Ministère de la Communauté française de Belgique 1985, p.42; Loyer, Francois, 'The Theatricality of Art Nouveau; Victor Horta's Hotel Tassel', in Loyer, Francois, and Dehaye, Jean, *Victor Horta Hotel Tassel 1893–95*, Brussels: Brussels aux Archives d'Architecture Modern, 1986, p.117.

2. Loyer, p.117.

3. Another possible source was Liberty prints, as van de Velde supplied wallpapers and textiles for the Tassel House. Some of the furniture was purchased at Bing's L'Art Nouveau, which had just opened.

4. Two letters dated 1895 confirm the window designed by Horta for the smoking room was fabricated by the Société Artistique de Peinture sur Verre Overloop et Cie, Brussels (Loyer and Delhaye, p. 130, FN. 23).

5. Horta, *Mémoires*, pp.48–49; Loyer, p.130, FN.24.

6. Bing, 1903, p.237.

7. Bing, 1903, p.238.

8. Bing, Samuel, 'La Culture artistique en Amérique' (Artistic America) (1895) *Artistic America, Tiffany Glass and Art Nouveau*, Cambridge Mass.: MIT Press, 1970, p.128.

9. de Toulouse-Lautrec, Henri, *At the New Circus, Papa Chrysanthemum*. https://www.musee-orsay.fr › at-the-new-circus-papa-chrysanthemum-22802

10. Brown, Alison, *Charles Rennie Mackintosh: Making the Glasgow Style*, Glasgow: Glasgow Museum, 2018, p.21.

11. Bing, 1895, p.183.

12. Many Guimard buildings can be found in the 16th arrondissement, an area rapidly developing into a fashionable suburban district. He was commissioned to design several single-family houses and

large apartment buildings in the neighbourhood by developers and landowners.

13. Launched in 1877, Lincrusta was the ingenious invention of Frederick Walton, a washable wall covering that replaced time-consuming and expensive plasterwork. Its name derives from Lin for Linum (flax, the basis of linseed oil) and Crusta (relief), with the inventor's name added to prevent imitations.

14. Guimard, Hector, *Castel Béranger*, exhibition catalogue, Munich: Métropolitain Bolivar/Villa von Stuck, 1999.

15. Mme. Guimard donated the dining room suite and interior wall panelling from l'Hotel Guimard to the city of Paris; it is displayed in the Petit Palais.

16. Kinchin, Perilla, *Tea and Taste The Glasgow Tea Rooms, 1875–1975*, Oxford: White Cockade, 1996, p.41.

17. Kinchin, p.86.

18. Kinchin, p.86.

19. White, Gleeson, 'Some Glasgow Designers and their work Part I', *The Studio*, Vol.11, No. 52, July 15 1897, pp.96–97. The execution of the murals was carried out by Messrs Guthrie, famed as makers of stained-glass windows.

20. White, p.99.

21. Kinchin, p.89.

22. Percy, Clayre and Ridley, Jane (eds.), *The Letters of Edwin Lutyens to his Wife Lady Emily*, 1985, 17th June 1897, p.49, following.

23. Percy and Ridley, Letter 1st June 1898, p.56, following.

24. Later repeated as an over-mantel for Elmbank, York.

25. Kinchin, p.97.

26. Kinchin, p.101.

27. The commission went to Anastasios Metaxas (1862–1937), who opted for a Greek Byzantine-style (1908 – inaugurated 1974).

28. Sarnitz, p.15.

29. Sarnitz, p.59.

30. Sarnitz, p.12.

31. Keiblinger, P.J., *Kirche am Steinhof*, Vienna: Ueberreuter Print, 2006, p.35.

32. Keiblinger, p.9.

33. Keiblinger, p.14.

34. Vergo, Peter, *Art in Vienna 1898–1918; Klimt, Kokoschka, Schiele and their contemporaries*, Oxford: Phaidon Press, 1986, pp.110–11.

35. Keiblinger, p.5.

36. Vives achieved fame with the Zarzuela, a lyric-dramatic genre that alternates between spoken and sung scenes, the latter incorporating operatic and popular songs, as well as dance.

37. Mackay, David, 'The Palau de la Música Catalana', *Domènech I Montaner Ano 2000*, Barcelona: Collegi d'Arquitectes de Catalunya, 2000, p.76.

38. Mackay, p.78.

39. The workshop operated from 1890 to 1984.

40. Franz, Eckhart G., (ed.), *Ernst Ludwig Grossherzogs von Hesses und bei Rhein, Erinnertes*, Darmstadt: Eduard Roether Verlag, 1983 (reprint), p.115.

41. Latham, Ian, *Olbrich*, London: Academy Editions 1980, p.48.

42. *Künstlerkolonie Mathildenhöhe Damstadt 1899–1914, The Museum Book*, Darmstadt: Institut Mathildenhöhe Darmstadt, 1999, p.73. The original artists were contracted for three years.

43. *The Museum Book*, p.74. After the exhibition, the Blue House and the Corner House were sold, the Grey House becoming the official residence of the court chaplain.

44. *The Museum Book*, p.75.

45. Ulmer, p.208.

WHILE THE FIRST WORLD WAR PROVIDES a clean break, Art Nouveau/Jugendstil ending and Art Deco and Modernism emerging in 1919, the decorative excesses of the style were challenged long before 1914. Wagner's Nutzstil or Use-Style, modern functionalism, found full expression in his Österreichische Postsparkasse (Austrian Postal Savings Bank) (1904–06 and 1910–12) deemed the first modern building in Europe. This was driven by his caveat 'the sole mistress of art is necessity'. The marble façade was easy to clean, as were the tile and glass surfaces used throughout the interior. In the austere but beautiful Kassenhalle (banking hall), glass blocks are set into the floor to light the level below, where the mail sorting rooms were located. The vast frosted glass skylight allows natural light to enter the heart of the building. Aluminium is used for the decorative elements inside and out, for the portico columns and the central-heating fans. The two great cast aluminium angels standing on the attica of the building, the work of Wagner's long-time collaborator Schimkowitz, seem to proclaim a new age.

Post-war Modernism was also foreshadowed by Adolf Loos (1870–1933), whose infamous essay *Ornament and Crime* (1913) advocated clean, uncluttered surfaces in contrast to the lavish ornamentation of the Wiener Werkstätte. Three crucial years spent in America (1893–96), working in New York and visiting the 1893 Columbian Exposition in Chicago, completely changed his outlook; useful things, like fountain pens and inkwells, did not need to be decorated. What was required were sleek lines and fine materials. The Looshaus (1909–11), on the Michaelerplatz directly opposite the Hofburg, the royal residence, exemplifies 'Wiener Moderne'. Built for Goldman & Salatsch Gentleman's Outfitters, the building is like a well-cut suit. While there are no frills, the materials and craftsmanship are of the highest quality. The shop front is clad in Cipollino marble, from the Greek

Wagner, Österreichische Postsparkasse (Austrian Postal Savings Bank), Vienna (1904/06 and 1910–12).

Loos, Looshaus (1909–11), Michaelerplatz, Vienna (1909–11).

island of Euboea; the window frames are bronze. However, the simple plaster façade of the residential floors caused an uproar. Lacking any conventional stucco ornamentation, it was nicknamed the 'House without Eyebrows'. This 'modern monstrosity' outraged Emperor Franz Josef, who refused to use the Hofburg entrance; window boxes had to be added to soften the austerity of the upper façade.

Materials of the highest quality also define the Palais Stoclet, Avenue de Tervuren, Brussels (1907–11), a Wiener Werkstätte masterpiece. Commissioned by the engineer, financier and noted collector Adolphe Stoclet (1871–1949), Palais Stoclet was the ultimate 'total artwork'. Conceived by Hoffmann, the sumptuous dining and music rooms exemplify the theatrical pretensions of the gesamtkunstwerk, celebrating sight,

Hoffmann, Palais Stoclet, avenue de Tervuren, Brussels (1907–11).

sound, touch and taste in a symphony of sensual harmonies. 'Smell' was taken care of by Madame Stoclet who arranged the flowers, apparently coordinating their colours with her husband's ties. After seeing Madame Stoclet in a Paul Poiret gown he considered inappropriate, Hoffmann designed her dress so that she would not clash with the living room décor. Loos' cautionary tale, *Poor Little Rich Man* (1900), warning that total unity could be taken too far, appeared to have come true. Certainly no expense was spared: Gustav Klimt designed the fabulous wall mosaics, *Expectation* and *Fulfilment*, of the dining room fabricated by Leopold Forstner[1]. Although described as a 'reformed interior', with minimal clutter, the lavish materials and angular furniture look ahead to Art Deco rather than Modernism.

The same can be said for 78 Derngate, Northampton (1916–17), Mackintosh's only completed project south of the Scottish border. Designed for local businessman Wenman Joseph Bassett-Lowke (1877–1953), who made his fortune manufacturing model railways, boats and ships, Derngate was remodelled during the difficult war years. A member of the Design and Industries Association, whose slogan was 'Fitness of Purpose', Bassett-Lowke sought to raise the standard of British industrial design. He chose an architect synonymous with modernity, although in articles published in *Ideal Home* Bassett-Lowke took the credit for his home's avant-garde bravado. The most audacious space is the tiny drawing room, originally painted black and decorated with a frieze of squared-headed trees in bold yellow with black-and-white chequerboard trunks. The equally bold screen, which conceals the staircase rising from the basement, is decorated with triangular patterns of yellow and white glass. Complementary geometric furniture, a smoker's cabinet, a display cabinet, settle and chairs, are lacquered black; the smoker's cabinet is inlaid with yellow Erinoid plastic triangles and lozenges[2]. While Bassett-Lowke was apparently colour-blind, Mrs Bassett-Lowke was not and the colour scheme had to be lightened, pale grey replacing the black (1920–22).

The guest bedroom is equally dramatic, the colour

Mackintosh, drawing room, 78 Derngate, Northampton (1916–17).

scheme dominated by dark blue. Mackintosh created a faux tester over the bed, bold stripes forming a large rectangle on the ceiling. Mrs Bassett-Lowke feared it might disturb Bernard Shaw's sleep, but he reassured his hostess that he slept with his eyes shut. However, in 1924, when Bassett-Lowke had the means to build a new house, Mackintosh had retired to Port Vendres, southern France to paint. Instead he turned to Behrens; New Ways, Wellingborough Road, completed in 1926 is deemed the first Modernist house to be built in Britain.

Legacy

When revered architectural historian Sir Nikolaus Pevsner and Sir James Richards published *The Anti-Rationalists* (1973), a series of articles, those who loved the New Art could at last rejoice. The 'Anti-Rationalists', numbering Guimard, Lechner, Gaudí and Mackintosh, were at last recognized as contributing to the search for new forms at the close of the nineteenth century. In his seminal *Pioneers of Modern Design from William Morris to Walter Gropius* (1936), Pevsner had dismissed Art Nouveau as weak and self-indulgent leading into a 'blind alley'. Within the context of 1970s post-Modernism, Art Nouveau/Jugendstil/Secession/Modernisme/Liberty could be repositioned as pioneering movements. Rather than being a dead end, the New Art is now seen to lead to the architectural innovations of the 1910s and the emergence of intellectual Modernism and fashionable Art Deco. Most importantly the values expressed in Art Nouveau and Jugendstil were recognized as valid: individualism, plastic and sculptural values, picturesqueness (asymmetry) and fantasy[3]. By the time *The Anti-Rationalists and the Rationalists* was published in 2000, it appeared 'the austere rationality of the modern movement is after all losing out'[4]. Looking at the buildings of Frank Gehry (1929–) and Zaha Hadid (1950–2016) this might well be true. In other words, the spirit of the New Art lives on.

Notes

1. Klimt's cartoons can be seen in the MAK, Vienna.
2. Bassett-Lowke sent Mackintosh booklets on Erinoid, a plastic material he recommended for the hall screen and as an inlay for furniture in the dining room.
3. Pevsner, Nikolaus, and Richards, J.M., (eds), *The Anti-Rationalists*, Toronto: University of Toronto, 1973, pp.1–7.
4. Pevsner, Nikolaus; Richards, J. M. and Sharp, Dennis, *The Anti-Rationalists and the Rationalists*, London: Architectural Press, 2000, Preface.

General

Amaya, Mario, *Art Nouveau*, London and New York: Studio Vista, 1966.

Arwas, Victor, *Art Nouveau: From Mackintosh to Liberty: The Birth of a Style*, London: Andreas Papadakis, 2000.

Arwas, Victor, *Art Nouveau: The French Aesthetic*, London: Andreas Papadakis, 2002.

Arwas, Victor, Paul Greenhalgh and Ghislaine Wood (eds), *Art Nouveau: An Architectural Indulgence*, New Architecture 6, London: Andreas Papadakis, 2000.

Becker, Vivienne, *Art Nouveau Jewellery*, London: Thames and Hudson, 1998.

Borisova, Elena A. and Grigory Sternin, *Russian Art Nouveau*, New York: Rizzoli, 1988.

Brohan Museum State Museum for Art Nouveau, Art Deco and Functionalism 1889–1939, Berlin: Brohan Museum, 1998.

Buffet-Challie, Lawrence, *Art Nouveau Style*, London: Academy Editions, 1983.

Duncan, Alastair, *Art Nouveau and Art Deco Lighting*, London: Thames and Hudson, 1978.

Duncan, Alastair, *Art Nouveau Sculpture*, New York: Rizzoli, 1978.

Duncan, Alastair, *Art Nouveau Furniture*, London: Thames and Hudson, 1982.

Duncan, Alastair, *Art Nouveau*, London: Thames and Hudson, 1994.

Escritt, Stephen, *Art Nouveau*, London: Phaidon, 2000.

Fahr-Becker, Gabriele and Gabriele Sterner (1982) *Art Nouveau An Art of Transition: From Individualism to Mass Society*, Woodbury, NY: Barrons Educational Series, 1982.

Fahr-Becker, Gabriele, *Art Nouveau*, Potsdam: h.f. Ullmann, 2015.

Greenhalgh, Paul (ed.) *Art Nouveau 1890–1914*, London: V&A Publications, 2000.

Harris, Nathaniel, *Art Nouveau Paintings, Jewellery, Sculpture Architecture*, Twickenham: Hamlyn, 1985.

Haslam, Malcolm, *In the Nouveau Style*, London: Bulfinch, 1990.

Howard, Jeremy, *Art Nouveau International and National Styles in Europe*, Manchester: MUP, 1996.

Madsen, S. Tschudi, *Sources of Art Nouveau*, Oslo: H. Aschehoug & Co., 1956.

Massini, Lara-Vinca, *Art Nouveau*, London: Thames and Hudson, 1984.

Russell, Frank, *Art Nouveau Architecture*, London: Academy Editions, 1979.

Sembach, Klaus Jurgen, *Art Nouveau; Utopia: Reconciling the Irreconcilable*, Koln: Benedikt Taschen, 1991.

Tahara, Keiichi, Philippe Thiebaut & Bruno Girveau, *Art Nouveau Architecture*, London: Thames and Hudson, 2000.

West, Shearer, *Fine de Siècle: Art and Society in an age of uncertainty*, London: Bloomsbury, 1993.

Brussels/Belgium

Cuito, Aurora and Cristina Montes (eds) *Victor Horta*, Krefeld: teNeues Media Publishing, 2002.

Dierkens-Aubry, Françoise, *The Horta Museum Brussels Saint-Gilles*, Brussels: Credit Communal, Cultura Nostra, Ludion, 1990.

Dierkens-Aubry, Françoise and Jos Vandenbreeden, *Horta – Art Nouveau to Modernism*, New York: Harry N. Abrams, 1998.

Dierkens-Aubry, Francoise and Jos Vandenbreeden, *Art Nouveau in Belgium: architecture and interior designs*, Ghent; Lannoo, 2001.

Dierkens-Aubry, Françoise, Christine Bastin and Jacques Evrard, *The Brussels of Horta*, Ghent: Ludion, 2007.

La Maison Cauche Entre reve et realite, Brussels: Edition Maison Cauche, 2004.

Loyer, Francois and Jean Delhaye, *Victor Horta, Hotel*

Tassel 1893–95, Brussels: AAM Editions, 1998.

Musee fin-de-siecle museum, Brussels: Royal Museum of Fine Arts Belgium, 2013.

Oostens-Wittamer, Yolande, *Horta The Solvay House Brussels 1894–1903*, Brussels: Diane de Selliers, 2005.

Robert-Jones, Philippe, *Brussels Fin de Siècle*, Cologne: Taschen, 1999.

Sembach, Klaus-Jurgen, *Henry van de Velde*, London: Thames and Hudson, 1989.

Tron, Nupur, *Victor Horta and the Frison House in Brussels*, Brussels: Sterck & De Vreese, 2019.

Paris/Nancy

Bing, Samuel, 'l'Art Nouveau' (1902) and 'l'Art Nouveau' (1903), Robert Koch, *Artistic America, Tiffany Glass and Art Nouveau*, Cambridge, Mass and London: MIT Press, 1970.

Daum, Noel, *Daum: Mastery of Glass from Art Nouveau to Contemporary Crystal*, Lausanne: Edita, 1985.

Debize, Christian, *Émile Gallé and 'école de Nancy'*, Metz: Editions Serpenoise, 1999.

Duncan, Alastair, *Louis Majorelle: Master of Art Nouveau*, London: Thames and Hudson, 1991.

Garner, Philippe, *Gallé*, London: Academy Editions, 1990.

Guide L'Ecole Nancy, Nancy: Presses Universitaries de Nancy, 1999.

Jullian, Philippe (1975) *Paris Exhibition 1900: The Triumph of Art Nouveau*, London: Phaidon, 1975.

Midant, Jean-Paul, *Art Nouveau in France*, Paris: Books and Co., 1999.

Petry, Claude, *Daum dans les Musees de Nancy*, Maxeville: Jean-Lamour, 1989.

Silverman, Deborah, *Art Nouveau in Fin-de-Siecle France: Politics, Psychology and Style (Studies in History of Society and Culture)*, University of California Press, 1992.

Weisberg, Gabriel, *Art Nouveau Bing: Paris Style 1900*, New York: Rizzoli, 1986.

Darmstadt/Germany

Hiesinger, Kathryn Bloom, *Art Nouveau in Munich: Masters of Jugendstil from the Stadtmuseum, Munich, and other public and private collections*, Philadelphia: Prestel/Philadelphia Museum of Art, 1988.

Kunsterkolonie Mathildenhohe Darmstadt 1899–1914: The Museum Book, Darmstadt: Institut Mathildenhohe Darmstadt, 1999.

Latham, Ian, *Olbrich*, London: Academy Editions, 1980.

Makela, Maria, *The Munich Secession Art and Artists in Turn-of-the-Century Munich*, Princeton, NJ: Princeton University, 1990.

Metzger, Rainer, *Munich Its Golden Age of Art and Culture*, London: Thames and Hudson, 2008.

Schulte, Birgit (ed.), *Henry van de Velde in Hagen*, Hagen: Neuer Folkwang Verlag im Karl-Ernst-Osthaus Museum Hagen, 1992.

Ulmer, Renate, *Jugendstil in Darmstadt*, Darmstadt: Eduard Roether Verlag, 1997.

Vienna

Borsi, Franco and Ezio Godoli, *Vienna 1900 – Architecture and Design*, London: Lund Humphries, 1986.

Branstatter, Christian (ed.), *Vienna 1900 and the Heroes of Modernism*, London: Thames and Hudson, 2006.

Kallir, Jane, *Viennese Design and the Weiner Werkstätte*, London: Thames and Hudson, 1986.

Pintaric, Vera Horvat, *Vienna 1900 – the Architecture of Otto Wagner*, London: Studio Editions, 1989.

Sarnitz, August, *Otto Wagner: Forerunner of Modern Architecture*, Koln: Taschen, 2005.

Thun-Hohenstein, Christoph, Elisabeth Schmuttermeier and Christian Witt-Dörring (eds), *Koloman Moser, Universal Artist between Klimt and Hoffmann*, exhibition catalogue, Vienna: MAK, Birkhäuser Verlag, 2018.

Vergo, Peter, *Art in Vienna 1898–1918; Klimt, Kokoschka, Schiele and their contemporaries*, Oxford: Phaidon, 1975.

Budapest/Hungary

Alofsin, Anthony, *Architecture as Language in the Habsburg Empire and Its Aftermath, 1867–1933*, Chicago: University of Chicago Press, 2006.

Bede, Bela, *225 Highlights Hungarian Art Nouveau Architecture*, Budapest: Corvina, 2015.

Éri, Gyöngyi and Zsuzsa O. Jobbágyi, *A Golden Age Art and Society in Hungary 1896–1914*, Budapest: Corvina, 1989.

Gerle, Janos, *Art Nouveau in Hungarian Architecture for Connoisseurs*, Budapest: 6BT. Kiado, 2013.

Kovacs, Daniel and Zsolt Batar, *Budapest Art Nouveau*, Budapest: Laszlo Kedves, 2012.

Taylor Jeffrey, *In search of the Budapest Secession: The Artist Proletariat and Modernism's Rise in the Hungarian Art Market 1800–1914*, St Helena CA: Helena History Press, 2014.

Barcelona

Castellar-Gassol, Juan, *Gaudí, the Life of a Visionary*. Translated by Paul Martin. Barcelona: Edicions de 1984, 1999.

Moderisme Route Barcelona, Barcelona: Institut del Paisatge Urba I la Qualitat de Vida, 2005.

Sala, Teresa M. (ed.), *Barcelona 1900*, exhibition catalogue, Brussels: Mercatorfonds, 2007.

The Sant Pau Modernista Precinct, Barcelona: Fundacio Privada, Hospital de la Santa Creu I Sant Pau, 2014.

Zerbst, Rainer, *Gaudí, 1852–1926: Antoni Gaudí i Cornet: a life devoted to architecture*, Koln: Taschen, 2002.

Italy

Bossaglia, Rossana and Valerio Terraroli, *IL Liberty A Milano*, Milano: Skira, 2003.

Guttry, Irene, Maria Paola Maino and Gabriella Tarquini, *Italian Liberty Style*, 20th Century Decorative Arts, Pero: 24 Ore Cultura, 2012.

Roiter, Fulvio and Guido Lopez, *Milano Liberty/Art Nouveau in Milan*, Milano: Edizioni CELIP Milano, 1993.

Speziali, Andrea (ed.) *Italian liberty. Una nuova stagione dell'Art Nouveau*, Flori: CartaCanta editore, 2015.

Speziali, Andrea (ed.), *Italian Liberty. Il sogno europeo della grande bellezza,* Flori: CartaCanta editore, 2016.

Speziali, Andrea, *Giuseppe Sommaruga (1867–1917). Un protagonista del Liberty*, Flori: CartaCanta editore, 2017.

Speziali, Andrea (ed.) *The World of Art Nouveau*, Flori: CartaCanta, editore 2017.

Squarotti, Silvia Barberi, *Il Liberty nei quartieri torinesi*, Torino: Daniela Piazza editore, 2012.

Baltic

Grosa, Silvija, *Art Nouveau in Riga*, Riga: Jumava, 2003.

Hämäläinen, Pirjo, *Jugend Suomessa*, Helsinki: Kustannusosakeyhtio Otava, 2010.

Krastiņs, Jānis, *Art Nouveau Architecture in Riga*, Riga: ADD Projekts, 2007.

Krastins, Jānis, *Art Nouveau buildings in Riga, A Guide to Architecture of Art Nouveau Metropolis*

Krastins, Jānis, *Riga. Jugendstilmetropole. Art Nouveau Metropolis, Jugendstila Metropole*, Riga: Baltika, 1996.

Pirjo, Hämäläinen, *Jugend Suomessa*, Helsinki: Kustannusosakeyhtiö Otava, 2010.

Rush, Solveiga, *Mikhail Eisenstein. Themes and symbols in Art Nouveau architecture of Riga 1901–1906,* Riga: Neputns, 2003.